ISSUES IN CONTEMPORARY AMERICAN JOURNALISM

Bringing together the diverse perspectives of over 20 leading journalism scholars, this collection provides an original insight into the history of American journalism and issues that exist and have existed within the industry for decades.

The culture of journalism is in constant flux, with both individual journalists and the news industry as a whole regularly finding themselves at the center of controversy. While heightened in recent years, such controversy is not new and could in fact be considered a hallmark of the profession. With this in mind, this book presents original perspectives into issues and debates regarding the role of journalism in America, journalistic objectivity and ethics, diversity and representation, war and conflict reporting, local news, fake news, and hostility toward journalists. Each of the seven sections begins with a topical overview and ends with a short essay written by a leader in the field.

Issues in Contemporary American Journalism is recommended reading for anyone studying the history and evolution of journalism in the US at an advanced level.

Hans C. Schmidt is an associate professor of communications at Penn State University, Brandywine, and holds a PhD in mass media and communication. He teaches journalism and media classes, and is author of numerous peer-reviewed academic journal articles. His scholarship is primarily focused on journalism, journalism education, and media literacy.

ISSUES IN CONTEMPORARY AMERICAN JOURNALISM

Edited by Hans C. Schmidt

Routledge
Taylor & Francis Group

LONDON AND NEW YORK

Designed cover image: © Getty Images | enot-poloskun

First published 2023
by Routledge
4 Park Square, Milton Park, Abingdon, Oxon OX14 4RN

and by Routledge
605 Third Avenue, New York, NY 10158

Routledge is an imprint of the Taylor & Francis Group, an informa business

British Library Cataloguing-in-Publication Data
A catalogue record for this book is available from the British Library

Library of Congress Cataloging-in-Publication Data
Names: Schmidt, Hans C., editor.
Title: Issues in contemporary American journalism / edited by Hans C. Schmidt.
Description: Abingdon, Oxon ; New York, NY : Routledge, 2023. | Includes bibliographical references and index.
Identifiers: LCCN 2022056475 (print) | LCCN 2022056476 (ebook) | Subjects: LCSH: Journalism--United States--History--21st century.
Classification: LCC PN4867.2 .I85 2023 (print) | LCC PN4867.2 (ebook) | DDC 071/.30905--dc23/eng/20230320
LC record available at https://lccn.loc.gov/2022056475
LC ebook record available at https://lccn.loc.gov/2022056476

ISBN: 978-1-032-32552-1 (hbk)
ISBN: 978-1-032-32551-4 (pbk)
ISBN: 978-1-003-31560-5 (ebk)

DOI: 10.4324/9781003315605

Typeset in Bembo
by SPi Technologies India Pvt Ltd (Straive)

CONTENTS

List of Contributors   *ix*
Preface   *xii*
Introduction   *xiv*

PART I
The Role of Journalism in America   **1**

1   A Brief History of Journalism in the United States   3
    Hans C. Schmidt

2   The Free Press: A Confusing History and Uncertain Future   15
    Gina Baleria

3   How Free and How Responsible? The 75th Anniversary of the
    Hutchins Commission Report   24
    Lois A. Boynton

    Essay: The Importance of Journalism Today   33
    Dane S. Claussen

PART II
Rethinking Journalistic Objectivity and Ethics   **37**

4   Journalism Ethics: Dilemmas and Decisions   39
    Maggie Jones Patterson

5 Journalistic Objectivity: A Gold Standard or Myth?   47
   E. S. McIntyre

6 How Journalistic Objectivity Turns Matters of Science into
   Matters of Politics: A Closer Look at Climate Change and
   COVID-19 Reporting   55
   Jason Turcotte and Nicolas Hernandez Florez

   Essay: When Objectivity Isn't Enough: A Case Study on
   Feminicidios, Violence Against Women, and Anti-Violence
   Activism   63
   Leandra H. Hernández

PART III
Diversity and Representation in Journalism   **69**

7 African American Newspapers: The Voice of the Community   71
   Masudul Biswas

8 It's Everybody's Problem: Why Journalism's Macho Culture
   Persists and How to Help Make it End   81
   Meg Heckman

9 Heroes and Villains? How US News Organizations are Shifting
   Their Representations of Protesters and Authorities   88
   Jennifer Brannock Cox

   Essay: The Uneven History of Diversity in Journalism   99
   Gwyneth Mellinger

PART IV
War and Conflict Reporting in a Multidimensional
World   **103**

10 The Complicated History of War and Conflict Reporting
    in the United States   105
    Hans C. Schmidt

11 Media, War, and the Propaganda of Pretext   116
    Oliver Boyd-Barrett

12   Challenges in Terrorism Coverage in the United States   125
     Yiyi Yang

     Essay: War Coverage: Perspectives from the Academy
     to the Field   131
     Sean Aday

PART V
Challenges and Opportunities for Local News   **135**

13   Local News in Crisis   137
     Bill Reader

14   Public Access Television: An Untapped Resource for
     Local News   146
     Antoine Haywood and Victor Pickard

15   The Engaged Student Journalist: A Teaching Hospital Model
     for the 21st Century   154
     Allison M. Frisch and Gina Gayle

     Essay: Building Better Competitive News Environments   161
     John-Erik Koslosky

PART VI
The Real Impact of Fake News   **167**

16   Understanding Fake News Today   169
     Larry J. King

17   The Return of Fake News   177
     J. D. Ponder

18   The Evolution of Fake News on Facebook: Truth Disagreements
     and a Loss of Common Knowledge   187
     Danielle R. Mehlman-Brightwell

     Essay: Inoculation Theory and Fake News   196
     Josh Compton

PART VII
**Journalistic Trust and Accuracy in an Era of Hostility
and Partisanship** **201**

19 Hostility Toward the Press: Background and Steps Forward   203
    Kelsey Mesmer and Kaitlin Miller

20 Participatory Journalism: A New Approach for Increasing
    Public Trust and Engagement   211
    Mirjana Pantic

21 Of Sounder Mind: Considering the Well-Being of Professional
    Journalists   218
    Avery E. Holton and Valérie Bélair-Gagnon

    Essay: Predatory Publishing: What Every Science Journalist
    Needs to Know   227
    Amy Koerber

Index   231

CONTRIBUTORS

Sean Aday is an associate professor of media and public affairs and international affairs at George Washington University, USA.

Gina Baleria is an assistant professor of journalism, media writing, radio and podcasting, and digital media at Sonoma State University, USA.

Valérie Bélair-Gagnon is an associate professor of journalism and mass communication and Cowles fellow in media management at the University of Minnesota-Twin Cities, USA.

Masudul Biswas is an associate professor of communication at Loyola University Maryland, USA.

Oliver Boyd-Barrett is a professor (emeritus) of journalism and communication at Bowling Green State University and Cal Poly Pomona, USA.

Lois A. Boynton is an associate professor of journalism and media at the University of North Carolina at Chapel Hill, USA.

Dane S. Claussen is the editor and executive director of Nonprofit Sector News in Moscow, Idaho, USA.

Josh Compton is a professor of speech at Dartmouth College, USA.

Jennifer Brannock Cox is an associate professor of communication at Salisbury (Maryland) University, USA.

Nicolas Hernandez Florez is a political science doctoral student at the University of Michigan, USA.

Allison Marie Frisch is an assistant professor of journalism at Ithaca College, USA.

Gina Gayle is an assistant professor at Emerson College, USA.

Antoine Haywood is a PhD candidate and Penn Presidential Fellow at the University of Pennsylvania, USA.

Meg Heckman is an assistant professor of journalism at Northeastern University, USA.

Leandra H. Hernández is an assistant professor of communication at Utah Valley University, USA.

Avery E. Holton is an associate professor of communication and department chair at the University of Utah, USA.

Larry J. King is a professor of communication at Stephen F. Austin State University, USA.

Amy Koerber is a professor of communication studies and associate dean for administration and finance at Texas Tech University, USA.

John-Erik Koslosky is an assistant professor of media and journalism at Commonwealth University of Pennsylvania, USA.

E. S. McIntyre is an investigative journalist and assistant professor of journalism at the University of North Carolina at Chapel Hill, USA.

Danielle R. Mehlman-Brightwell is an assistant professor of public policy and communication at the University of Pittsburgh at Greensburg, USA.

Gwyneth Mellinger is a professor at James Madison University, USA.

Kelsey Mesmer is an assistant professor of journalism at Saint Louis University, USA.

Kaitlin Miller is an assistant professor of journalism and creative media at the University of Alabama, USA.

Mirjana Pantic is an assistant professor of media, communications, and visual arts at Pace University, USA.

Maggie Jones Patterson is a professor of journalism at Duquesne University, USA.

Victor Pickard is a professor of media policy and political economy at the University of Pennsylvania, USA.

J. D. Ponder is an associate professor at Kent State University, USA.

Bill Reader is a professor of journalism at Ohio University, USA.

Hans C. Schmidt is an associate professor of communications at Penn State University, Brandywine, USA.

Jason Turcotte is an associate professor of communication at Cal Poly Pomona, USA.

Yiyi Yang is an assistant professor of communication studies at the University of North Carolina Wilmington, USA.

PREFACE

If you take some time to travel across the country, it quickly becomes apparent just how vast this nation is. It also becomes apparent that this is a nation defined less by its similarities than by its differences. The differences are geographic: rolling hills, soaring mountains, boundless coastlines, frozen tundra, vast planes, barren deserts. The differences are cultural, in the cars we drive, the food we eat, the jobs we hold, the homes we live in, the languages and dialects we speak, the clothes we wear, the faiths we hold, the politics we espouse, the people we love.

With such profound differences, what is it that makes these 50 states united? In a legal sense, of course, there is the constitution that binds this place and people together into the nation – the idea – that is America. But law alone does not create our national identity. Indeed, our sense of nationhood is formed as much by our shared information as it is by our shared laws; it is this which makes the nation truly national.

Today, our national media connects us – the US – together. Thanks to our media, we can feel connected to people, places, and events that are thousands of miles away. Our news provides a shared common denominator.

It's easy to take our news media for granted, but we shouldn't; it hasn't always existed, and the very principle of an independent press has been fought for – and fought over – for centuries. At times, its evolution has been rocky. At times, it has been painful. But, over the course of a few hundred years – driven by innovations in technology and practice – we have come to have a system of journalism just as extensive as this great land in which we live.

This book seeks to explore the background of contemporary news media, and investigate some of the challenges and opportunities that exist within journalism and news media today. I approach this consideration as a former journalist, a journalism professor, and – fundamentally – as a person who has always wanted to be informed about what is happening around me. I hope this book helps you to, similarly, develop an appreciation for the importance of news media today, and think critically about ways in which our news media can improve, and better serve us in a dynamic, diverse, and exciting future.

INTRODUCTION

Hans C. Schmidt

> Were it left to me to decide whether we should have a government with-
> out newspapers, or newspapers without a government, I should not hesi-
> tate a moment to prefer the latter.
>
> — *Thomas Jefferson*

A common perception exists that, once upon a time, the news was always factual, independent, trustworthy, and created by altruistic journalists who operated
free from commercial or political influence. In reality, though, such a fabled time
never existed. Journalism has always been controversial, criticized by governments,
businesses, and everyday people alike. And it has long been a profession that has
looked inward, and asked itself questions about what journalism really is, and what
journalism should aim to be.

Yet, for all the time we, as a society, spend criticizing the news, we also take it for
granted, and overlook just much we rely on it. For many of us, the day's headlines
are among the first things we see every morning and the last things we see at night.
News is everywhere. Its omnipresence makes it almost invisible, as if somehow "the
news" simply exists in the ether, as natural as the air we breathe and as impersonal
as the Wi-Fi signal or broadband connection on which it is delivered. But, in fact,
such content does not spring out of thin air. It does not necessarily exist. It does
not automatically appear.

Instead, this content that we take for granted is the product of many people,
many institutions, and much hard work. The content we see — and rhetorically
combine into an imaginary monolith we call "The Media" – is the result of a mul-
titude of decisions, made by people who have a wide range of motives, opinions,
perspectives, and biases. The decisions these people and institutions make — and the
content that results – affects us in dramatic and profound ways. Indeed, journalism
functions as one of the primary ways in which we all come to understand and

contextualize the world in which we live. Without it, our worldview and under-standing would be limited to those relatively few things we personally experience directly, and which we observe with our physical senses. Instead, our media give us a connection to the broader world, and allow us to be global citizens regardless of geography.

This connection – and the collective knowledge that news media offer – can be a great and unifying thing. But – of course – there is a downside as well, and news can be just as harmful as it is helpful. The news content we consume can both feed and poison, nourish and pollute. Therefore, it is critically important that we – as individuals and as a society – take time to carefully consider the institutions of jour-nalism, the issues and problems that exist, and the opportunities for improvement that can be fostered.

This book is intended to encourage such an analysis by providing a general overview of American journalism. Admittedly this is an enormous topic, and it is well beyond the scope of this book to reasonably offer a comprehensive analysis of every concern facing this nation's press. However, this book does intend to serve as a resource by providing a survey of several critical issues, topics, and challenges that have affected journalism in the past and that continue to affect news media today. Instead of trying to point out ways in which contemporary journalism has lost its way or falls short of some fabled "golden age," it aims to provide perspective and directions for improvement and progress.

In the first part, we consider the role of journalism in America. Chapter 1 presents a brief history of American journalism, and focuses on explaining the four eras of journalism in the United States: the partisan press, penny press, 20th-century press, and the evolving 21st-century news media. After presenting this general overview, Chapter 2 moves into a consideration of press freedoms – or the lack thereof – both historically and in the present day. This chapter, written by Gina Baleria, explores how the concept of a free press has been understood differently over time, considers how funding, audiences, politics, and social constructs have affected the exercise of a free press, and makes suggestions for how the past can inform the way we envision a free press operating in the future. Chapter 3, written by Lois A. Boynton, similarly explores issues of professional practice, and focuses on the legacy of the Hutchins Commission Report and its lasting impact on professional standards, expectations, and goals. The first section concludes with a supplementary essay, in which Dane S. Claussen explores the critically important role of journalism in society.

Part II explores journalistic ethics and objectivity. In Chapter 4, Maggie Jones Patterson explores an ethical dilemma in the age of visually-driven news, and addresses ethical challenges related to photojournalism and photographic depictions of news events. In Chapter 5, the consideration of ethics shifts toward a considera-tion of the appropriateness of journalistic objectivity in an era of politicization, mis-information, and disinformation. E. S. McIntyre dives into the topic by exploring what journalism aspires to be and is capable of, questioning if objectivity should be held up as the gold standard, and ultimately arguing that a model of accuracy and transparency is better suited to the modern world. Chapter 6, by Jason Turcotte and Nicolas Herrandez Florez, addresses unintended negative consequences of objective reporting, and focuses on how efforts to present stories impartially can unwittingly lead to the politicization of news, especially in the context of scientific and medical reporting. This part concludes with an essay, in which Leandra H. Hernández explores other potential harms of journalistic objectivity, and presents instances where society could be better served if journalists act as moral witnesses rather than objective reporters.

The third part addresses problems associated with diversity and representation, which have long plagued the news industry. The section begins with Chapter 7, in which Masudul Biswas explores the role of African American newspapers, and explains how these publications have had an impact both historically and in the present day. Chapter 8 addresses what Meg Heckman has referred to as "the pink ghetto," and the limited professional opportunities and institutional obstacles that have existed for women journalists. In Chapter 9, Jennifer Brannock Cox explores how social justice movements and activism are covered in the American press. The part concludes with an essay by Gwyneth Mellinger, who explores how issues related to diversity in news during the 20th century inform contemporary professional practice.

Part IV turns our attention to the way in which wars and conflicts are covered in news media. Chapter 10 begins the section with an overview of the complicated history of war reporting in the United States, and explains how the relationship between journalists, governments, and society have changed during each war since the founding of the republic. Chapter 11 addresses war propaganda and disinformation, and Oliver Boyd-Barrett focuses on the way in which media are often manipulated to promote fabricated or false pretexts as a justification for war. Chapter 12, by Yiyi Yang, moves into a consideration of the complexities associated with reporting on terrorism. The part concludes with an essay, in which Sean Aday discusses some of the problematic frames typically used in war and military reporting, as well as ways in which such reporting can be improved.

The fifth part brings journalism back to its roots with a consideration of local news, one of the most important but often overlooked types of journalism. Chapter 13 begins this section by discussing the crisis in local news, and Bill Reader explores the extent to which local news has diminished in recent years, as well as the many negative implications of these cuts. Chapter 14 presents one potential solution to the problem, and Antoine Haywood and Victor Pickard suggest public access television as a potential way to help keep communities connected to news that is of critical importance to their lives. In Chapter 15, Allison M. Frisch and Gina Gayle present a different potential solution, and suggest that journalism schools could model themselves after teaching hospitals, and use academic resources to both train students and provide critical information for nearby communities. The section concludes with an essay by John-Erik Koslosky which uses one Pennsylvania county as a case study to demonstrate the issues facing much of the country today.

The sixth part considers fake news. While the term "fake news" has become well known in recent years, there is nothing new about it; fake news has been a problem for as long as journalism has existed. The section begins with Chapter 16, in which Larry J. King explains a history of fake news, and presents ways in which fake news can be defined and classified. Chapter 17 builds on this, and J. D. Ponder also considers both the background of fake news, and potential ways to address the problem. Chapter 18 addresses another angle to the topic, and Danielle R. Mehlman-Brightwell discusses fake news on social media and explains industry and legislative efforts to stem the problem. This part concludes with an essay by Josh Compton, in which he draws on inoculation theory as a frame for effectively combating fake news.

The final, seventh part of the book expands into a discussion of journalistic truth and accuracy during a time of widespread public mistrust of and hostility toward the press. Chapter 19 begins the section, and Kelsey Mesmer and Kaitlin Miller present historical and contemporary anti-press sentiments, and some strategies that journalists and news organizations are now using to mitigate the problem. In Chapter 20, Mirjana Pantic considers how participatory journalism and user engagement can be used to engage the public and rebuild trust. Chapter 21 discusses the impact of harassment on journalists, and Avery E. Holton and Valérie Bélair-Gagnon address how an increased focus on mental health and wellness can help journalists better cope with such pressures. Finally, an essay by Amy Koerber wraps up the part, and addresses how the related topic of predatory publishing further clouds the public's understanding of issues, and can have a detrimental effect on medical and science journalism.

Clearly, there are many challenges facing the news industry. But journalism is as important today as it has ever been. Furthermore, as explored throughout the chapters in this book, many opportunities exist for the future. Journalism is dynamic; it has always been changing, adapting, and adjusting. At times, the going has been difficult. But it is an enduring profession; people want to know about their world, and as such it is important to continually learn from the past, consider the present, and look ahead to the future.

PART I

The Role of Journalism in America

There are few institutions as central to this nation as is journalism. Sometimes called the fourth estate, the press occupies an informal role as one of the central components of American democracy and public life. The term – the fourth estate – is quite old; originally it referred to the European concept that the clergy, nobility, and commoners constituted the three estates of society, and suggested that the press operated as an adjunct to them. Today it more commonly references the press' role alongside the three branches of government. It's no exaggeration. Journalism really is just that important: it's hard to imagine the American Revolution occurring were it not for a lively 18th-century press. The nation's founders recognized just how important the press was to national independence, and enshrined the right to free expression in the Bill of Rights. Indeed – with the possible exception of the Constitution itself and the government it empowers – not much is more American than news media.

Yet journalism is not without its problems, and any consideration of the topic requires a careful reflection of ways in which this critically important institution can serve us all better. To that end, the chapters in Part I provide a fitting introduction to American news media, and some of the most important elements associated with it.

DOI: 10.4324/9781003315605-1

1

A BRIEF HISTORY OF JOURNALISM IN THE UNITED STATES

Hans C. Schmidt

The institution of journalism – as we know it today – may only have existed for a few hundred years. But the idea of sharing news, in some form, is as old as time. People have always wanted to know what was happening, and information about new events and developments has always been shared. For much of human history, however, the distribution of this information was largely an informal process; most stories and gossip could be shared in conversations between friends and acquaintances, and official decrees or proclamations could be announced by government officials or town criers. In small city-states or walled cities, this posed little challenge, and news could travel easily by word of mouth. But, as nations grew to encompass more territory, formal systems for sharing information became necessary. Accomplishing this task was beyond the means of a single voice or emissary. Thus, as nations evolved and societies grew larger, so too did the importance of written news.

The Precursors

Many trace the history of journalism to Roman newsletters, which date back as early as the fifth century BCE. In their early form, these prototypical newsletters were official reports about Senate actions that were handwritten and posted for public viewing. The newsletters were written, at first, by educated slaves; later, the job became more professional and was formalized by Julius Caesar who, shortly after becoming consul in 60 BCE, decreed that Senate proceedings should be published on a daily basis. Thus was born the precursor to a daily newspaper: *Acta Diurna*, or *Daily Acts*.

Over the course of the next 1000 years, societies continued experimenting with different means of sharing news, and eventually English-language news distribution

DOI: 10.4324/9781003315605-2

started to develop as well. At first, English-language newsletters were handwritten and funded by wealthy landowners who wanted to stay apprised of affairs in London. As the popularity of these manuscript-style newsletters grew and demand increased, it became apparent that some level of mass production would be necessary. To this end, in 1622, Nathaniel Butler – who owned a printing press – launched what is generally considered to be the first English-language news publication printed on a regular basis: the *Weekly News*. It took several decades to come up with a fitting name for such a printed news periodical, but by 1670 the term "newspaper" had come into use, in reference to *The Oxford Gazette*, later renamed *The London Gazette*. The *Weekly News* and the *Gazzette* didn't last, but the name did. Newspapers had been born.

The American Colonial Press

The earliest newsletters in the American colonies were published on a sporadic basis. Most settlers were extremely isolated, and so it could easily take several weeks or months for a publisher to accumulate enough news items to warrant printing. Among these was Samuel Green's *The Present State of the New-English Affairs*, which first appeared in 1689 and which consisted of one single page of articles, most of which had previously been published in London periodicals.

The emergence of these publications raised concerns among the colonial authorities in Massachusetts, and starting in 1689 the government began requiring all publishers to apply for "Published by Authority" status. It was in this era – long before the idea of a free press emerged – that the short-lived *Publick Occurrences Both Forreign and Domestick* was born. Unlike its contemporaries, *Publick Occurrences* intended to be published at regular monthly intervals – or more frequently if events warranted – and as such is generally considered to be the first true newspaper of the American colonies. The newspaper, published by Boston's Benjamin Harris, appeared on September 25, 1690 as a four-page publication, with one page left blank. Yet the newspaper lacked governmental sanction, and as such was ordered to cease operations after just one issue.

Facing stiff opposition from colonial authorities and church officials, little opportunity for innovation existed, and it took nearly 15 years before the next attempt was made to publish a newspaper. By 1704, however, conditions had changed just enough to warrant to launch of the North America's first continually published newspaper: *The Boston News-Letter*. With John Campbell as publisher, the paper was successful – at least in that it was not closed – and continued publication long after Campbell's retirement in 1722.

While important to the history of journalism, these groundbreaking publications had many challenges, including limited funding, a small readership, and governmental censorship. Nevertheless, news publishing continued, and more papers were launched. Among them was William Booker's pro-government *The Boston Gazette*, launched in 1719, and James Franklin's *The New-England Courant*, launched in

1721. Franklin was a controversial figure, and he attacked prominent government and church officials and governmental policies. Especially irksome to authorities at the time was his opposition to smallpox vaccination efforts.

This controversy – and the contentious relationship that existed with governmental authorities – presented an opportunity for James' soon-to-be-famous brother, Benjamin, who at the time was nothing more than a publisher's apprentice. The elder Franklin brother had so enraged the authorities that the government declared him no longer printer of the *Courant*. In order to continue publication, and legally evade the order, Franklin formally named his brother, Benjamin, as a replacement publisher. Yet Benjamin Franklin had bigger ambitions, and moved to Philadelphia to step out of his brother's shadow and enter the world of publishing on his own. Together with a business partner, Franklin took over the failing *Pennsylvania Gazette* in 1729; the following year, Franklin became sole publisher.

The paper was highly influential in the American colonies, and, unlike most of its competition, was also a business success. Franklin innovated in a number of ways. For instance, Franklin's *Gazette* was the first to print a newspaper cartoon: the famous "Join or Die" woodcut. In order to encourage support for strengthening colonial defenses and preparing for a potential war with the French in 1754 he printed a cartoon showing a snake cut into eight pieces – each representing a colony – along with the caption "Join or Die." The insinuation was clear: the colonies needed to unite in common defense. Both the cartoon and the caption resonated with the public, and soon became famous – an 18th-century meme – and were republished in other papers throughout the colonies.

The cartoon's influence was not confined to the 1750s. The cartoon snake resurfaced 11 years later to rally Americans against the British Stamp Act, and then again in the runup to the Revolution. Its appearance varied; at one point it appeared united, as one complete snake, and then eventually both coiled and uncoiled. In its uncoiled form, it was an inspiration for the first Continental Navy ensign, and in its coiled form it was the inspiration for the Gadsden Flag, adopted for use by the Continental Marines starting in 1775.

During this pre-revolution time, the newspaper industry was also expanding in other cities along the east coast. The first newspaper in New York – the decidedly pro-British *New York Gazette* – had been established as early as 1725 by William Bradford. Among his notable competition was John Peter Zenger, who launched the anti-British *New-York Weekly Journal* in 1733, and played a key role in influencing future press rights.

After publishing an article that drew attention to the corrupt administration of colonial Governor William Crosby, Zenger was imprisoned, and in 1734 he was charged with seditious libel. The charge was a serious one. Legal precedent at the time held that printing any criticism of government officials – even if the criticism was based on fact – was criminal behavior. In his defense, lawyer Andrew Hamilton admitted that Zenger had published the allegedly libelous articles, but argued that the law should be interpreted to mean that content was libelous only if it was untrue, and that there was nothing wrong about factually exposing corruption.

It was a risky argument to make, but the jury agreed that truth – even if critical of government – was not seditious or libelous if its publication was justifiable and in the public's interest. It was the first such decision in known history and set the precedent for future constitutionally guaranteed rights to a free press.

The Divisive Press and the Early Days of the United States

After the Revolutionary War, the precarious ties between the former colonies were tested, and political fighting escalated to new levels. This was reflected in the press. The power of the press to influence public opinion was recognized, and, through the 1780s, most newspapers became heavily affiliated with regional political platforms. Additionally, the newly formed political parties launched their own newspapers, in which they published extensive commentary and attacks on political rivals.

Such fierce attacks and the dramatic politicization and polarization of the young Republic's newspapers no doubt contributed, in part, to the passage of the Alien and Sedition Acts in 1798. The new legislation was a wholesale attack on the idea of a free press – even though it was passed into law by some of the same individuals who had, just a few years earlier, been signatories of the Constitution. The law stated that written or spoken content that was found to contain "false," "scandalous," or "malicious" statements, or any statements against a branch the US government, would be subject to up to two years' imprisonment and a $2000 fine.

The Alien and Sedition Acts were so broad that they, inevitably, led to the imprisonment of outspoken newspaper publishers. However, they were also politically controversial, and when Thomas Jefferson assumed the Presidency following the election in 1800, he allowed most components of the legislation to expire and issued pardons to some individuals who had been convicted.

After this, the news industry simply became even more politically partisan. This was due, in no small part, to the steady revenue stream that came from aligning with a party. Some prominent politicians – including some of the nation's founding fathers – even went so far as to start their own newspapers. Others shamelessly used government funds to finance the operations of a loyal publication.

The political parties made full use of partisan newspapers, and used them to plant stories, secure endorsements for party-backed candidates, engineer phony grassroots support, attack politicians and their families, and publish distorted and untrue reports. But, aside from such political attacks, most of the news was stale; actual reporting was very uncommon, and publishers largely relied on news items provided by friendly politicians to fill their pages, offering little variety and almost no news of local interest.

This is not to say that every news operation was politically partisan. There were outliers. For instance, there were a few religious papers, literary newspapers, commercial newspapers, and, starting with *The Emancipator* in 1820, some abolitionist newspapers which crusaded to end slavery.

The Penny Press and Emerging Mass Media

In 1800, the population of the US was slightly above 5 million; by 1830, it had increased to nearly 13 million. Cities were growing, and the nation was expanding westward. Education was improving, and more people were learning to read. Mail delivery was becoming faster and more reliable, and new mechanized printing technologies were being developed. This combination of factors made possible the idea of reducing the price of newspapers.

What was the magic price-point? One cent.

Nevertheless, figuring out a business model that would sustain such a low price was difficult, especially considering that the typical newspaper in the 1820s cost six times as much. Most publishers balked at the idea of selling a newspaper so inexpensively. Those who wanted to innovate, however, came to understand that the only way to drive the price down so low would be by massively increasing the readership. To do that, newspapers would need to publish content that was interesting and useful to common folk, and not just those engaged in political life.

While a few publishers briefly experimented with cheap papers, Benjamin Day was the first to figure it out in a sustainable way. Aptly named *The Sun* and carrying to motto of "It Shines for All," Day's publication first appeared in 1833 in New York at the price of one cent per issue. Day had a vision and understood mass media – a concept that hadn't really yet developed – in a way that his competitors did not. Instead of catering to the affluent and politically-connected elites – as did the six-cent competitors of the time – Day aimed to create content for the masses of everyday and working-class people. Its columns were replete with local news, including police and crime reports, as well as gossip. The model worked, and by the end of the decade *The Sun* was New York's largest newspaper, with a daily circulation of about 130,000. Before long other publications modeled after *The Sun* were launched in New York, Philadelphia, Boston, and other large East Coast cities.

The next leap forward came with James Gordon Bennet's launch of *The New York Herald* in 1835. Priced at one penny at first (later increased to two cents). Bennett entered a crowded field; in 1835 there were 15 daily papers, 11 semi-weeklies, and 31 weeklies in New York. But Bennett differentiated himself, publishing extensive police reports, court news, scandal, attacks on religion, and the nation's first daily financial reports of the Wall Street stock market. A constant innovator, he focused on timeliness to an unprecedented extent, employing correspondents and making use of faster steamships for transatlantic news. Along with his penny paper rivals, he also expanded advertising and innovated with new distribution methods, employing newsboys to hawk the newspapers on street corners throughout the city.

Such newspapers were overwhelmingly popular; the penny press model soon came to dominate the news market in most major cities, and the news industry grew by leaps and bounds during the second half of the 19th century.

Pulitzer, Hearst, and the Late 19th-Century Press

Journalism in America was on the move during the later decades of the 19th century. Preferences had changed; the public had developed a thirst for exciting, dramatic, up-to-date news, and newspapers were delivering just that. News was faster than ever, largely due to the invention of the telegraph and the formation of press associations like the Associated Press that allowed content to be shared between geographically dispersed publications.

It was in this era that Joseph Pulitzer would make his mark. Born in Hungary, Pulitzer was recruited to emigrate to the United States to fight for the Union in the Civil War. He arrived in 1864, and joined a cavalry unit. After the war, Pulitzer began his new life in America. It was not an easy life; he spoke little English, and worked in various jobs before eventually moving to St. Louis, then the edge of the western frontier, where he began working as a journalist. Pulitzer was talented, and by the age of 25, he was named publisher of the *St. Louis Post-Dispatch*, of which he soon became owner. As publisher and owner, Pulitzer began experimenting with new editorial techniques, using his newspaper to champion the everyday person and exposing corruption. Pulitzer's populist newspaper model succeeded, and in 1883 Pulitzer traveled back to New York. There, he purchased the struggling newspaper *The World*, which at the time had a circulation of less than 10,000.

Pulitzer remade *The World* in the image of the *St. Louis Post-Dispatch*; he mixed crusades against corruption and monopolies with sensational features, staged news stunts, and made use of illustrations and cartoons, which had been absent from most of the competition. It was a paper with a mission, as outlined in Pulitzer's first editorial as *The World*'s owner:

> There is room in this great and growing city for a journal that is not only cheap, but bright, not only bright but large, not only large but truly democratic – dedicated to the cause of the people rather than that of purse-potentates – devoted more to the news of the New than the Old World – that will expose all fraud and sham, fight all public evils and abuses – that will serve and battle for the people with earnest sincerity.

The model was tremendously successful; by the end of the century, *The World* had a circulation exceeding 600,000 and had established itself as the most-read newspaper in the country.

Still, Pulitzer faced competition, the sternest of which came from William Randolph Hearst, who purchased the *New York Journal* in 1896 after successfully running the family-owned *San Francisco Examiner*. The rivalry was personal; the *Journal* had been founded by Pulitzer's brother, Albert. With a sizeable inheritance to spend – his father was a mining tycoon – Hearst quickly attacked the leading competition, hiring many of Pulitzer's best staffers, and even giving out promotional copies of his paper for free. Where Pulitzer built a legacy, Hearst built a media empire, expanding with newspapers in numerous cities across the country, launching magazines, a newsreel service, and an enduring syndicate business.

As a result, toward the end of the century Pulitzer and Hearst became locked in a circulation war. In a quest to gain readers at any cost, both papers devolved into the worst practices of yellow journalism, replete with sensationalized and even fabricated news. Pulitzer's paper eventually stepped back from the sensationalism, and towards the end of Pulitzer's life he returned *The World* to its original focus on improving social conditions, funded endowments to establish the Columbia School of Journalism and the Pulitzer Prizes, and worked to improve the overall professionalism of journalism.

The Birth of 20th-Century Journalism

The excesses of the gilded age and turn-of-the-century journalism – characterized by yellow journalism – were not to last. By the beginning of the 20th century, newspapers were very popular, but even Joseph Pulitzer was starting to recognize the danger of continuing down the path of sensational populism.

Similarly, public preferences were starting to shift toward a more responsible and respectable form of journalism, and the style of reporting that was exemplified by *The New York Times*. The *Times* had been in existence for decades – it had first appeared in print as the *New-York Daily Times* on September 18, 1851 – and was known for its focus on information, presenting facts, and dispassionate, impersonal reporting. After the death of its founding editor Henry Jarvis Raymond, however, the paper dwindled in popularity and became unprofitable. Thus, an opportunity existed when Adolph Ochs – who owned the *Chattanooga Times* – came to New York. Ochs formed a corporation and purchased the *New-York Times* in 1896. Yet Ochs, and the *Times*, faced a challenging situation. The newspaper was respectable, but it was also struggling. It was still the peak of the yellow journalism era, sensationalism was popular, and there was no chance that Ochs and the *Times* could beat Pulitzer and Hearst at their own game.

Instead, Ochs doubled down on the model of respectability and serious reporting, in the hopes that his competing model for news would be seen as a viable alternative. Ochs' editorial statement, published when he assumed control of the *Times*, is famous today, and in it he outlined his plan "to give the news impartially, without fear or favor" in a concise and dignified fashion. Soon thereafter, he also adopted the newspaper's lasting motto: "All the News That's Fit to Print."

The motto was, largely, aspirational. But it also identified a clear difference between the *Times* and its yellow competitors: while competing newspapers were playing up salacious stories, exaggeration, lurid crime, scandals, and sensationalism, the *Times* would provide a dignified forum for the presentation of factual information.

It proved an uphill battle: in 1896, when Ochs took over the *Times*, his paper's circulation was inconsequential in comparison to his competitors: *The New York Times* sold just 9,000 copies daily, compared to *The World* and the *Journal*, which boasted daily circulations of 600,000 and 430,000 respectively. But the *Times* did slowly gain more readers, and when, two years later, the price was dropped from three cents per issue to one cent, circulation shot up; Ochs hit the sweet spot of giving the public the news content they increasingly wanted, at a price that they were willing to pay. Circulation tripled within a year, and by 1900 the *Times* had a daily circulation of 82,000.

The New York Times model of news gathering had become a new professional standard, and – while it took some time for the public to fully embrace the new model for journalism – it was one that was lasting. Today, *The New York Times* is as, or more, popular than ever, while the news titans of those early years – *The World* and the *New York Journal* – have long since ceased publication.

The Rise of Broadcast News

Before 1920, news was synonymous with print. This changed with radio. The technology itself had been around for decades; wireless telegraph transmission was demonstrated in 1895, and an experimental broadcast of music and voice occurred just 11 years later. Yet, it was not until 1920 that the nation's first radio station, KDKA in Pittsburgh, received a license to operate as a commercial broadcaster. When the station first went on the air, in November of that year, what was the very first type of content it broadcast? News. Specifically, the inaugural broadcast featured the results of that year's presidential election.

At first, radio stations relied on newspapers for content. But, eventually, as radio networks grew in size and stature, they began experimenting with their own, independent news-gathering operations. Such operations rose in prominence during World War II, as radio worked to meet the public's demand for information. This expansion of broadcast news continued in the postwar years, when American news media – like much in the country during that time – experienced a burst of growth. Some of the biggest opportunities were in a new medium: television.

The technology had been in existence in a functional but rudimentary form since 1939. But, with the conclusion of World War II, television took off. By the end of the 1950s, nearly 90% of American households owned a television set, and fledgling television broadcasters, stations, and networks began experimenting with news programs. Early television news programs were short – just 15 minutes per day – and were funded directly by sponsoring companies for whom the shows were named, leading to awkward program titles like *Camel News Caravan*, funded – of course – by Camel cigarettes.

Also, because television broadcast over the public airwaves, the Federal Communications Commission (FCC) had the ability to impose regulations, including the fairness doctrine, which required broadcasters to give equal airtime to opposing viewpoints and prohibited broadcasters from advocating for any one point of view.

The television news business was expensive, but networks pressed ahead nevertheless. It did not hurt the fledgling TV news operations that so much was happening in the world. The nation was in love with their new TVs, and Americans found gripping coverage of the Army–McCarthy hearings, the Korean War, and the Vietnam War. Americans watched Martin Luther King deliver now-famous speeches, and were glued to televised coverage of President John F. Kennedy's assassination. Later there was the space race, and the first moon landing – broadcast on live TV to viewers back on Planet Earth. The groundbreaking broadcasts of these events remain breathtaking to this day, and the public developed a new desire to see important events happening, live, for themselves and from their living rooms.

Before long, the public was hooked on visually-driven TV news. Networks responded, and began developing longer news programs, new formats, and better-produced shows. Further, the Corporation for Public Broadcasting was established as a not-for-profit news alternative. The result was a growing presence of news in society. Most of that news was relatively uncontroversial. The fairness doctrine meant that TV news presented a balance of perspectives. This was the era of true mass media, and attracting massive audiences – and the ensuing advertising revenue – was the name of the game. If the goal was to build as large an audience as possible, then it only made sense to create content that most would not find offensive, troublesome, or alienating.

While the push for balanced coverage – sometimes called the period of "great consensus" – did at times created false equivalencies, much important and even risky journalism emerged during this era. Notably, reporting during the Vietnam War played a critical role in exposing how misguided and mismanaged the war had become. Investigative reporting that uncovered and exposed the Watergate scandal led to the resignation of President Richard Nixon and inspired a generation – or more – of journalists to come. Coverage of events related to the Civil Rights Movement helped to bring public attention to social inequities.

From a business perspective, the news industry did exceptionally well through the middle decades of the 20th century. Further, newspapers were increasingly forming large chains and media conglomerates, which were very profitable. The Gannett newspaper chain, for instance, went public in 1967 and earned a profit every single quarter for 18 years, with a 21% average rate of return (Bagdikian, 2004). So, too, in radio and television – the dominant electronic medium – where stations were increasingly being purchased by conglomerates.

Meanwhile, though, changes were afoot that would completely change the industry. In 1987, the FCC repealed the fairness doctrine, giving broadcasters free rein to pursue political agendas. This, combined with the rollout of cable television, upended the traditional model of broadcasting and offered new opportunities for specialized stations and content. The stage was set for the birth of cable news and the 24/7 news environment. News was never to be the same.

Cable TV, the Web, and the Never-Ending News Cycle

The Cable News Network – CNN – launched by Ted Turner on June 1, 1980 was the first news operation to offer nonstop news, all day, every day. The idea was revolutionary for a TV landscape in which daily broadcast news programming typically consisted of comparatively short morning and evening network and local news programs.

Faced by the staggering expenses associated with providing continuous coverage and content, it took five years for the network to finally turn a profit. But it continued growing and by the end of the 1980s, CNN was a household name, reaching 53 million homes in the US, broadcasting internationally, and boasting news-gathering operations as large or larger than established competitors in the networks and print (Whittemore, 1990). If there was any question regarding cable news' staying power, the proof came in the 1991 Gulf War. The American public was glued to their televisions as they watched images of guided missiles hitting targets, tanks rolling across the desert, fighter jets screaming down the runway, and warships launching naval artillery barrages. Ratings soared.

With higher ratings and higher profits came competition, and 1996 saw the launch of two competitors for CNN: Fox News and MSNBC. Fox's model was clear from the start: it would copy talk radio, and would save money by replacing CNN-style on-location coverage with extensive commentary, typically infused with a conservative or pro-Republican ideology. MSNBC launched with a model that aimed to combine the news-gathering operations of NBC with a commentary-heavy programming lineup. More progressive-leaning than Fox News, MSNBC was not, however, initially intended to be the liberal anti-Fox cable channel. But, over time – as MSNBC struggled to find its audience – the network settled on doing just that: if Fox was attracting an audience on the political right, MSNBC would focus on an audience to the political left.

Thus began a new move toward audience segmentation. While national news media since World War II had prioritized attracting the largest audience possible with middle-of-the-road content, cable quickly upended this model and created an opportunity to offer a different product to different people: news could now be specifically targeted toward different preferences and viewpoints. While such segmented channels would not deliver as massive an audience to advertisers, they offered something different: the promise that those who were in the audience had some shared commonalities. Thus, sponsors could use segmented media to target their advertising toward demographic groups that were most interested in the products or services that were being sold.

The new business model worked in cable. And, in the years to follow, it would prove to work even better on the web.

While the internet had existed in some sense since 1969, albeit just for government and research purposes, and had been accessible to tech-savvy private individuals since the late 1970s, online connectivity really started to enter the mainstream after the launch of the World Wide Web and the release of the first publicly available web browser, Mosaic, in 1993. The web's user-friendly graphics-based interface allowed for easy use. Furthermore, with the web, barriers to entry for publishers were dramatically lessened. Before the web, newspapers and magazines required a complicated manufacturing and distribution system. Television operations were similarly expensive. With the web, however, a news organization could be started relatively inexpensively. With the reduced cost of web publishing, websites could be launched that would cater to narrower and narrower segments of the population, and gear content toward very specific demographic groups.

Yet, even as upstart online news operations launched and found success, traditional news organizations remained unconvinced about the importance of the new medium, and were hesitant to invest resources in new digital platforms. Additionally, legacy news organizations had earned unrealistically high profits for decades, and had done so by prioritizing short-term profit over long-term investments. As such, they were unprepared when public preferences and advertising revenue started shifting from print to digital. Additionally, and importantly, the national political landscape was also becoming increasingly divisive; people were aligning with political movements and becoming less and less interested in content that did not directly reflect their worldview.

The combination of these factors proved painful to the news industry overall, and lethal to many news organizations. The newspaper industry was hit especially hard. Between 2005 – the industry's all-time most profitable year – and 2010, revenue was in freefall, dropping 40% in just five years (Pew Research Center, 2021). News organizations responded by cutting budgets and laying off staff. The result was a downward spiral: declining circulation led to lower revenue, which led to budget cuts, which led to reduced news content and quality, which, in turn, led to the further loss of readers.

Thousands of newspapers closed or ceased publication.

Eventually, the industry started to adapt, and many news organizations have now made a successful digital transition. Notably, *The New York Times* boasts a growing readership and increasing subscriptions. *The Wall Street Journal* and *The Washington Post* also have maintained or grown their presence and news operations. But these are elite news media. The future of smaller news organizations is much less certain.

Clearly, times are changing; one era of news is ending, and another is dawning. These changes to the world of journalism are just as profound today as they were during the time of Benjamin Franklin, Benjamin Day, Joseph Pulitzer and Adolph Ochs.

Certainly, this next era of journalism will be a digital one. More importantly, it will most likely be an era characterized by niche news content and micro-segmentation. And it will likely be an era of nearly continual innovation and change. Yet the fact that contemporary journalism is in a state of flux should come as no surprise. Journalism has always faced challenges and threats – whether from censorship, financial pressures, or technological limitations – and it has always needed to adapt – to new governments, social trends, urbanization, industrialization, and formats. And adapt it has.

Of course, many questions exist as we look toward the future. Will people pay for journalism again? Will advertising return? Will new funding models be developed? Will journalism become a not-for-profit enterprise? Will journalism be guided by ideals of objectivity, advocacy, or partisanship? Will reporting become automated? Is citizen journalism the future?

Will people care?

Many of these questions are difficult, if not impossible, to answer. But the last question – will people care? – does have an answer: yes. For all our cynicism, people still want to know what is happening in the world. People care today, just as people have always cared. Thousands of years ago people cared enough to post reports in public squares, and copy pages by hand. Hundreds of years ago people cared enough to haul printing presses to far-flung continents on sailing ships. People cared enough to lay telegraph cables across vast oceans. People cared enough about the news to send satellites into orbit to deliver it faster. And, notably, people still care enough about news to want to limit it, to censor it, and to prevent its spread.

And as long as people care – which they will – journalism will continue to develop and evolve to meet the needs of the future.

References

Bagdikian, B. H. (2004). *The new media monopoly: A completely revised and updated edition with seven new chapters*. Beacon Press.

Pew Research Center. (2021, June 29). *Newspaper fact sheet*. https://www.pewresearch.org/journalism/fact-sheet/newspapers/

Whittemore, H. (1990). *CNN, the inside story*. Little, Brown.

2

THE FREE PRESS

A Confusing History and Uncertain Future

Gina Baleria

When we think of a free press today, we may think of the intrepid journalist, tasked with holding power to account, bringing issues to light for the public, and asking tough questions to get at a story. We may also think of an information seeker or the cable news talk show host stoking fear or spouting opinions that may – or may not – be supported by facts. The concept of a free press may also bring to mind the citizen journalist sharing content on social media, circumventing gatekeepers at so-called traditional media outlets, and perhaps sharing a perspective not generally seen in daily news. Or, we may expect news outlets to cover local stories that inform us and help us engage with our communities.

Such expectations for the news media of today can trace their roots to the late 18th century, when the Constitution and Bill of Rights – which included language protecting press freedom – were passed and ratified. But in many ways, the news media of today looks very different from the press that existed on September 25, 1789.

The Press of the Late 1700s

One major difference between the press of the 1790s and today is that the only form of mass media then involved paper. In a world without TV, digital, or social media, people used printing presses to create and distribute pamphlets, newspapers, and newsletters. The technological advances that made timely news gathering, content creation, and distribution easier and more streamlined had not yet been invented. Thus, the press of the late 18th century did not have the technology to get information out quickly, follow breaking news, or communicate immediately across distance.

More importantly, content considered news was somewhat different. 18th-century newspapers often published reprints of news from papers in London or other cities; literary entries; opinion, analysis, and propaganda about issues of the day; letters and correspondence; information gleaned from people arriving by ship

DOI: 10.4324/9781003315605-3

from Europe; and even gossip. Timeliness was not a priority. Indeed, much information was weeks or months old by the time it was published.

Newspapers were often published by one person, who served as publisher, writer, printer, and content curator. That person may or may not have prioritized what we've come to know as journalistic integrity, and news reporters were not yet a common feature of the press.

Press outlets of the late 18th century were mostly funded by wealthy, influential subscribers and patrons who often had specific political leanings. Thus, content would have focused on topics and perspectives of interest to this audience. In larger towns, content likely took a side on political issues. The press the framers were familiar with provided "a forum for the intense, usually acrimonious discussion of… issues and personalities" (Clark, 2005, p. 84).

Bias was explicit and expected. The idea of an "objective" journalist gathering news from all relevant sides was not to become standard (for better and worse) until the 20th century. While this partisan content of the late 18th and early 19th centuries could be problematic, it also offered elite US citizens a way to learn more about their own perspectives and gain understanding of other perspectives. This is different from today, when we often consume only the perspective with which we agree.

The Constitutional Framers and "the Press"

What, then, did the framers of the Constitution and Bill of Rights envision when they gave protections to "the press" – the only industry given any protections in the US founding documents?

Many references to "the press" at that time referred to the actual mechanism of printing newspapers – referencing the ability to disseminate information. But we also see increasing references to the press as playing a role in government scrutiny based on quotes from thinkers of the day, whose perspective was that of a people seeking to get out from under the thumb of a colonial power and resist the tyranny they felt they experienced as a British colony.

The impetus to protect "the press" likely came in part from efforts by the Crown to impose licenses on papers, which, in essence, amounted to censorship, because licenses would only be granted to publications friendly to Crown interests. In addition, the framers also saw newspapers as providing a forum for debate and discussion, making the press a valuable tool for grappling with policy debates and perspectives.

Many Constitutional framers spoke in support of the press, including Benjamin Franklin, John Adams, James Madison, George Mason, Alexander Hamilton, and Thomas Jefferson, who said, "Our liberty depends on the freedom of the press, and that cannot be limited without being lost" (Jefferson, 1606–1827).

Jefferson and others saw the press as an "agent" of the people; a way for "citizens" to have their voices heard by those in power – an important component of democracy.

> I am… for freedom of the press, and against all violations of the constitution to silence by force and not by reason the complaints or criticisms, just or

unjust, of our citizens against the conduct of their agents… Our first object should therefore be, to leave open to (them) all the avenues to truth. The most effectual hitherto found, is the freedom of the press.

(Jefferson, 1606–1827)

This concept is reflected in an early draft of the First Amendment, written by James Madison, which read, "The people shall not be deprived or abridged of their right to speak, or to publish their sentiments; and the freedom of the press, as one of the great bulwarks of liberty, shall be inviolable" (Annals of Congress, 1789).

Adams and others linked a free press to national security. Wrote Adams, "The liberty of the press is essential to the security of the state" (Adams, 1780). And George Mason wrote that the press, "can never be restrained but by despotic governments" (Mason, 1776).

These quotes illustrate that one view of the press at the time the US Constitution was written revolved around seeking and printing "the truth" and ensuring an unfettered voice that represented and spoke to "the people." As to exactly who was included in "the people" in late-18th-century US, it was not inclusive. "The people" was primarily limited to landowning, white men. Women were not given any rights in the US Constitution; Blacks were referred to as not "free" and deemed three-fifths of a person; and indigenous people were listed alongside foreign nations when discussing commerce, were treated as *other*, and thus not included in "the people."

We also know the press was seen as contentious, and even those generally supportive of a free press sometimes expressed frustration.

Said Jefferson: "Nothing can now be believed which is seen in a newspaper. Truth itself becomes suspicious by being put into that polluted vehicle" (Jefferson, 1606–1827).

This sentiment is also heard today among those who dislike coverage focused on their actions and activities. But, then and now, cries of fake news often come in an effort to obfuscate and discredit, as journalists engage in strong journalism and come closer to the truth.

But, even in the late 18th and early 19th centuries, an imperfect press garnered support as an important instrument to the persistence of democracy. Said First Amendment author James Madison, "To the press alone, chequered as it is with abuses, the world is indebted for all the triumphs which have been gained by reason and humanity over error and oppression" (Madison, 1723–1859).

These quotes illustrate that the tensions that exist today are not new, indicating the enduring importance of the First Amendment to press protection.

What Does "The Press" Mean?

There is an open question as to what exactly the framers meant by the word "press." As discussed above, there are indications that "press" referred simply to the apparatus used to print pamphlets and newspapers, and perhaps the person who managed that printing press – i.e. the publisher (Clark, 2005) – rather than the journalism profession. Indeed, many historians believe "freedom of the press" may simply have been a response to England's earlier efforts to license – and thus censor – newspapers as a way to control content, and a warning to Congress to avoid future action that could constitute prior restraint or censorship.

This perspective is illustrated in an oft-cited quote from 18th-century English Jurist William Blackstone (1770), whose writings on common law influenced many framers: "The liberty of the press is indeed essential to the nature of a free state; but this consists in laying no *previous* restraints upon publications, and not in freedom from censure for criminal matter when published."

We see echoes of this sentiment in discussions today over whether and why content should be removed or people's accounts suspended on social media. These discussions often center around how and whether to apply the First Amendment, and reveal both astute analysis and a lack of understanding about how the First Amendment works.

However, by the late 1700s, there was some use of "the press" to refer to doing journalism, and the idea of the press as a watchdog that holds power to account and seeks to enlighten the public. Journalism was coming to be seen as "an institution of moral significance" (Clark, 2005, p. 63). Thus, by the time the Bill of Rights was drafted, some framers had begun to view the press as not just as a mechanical device, but an "institution" that was "organized" and served a function in a democracy.

Indeed, writings of the time indicate that the framers saw the press as a conduit and provider of knowledge to the public. For example, James Madison wrote, "Knowledge will forever govern ignorance; and a people who mean to be their own governors must arm themselves with the power which knowledge gives" (Madison, 1723–1859). That power included the institutional "press."

Thomas Jefferson saw the press as an "avenue of truth" that could prevent "violations of the Constitution" (Jefferson, 1606–1827) and thus in need of constitutional protection.

While the US Supreme Court has tended to treat press and speech as one in rulings involving the First Amendment, some scholars argue that the framers listed "speech" and "press" separately, because they intended the two concepts to be distinct (Campbell, 2017; Shiffrin, 2016; West, 2010).

No matter what the framers intended, the fact is that legal and journalistic landscapes have evolved, and case law has sent the concept of Freedom of the Press in a specific direction. It is important for us to both understand our journalistic and constitutional history, as well as consider how journalism can best serve the public interest moving forward and how the courts can protect it.

The Court's First Test of Freedom of the Press

Though "the press" is explicitly named in the First Amendment as distinct from speech, religion, assembly, and redress of grievances, the courts – in particular, the

US Supreme Court – have lumped "the press" with "speech" and generally have not given "the press" any special protections when considering First Amendment cases.

Some scholars say this trend is problematic, given the explicit mentions of "the press" in early drafts of the First Amendment. They argue streamlining the First Amendment to say "Freedom of Speech, or of the press" may have made sense to those at the time who had a common language about the meanings of "press" and "speech," but it has led to a loss of distinction between the two concepts today.

In addition, the explicitly named "freedom… of the press" faced its first challenge just seven years after the Bill of Rights was ratified. At that point, Federalists controlled all three branches of government and passed the Alien & Sedition Acts of 1798. In addition to allowing deportation of foreigners and limiting immigrant voting rights, one of these four laws prohibited public criticism of government, including "writing, printing, uttering or publishing any false, scandalous and malicious writing… against the government of the United States" (National Archives, n.d.). This law took direct aim at several First Amendment protections, including the right to peaceably assemble, seek redress of grievances, and of course free speech and a free press.

Under the Sedition Act, nearly two dozen news editors were imprisoned, all from the opposing Democrat-Republican party. However, no case was ever appealed to the Supreme Court, because its role in judicial review was not yet established. In its absence, multiple lower courts upheld the Alien and Sedition laws as constitutional. Only when Thomas Jefferson followed John Adams as president did he release jailed editors and convince Congress to let the acts expire in 1801. No federal court precedent was set.

The Evolution of the First Amendment, and from the "Press" to the "News Media"

Throughout the 19th century, the audience and profit motives of the burgeoning news industry changed, leading to shifts in what was covered and how. At the same time, courts were nearly silent on the issue of press freedom. The US Supreme Court did not take any cases involving Freedom of Speech or the Press during the 19th century. And, at the state level, courts were more apt to limit and curtail press and speech freedoms than protect them.

Early-19th-century court and legislative restrictions on speech and the press focused largely on speeches and writings that challenged government and industry, including content that encouraged unionization and workers' rights or criticized the government during wartime. Especially targeted were anti-slavery, abolitionist publications, often in Southern states.

At the same time, mainstream newspapers were evolving. In the early 19th century, the political calculus of existing publications had shifted from being pro- or anti-royalist to focus on the politics of the new nation, prompting many papers to express allegiance to either the Federalists or Democratic-Republicans, the two political parties of the day.

But by the 1830s, both technology and the US cultural landscape had shifted. Societally, more immigrants were arriving, many from countries in Europe beyond England, and these new Americans sought different information than readers in past decades. At the same time, news publishers began hiring reporters to gather or cover news. Content in mainstream newspapers shifted from political and business-oriented to happenings within a community, as news publishers sought to give their growing and changing audience what it wanted. Newspapers began covering things like crime, trials, and fires more often. But, as with the publishers of decades earlier, they still included gossip. It was these papers that laid the groundwork for the journalism that took hold in the 20th and early 21st centuries.

In addition to cultural and societal shifts came new technologies, such as the steam printing press, which allowed for cheaper, faster printing; and the camera, which, along with drawings, led to more visuals in newspapers. Mass printing led to the penny press era, when cheaper prices allowed more people to buy a newspaper every day.

Just a few years later, the telegraph allowed for instant transmission of messages over long distances, impacting news coverage in the 1840s the way Twitter changed the game in the 2000s. Thus, breaking news began. By the late 19th century, the typewriter allowed for faster writing of stories, and the telephone allowed reporters to reach sources much more quickly. Through all this, national case law involving Freedom of the Press and Speech remained nonexistent.

The Modern First Amendment and the "Objective" Journalist

Though 19th-century developments laid the groundwork for what we consider modern mainstream journalism, it was not until the 20th century that journalism and First Amendment law familiar to us today began to take shape.

By the late 19th century, the penny press had given way to yellow journalism, in which newspapers published more and more sensational content to sell papers. The profit motive began to outweigh the journalistic imperative.

Partially in response, and partially in tandem with developments in science, the 20th century brought the dawn of the muckrakers, investigative journalists focused on precision, holding power to account, and engaging in an objective journalistic process inspired by the scientific method. While journalists in this period shined light on societal ills and prompted those in power to address major issues, the muckrakers' approach inadvertently led to a misnomer that persisted and dogged journalism for the next 100+ years: the "objective journalist."

The muckrakers applied an objective process to their work, because they recognized no human being could be objective. We are, by nature, biased. However, the general public conflated the process with the person and began identifying journalists as objective, neutral arbiters of information in society.

While objectivity took hold at mainstream outlets, including popular magazines and daily newspapers, alternative press outlets continued doing what we now call advocacy or social justice journalism. But some began questioning any outlet that did not adhere to the goal of presenting "objective" news.

First Amendment Law Takes Shape

The first Freedom of Speech and Press case did not come before the high court until 1907, 116 years after the Bill of Rights was ratified. From 1907 to 1931, press and speech lost, as the Supreme Court upheld convictions, injunctions, and limits time after time, including upholding a second Sedition Act, which came before the court in 1918.

Finally, in 1931, in *Near v. Minnesota*, the high court ruled in favor of speech and the press, invalidating an injunction against a newspaper, because it amounted to censorship and prior restraint, which are prohibited under the First Amendment. Then, in 1936, in *Grosjean v. American Press Co.*, the court invalidated a tax levied on a newspaper, saying taxes might limit circulation of information in violation of the First Amendment. But it was not all smooth sailing. In 1938, the court banned *Life* magazine for publishing "indecent" content. That content? Images from a public health film entitled, "The Birth of a Baby."

One major feature of these Supreme Court decisions is that justices conflated speech and press, and so press protections were subsumed by protections involving speech. Thus today, there are in essence no distinct protections for "the press" guaranteed by the federal courts. There are some laws at the state level protecting journalists from things like newsroom searches and seizures, and forced disclosure of anonymous sources, but these laws may not apply at the federal level and have not been guaranteed by the US Supreme Court. A different composition of lawmakers in a given state could pass laws doing away with press protections. Supreme Court rulings explicitly protecting "the press" could provide increased stability and consistency.

Instead, Supreme Court decisions have only added to the debate about what the framers meant by "the press." In their writings, Supreme Court justices have acknowledged the special role of the press, focusing on its functions as a check on government activities and informer of the public. In *Branzburg v. Hayes*, Justice Byron R. White acknowledged, "news gathering is not without its First Amendment protections," and "without some protection for seeking out the news, freedom of the press could be eviscerated" (*Branzburg v. Hayes*, 1972), but this sentiment was not paired with a favorable ruling. In his dissent in *Citizens United v. Federal Elections Commission*, Justice John Paul Stevens argued that the First Amendment does presume some "identity-based distinctions," so we do not "treat a local nonprofit news outlet exactly the same as General Motors" (Stevens, 2010). But these acknowledgements have not yet led the high court to rule distinctly on press grounds. Rather, each ruling on a press case is couched in terms of speech.

While the prevailing wisdom is that case law is now too established to untangle and defining the press may be too confining in the current digital media landscape – in which anyone may lay claim to the moniker of journalist or the act of doing journalism – some argue that the framers listed "the press" separately for a reason (Campbell, 2017; Shiffrin, 2016; West, 2010). In an article for the *California Law Review*, Sonja R. West (2010) wrote that justices need to consider an understanding of the Press Clause as distinct from speech, as a way to protect and defend journalism.

> This marginalization of the Press Clause is contrary to both the clear meaning of the words and to a common intuition that there does exist a "press" that performs a special role in our democracy... Unlike other speakers, the press dedicates significant time, resources, and expertise to the journalistic missions of checking the government and informing the citizenry on matters of public concern. While individual speakers might, at times, act in "press-like" ways, only the press is consistently devoted to these endeavors, which at their core strengthen our democracy.
>
> *(p. 1025)*

West points out that states have been able to define "the press" to issue press passes, apply shield laws, determine access rights, and the like, but these protections do not exist at the federal level. In addition, members of "the press" currently have no federal protections against prosecution for actions taken while engaging in essential news-gathering activities, such as going undercover or engaging in minor deception or surreptitious recording. Carving out press protections in the area of news-gathering, argues West, can define and make distinct the Press Clause.

Where Does Journalism Go from Here?

More than 230 years have passed since the Bill of Rights gave explicit protections to "the press." Recently, journalism in the US has seen both a renewed acknowledgment of its importance to the functioning of a healthy democracy, and also attacks on its legitimacy by those who seek to control the narrative and delegitimize reporting that holds power to account and informs and enlightens the public.

At the same time, digital and social media have opened up communication channels to everyone. This has allowed sharing and consuming critical alternative narratives that increase our understanding and contribute toward societal and cultural inclusion. But this has also allowed misinformation and disinformation to flourish, leading to a more fractured and polarized populace.

Exacerbating these issues is corporate consolidation, in which a handful of companies and hedge funds own the bulk of US media outlets. As corporate owners siphon profits out of communities, many also cut resources, leaving local and regional news outlets unable to effectively cover their communities. This has left information vacuums often filled by partisan content and misinformation, leading to a less informed public and increased polarization. This threat to a "free press" must be part of our conversation to ensure the health of our news and information infrastructure moving forward.

People living in the late 18th and early 19th centuries faced analogous issues: a polarized populace, efforts to control the flow of information, and a lack of inclusion for anyone who was not a white, land-owning man – including women, indigenous people, African slaves, Mexicans living on land the US wanted to claim, and eventually immigrants from Southern and Eastern Europe, China, Japan, and elsewhere.

Given our current context, it seems that now is an opportune moment to revisit the Press Clause and come to an understanding of what the framers meant when they explicitly named "the press" as deserving of protection. We must also define what we want from our news media today, and how we can best protect journalists, so they can inform, enlighten, and protect us.

References

Annals of Congress, 1st Congress. (1789). http://memory.loc.gov/cgi-bin/ampage?collId=llac&fileName=001/llac001.db&recNum=227

Adams, J. (1780). *Massachusetts constitution article XVI*. Retrieved May 6, 2022 from: https://malegislature.gov/laws/constitution

Blackstone, W. (1770). *Commentaries on the laws of England* (Vol. 4). Harvard University.

Branzburg v. Hayes, 408 US 665 (1972). https://www.loc.gov/item/usrep408665/

Campbell, J. (2017). Natural rights and the first amendment. *Yale Law Review*, *127*(2), 246–489.

Clark, C. (2005). The press the founders knew. In T. Cook (Ed.), *Freeing the presses: The first amendment in action* (pp. 60–88). Louisiana State University Press.

Jefferson, T. (1606–1827). *The Thomas Jefferson papers at the Library of Congress: Series 1: General correspondence. 1651 to 1827*. https://www.loc.gov/collections/Thomas-jefferson-papers/

Madison, J. (1723–1859). The James Madison Papers at the Library of Congress. Retrieved May 10, 2022 from: https://www.loc.gov/collections/james-madison-papers/

Mason, G. (1776). *Virginia Declaration of Rights*. https://constitutioncenter.org/learn/educational-resources/historical-documents/the-virginia-declaration-of-rights

National Archives. (n.d.). *Alien and sedition acts (1798)*. National Archives and Records Administration. https://www.archives.gov/milestone-documents/alien-and-sedition-acts.

Shiffrin, S. (2016). *What's wrong with the first amendment?* Cambridge University Press.

Stevens, J. P. (2010, January 21). *Citizens United v. Federal election commission*. Legal Information Institute. https://www.law.cornell.edu/supct/html/08-205.ZX.html

West, S. (2010). Awakening the press clause. *UCLA Law Review*, *58*, 1025.

3

HOW FREE AND HOW RESPONSIBLE?

The 75th Anniversary of the Hutchins Commission Report

Lois A. Boynton

Spring 2022 marked the 75th anniversary of the Commission on Freedom of the Press report, *A Free and Responsible Press* (1947). The Commission, comprising 13 intellectuals, began deliberations in late 1943 to assess "the present state and future prospects of the freedom of the press" (p. v) and issued its findings and general recommendations for the press, government, and public in 1947. The "press," according to the Commission, referred to the breadth of mass communication channels – radio, movies, newspapers, magazines, and books. This designation earned the group both ire and ridicule from critics for including non-print media in their definition. This chapter provides an overview of the Commission's charge and summary report, resulting criticism, and the relevance of its insights in the 21st century.

Creating the Commission

Media mogul Henry Luce penned a lengthy commentary, "The American Century," for *Life* magazine's February 17, 1941, issue, in which he admonished Americans to shed their inward navel gazing and shift their focus to promoting the virtues of democracy worldwide. In part, he hoped to encourage American support of European allies in a second global war. Ten months later, the US was shocked by Japan's attack on Pearl Harbor, marking America's entry into World War II. About one year into that war, Luce conversed with former college classmate Robert Hutchins, University of Chicago chancellor, about concerns that American press freedoms were at risk in a world reeling from totalitarian takeovers by Hitler and the Communist powerhouse USSR, which had enveloped most of Eastern Europe and parts of Asia by 1922.

The Commission on the Freedom of the Press was thereby formed, with Hutchins as its chair. The 13 white, elite men hand-selected by Hutchins began their three-plus years of deliberations funded by Luce's company, Time Inc. ($200,000),

DOI: 10.4324/9781003315605-4

and Encyclopedia Britannica ($15,000). The University of Chicago managed the funding – more than $3 million in today's dollars – and Hutchins declared benefactors had no influence over the Commission's deliberations and findings.

The Commission included academics from a range of disciplines, a former assistant secretary of state, and the Federal Reserve Bank chair. Four international advisors represented Canada, France, China, and Germany. A staff of four assisted members in their activities. Only one – advisor Kurt Riezler, a German immigrant – had newspaper experience.

Life and Times of the Commission's Work

There is value in briefly contextualizing the social-economic-political climate of the time – the Commission deliberated while the world was in the throes of global conflict, and its final, 139-page treatise was published two years after the war ended and the Cold War began. Mass communication saw expansions of radio and movies during the war; for example, Voice of America began in 1942 as an anti-Nazi propaganda outlet in Europe. That same year, lack of trust in Japanese immigrants was codified through Executive Order 9066, which established relocation camps where nearly one-quarter million people lived throughout the rest of the war. With the federal debt growing, 1943 Americans faced wage freezes, and a new income withholding tax affected their paychecks. Rationing – from gasoline to tires to women's silk stockings – set in, and Americans made sacrifices for the war effort. The government issued war bonds, as during World War I, to raise billions of dollars needed for weaponry, supplies, and soldiers. Government sought mass media's support in promoting the nationwide effort.

About a month before war in Europe ended in May 1945, President Franklin D. Roosevelt died and Vice President Harry Truman assumed the presidency. Japan surrendered four months later, after the US dropped two atomic bombs on the island nation. A whole new world of television entered the mainstream post-war, with the Federal Communications Commission issuing the first TV broadcast licenses and associated regulations to ensure this new medium prioritized serving the public interest.

In 1946, expanding Communism reinvigorated the uneasiness some Americans felt about fellow citizens. As the Commission issued its report in 1947, Congress launched the House Un-American Activities Committee to tackle the "Red Menace," grilling innumerable Americans – public officials, public figures, and ordinary citizens – presumed to be communist sympathizers who would destroy the very fabric of our free society. The new world order, replete with weapons of mass destruction, called for cool heads to prevail.

"Is the Freedom of the Press in Danger?" (Commission, 1947, p. 1)

It is no wonder, based on this context of fear and trepidation, that the Commission (1947) resoundingly believed freedom of the press was in danger. They added, however, that the danger itself was nothing new, as a free press will always face threats by those who would control access to ideas; indeed, even the press might misuse its power. In all, the Commission consulted nearly 60 men and women who worked in mass communications and they also interviewed another 225 people in industry, government, and NGOs. Over three years, members gathered 17 times for two- to three-day meetings. They argued, wrote, and gathered their perspectives into 176 documents. Despite their range of ideology, the Commission released a unanimously approved summary report; it also listed six forthcoming publications with specific emphases on movies, radio, international communication, and a philosophical framework on press freedom.

As may be expected, the report came across as an erudite treatise on the importance of a free press, the impact of technological innovations, cautions about the dangers of near-monopoly ownerships, and admonitions for the press to act responsibly and in the best interests of democratic society.

What a Free and Responsible Press Must Do

The Commission (1947) identified five requirements, emphasizing the significant role the press holds in responsibly informing public opinion:

"A Truthful, Comprehensive, and Intelligent Account of the Day's Events in a Context Which Gives Them Meaning" (p. 21).
The Commission validated basic news media foundations of accuracy, reliable sourcing, and separating fact from opinion, the latter of which was no easy task. Inherent biases could affect how journalists reported; even eyewitness accounts could be tainted by underlying prejudices. What appears on its face to be true must be investigated deeply to discover crucial contexts that aid citizens in understanding their civic responsibilities at home and what transpires globally.
"A Forum for the Exchange of Comment and Criticism" (p. 23).
This requirement epitomizes the marketplace of ideas, the notion that truth will emerge as a variety of viewpoints are freely shared and debated. Mass media must ensure no group is insulated in ways that preclude mutual understanding. The risk of confirmation bias raised an alarm that prejudices flourish if societal groups remain isolated within their own beliefs. Making idea-sharing even more challenging was the waning number of independent newspapers and magazines, and the surge in chain ownerships. They feared for average news consumers who needed diverse, reliable information. Importantly, the press played a significant role ensuring citizens could effectively participate in the democratic process.
"The Projection of a Representative Picture of the Constituent Groups in the Society" (p. 26).
This requirement presents a conundrum grounded in the inequity experienced by American minorities. The US was deeply – and legally – segregated, Jim Crow laws thrived, and whites enjoyed privileges not attainable by other races and ethnicities. Internment camps sequestered Japanese Americans throughout the war, and the military was not integrated until 1948, a year after the Commission

published its report. Mass media could help or hurt racial progress. Their power could reinforce erroneous depictions of an increasingly diverse country; stereotypes of minority groups perpetuated these images, whether used explicitly or implicitly. Commissioners did not advocate ignoring any group's faults; rather, they encouraged reporters provide a full picture of values and circumstances, a rather progressive – perhaps naïve – notion for the time, 17 years before the Civil Rights Act passed.

"The Presentation and Clarification of the Goals and Values of the Society" (p. 27).

This stipulation stressed how the press helps ensure democracy functions effectively – informing people of their civic responsibilities and educating them about the issues at hand. Unfortunately, the Commission said, the press often sacrificed its role of reinforcing democratic ideals by ceding pages and air time to entertainment, gossip, and profitable advertising. The Commission (1947) further fretted that the definition of news had eroded, with mass media emphasizing "the exceptional rather than the representative, the sensational rather than the significant," to gain as many readers and viewers as possible (pp. 56–57).

"Full Access to the Day's Intelligence" (p. 28).

In short, the press must make publicly available an array of perspectives, whether or not readers and viewers availed themselves of the information. Some Commission trepidations eerily foreshadowed today's concerns that having more and varied communication channels may not contribute to the public being better informed on civic matters or willing to entertain viewpoints other than their own. While more Americans were able to read, the number of daily newspapers continued to drop. The vast majority of communities had only one newspaper, and only metropolitan areas had competing dailies. Noteworthy, although dropped in a footnote: the only unchanged categories were foreign language and African-American newspapers. The growth of women's magazines in the early 1900s had stalled, a few large corporations published the lion's share of American magazines, and the bulk of book publishing coalesced around a handful of publishing houses.

The Commission (1947) acknowledged the economic–civic responsibility conundrum facing the press, "caught between its desire to please and extend its audience and its desire to give a picture of events and people as they really are" (p. 57). These hurdles necessitated the press employ communication powers responsibly and reduce the risk that owners would prioritize perspectives they favored.

Professional Responsibility

The Commission urged the press to assume responsibility to serve the public interest and follow the foundations of established professions like law and medicine: training in specialized knowledge, public service over self-service, and self-regulation through enforceable ethics codes typically managed through professional associations. There is no licensing in mass communication and code enforcement is limited, thanks to the First Amendment. Whereas lawyers could lose their privilege of practicing law, the First Amendment precludes denying any communicator the right to speak or write. Instead, communicators could self-regulate through professional associations. Newspapers had a few such associations that could steer self-regulation, but the Commission believed self-interest took the upper hand.

Additionally, two schools of thought dominated proper education of future journalists. Many editors and publishers eschewed hiring college graduates, believing novice journalists would best learn their trade through on-the-job experience and interacting with seasoned reporters and editors. Others, including the predominantly academic Commission, saw value in a broad liberal arts education and challenged university journalism programs to train future reporters to think critically about cultural, economic, and democratic ideals. College degree or not, editors and publishers must properly prepare reporters to understand the complexity of domestic cultural differences and avoid perpetuating racial discord.

The Time Has Come

There is no doubt the Commission preferred that the press should police itself, but it also stressed that citizens, and to a lesser extent government, must watch the watchdog and hold it accountable to its professional obligations. The First Amendment precluded most government interference. Instead, the Commission reminded government officials of their obligation to ensure open communication through various print, audio, and video channels. At minimum, the government should not hinder the press in adopting technology advancements in their service to public good. The Commission left open the possibility that government could communicate directly with the public as long as it was to inform rather than for self-promotion, perhaps a nod to the 1913 Gillett Amendment, which curtailed government agency use of taxpayer money for undesignated publicity efforts.

The Commission (1947) conceded press's economic success lay with keeping readers and viewers happy; however, they also believed investing in "good practice in the interest of public enlightenment is good business as well, … We suggest that the press look upon itself as performing a public service of a professional kind" (pp. 91–92). In particular, the Commission urged media owners to nurture employees toward a goal of professionalism: pay staff livable wages and offer educational opportunities to enhance skills and reinforce their public service obligations. They admonished the press several times for its lack of professional discipline, which led to unacceptable sensationalism and inaccuracies; they urged radio stations to rein in advertiser influence.

Citizens, in addition to deciding what media to consume, should engage in public discourse and hold the press accountable to serve a democratic society's needs. It's not surprising the Commission, top-heavy with academics, would see educational institutions as problem solvers, particularly in equipping current and future journalists with general education and liberal arts foundations. They encouraged educators to conduct research and publish studies about media roles, effects, and accountability. The final recommendation was to develop a nonprofit organization, independent of both media and government, to assess how well the press performed its civic responsibilities.

Even with directives for government and citizenry, the Commission wanted the press to remain free of unnecessary constraints, but not without accountability. They preferred press self-regulation while warning that others – whether government or public interest groups – would step into a regulatory role if media failed in their civic responsibilities.

Perspectives: Criticizing the Critics

Following the report's release, large newspapers, including *The New York Times* and *Christian Science Monitor*, applauded the Commission's efforts and agreed with the report's contention that press power requires an equal commitment to responsibility. That contention, however, seemed elementary to some journalists, and many Commission contemporaries – particularly journalists – expressed disappointment in the final report. "There is nothing new in this," wrote the *Indianapolis Star* in a March 28, 1947, editorial. "These findings are true of the American press. They are also true of every other American institution. Any group within a democracy has public responsibilities as well as public rights" ("Press Reaction," 1947, p. 16).

In July 1947, the prestigious *Nieman Reports* published excerpts from several newspaper editorials and reviews that judged Commission findings ("Press Reaction," 1947). Both tepid and defensive reactions are understandable – journalists did not appreciate being called liars who misrepresented public issues, sensationalized mediocre topics, and were willing – even eager – to sacrifice substance for profits. *Louisville Courier Journal's* Barry Bingham questioned the report's "curious inconclusiveness," adding, "It makes a case against the press with dignity and seriousness. When it comes to describe the remedies, however, it ladles out great masses of confusion" (p. 16). Some media, Society of Nieman Fellows chair Louis Lyons wrote, appeared thin-skinned and unwilling to countenance any outsider criticism. He further complained about newspapers that did not provide adequate facts or context to readers; rather, they chose to butcher the report in editorials. A lack of research or substantiated proof of Commission critiques irked other editors. "The doubt arises from the fact that the commission has made its report so generalized that it runs the risk of distortion and over-emphasis," wrote the *New Philadelphia* [Ohio] *Times* (p. 17).

While the Commission believed the press should police itself, some critics, including political journalist Walter Lippmann, called for "personal detachment" by media outsiders. Others agreed, while also chastising the Commission of nonjournalists for being oblivious to how press operate. Certain critics found joy in taking pot shots at the ivory tower and its "long and tortuously-reasoned report," as described in a *Buffalo Evening News* March 29, 1947, editorial. "In practical, constructive value, the report isn't worth a thin dime... The average college professor knows as much about editing and publishing a newspaper as a Florida alligator knows about atomic energy," wrote the *Tampa Morning Tribune*. The *Portland Oregonian* added this gem: "The thirteen philosophers, professors and scholars under the chairmanship of Robert M. Hutchins, have produced a volume almost certain to cause the casual reader to fall asleep" ("Press Reaction," 1947, pp. 18, 19).

Somewhat unexpectedly, among the harshest critics was Henry Luce, the benefactor and odd couple friend of Hutchins who put up the lion's share of the Commission's funding. In his colorful margin notes, Luce took at jab at an early draft: "after 2nd reading I think the whole thing so naïve & unsophisticated I say to Hell with it," and, "is this the best philosophy can do?" (Bates, 2018, p. 820). Some researchers believe his criticism stemmed from disappointment that the report over-emphasized media flaws and concentrated news outlet ownership without also taking a stand against government interference. Historian and legal scholar Stephen Bates (2018) found evidence painting a fuller picture. A devout Christian, Luce had pushed commissioners to acknowledge "a publisher's moral responsibilities" (p. 816); he insisted – unsuccessfully – the report recognize "man is responsible to his Creator" (p. 824).

Academic Legacy

Although media contemporaries spurned "A Free and Responsible Press," it set in motion a new yet normative approach, conceptualized 10 years later by academician Theodore Peterson (1962) – social responsibility of the press theory. Whereas the libertarian press theory draws from the First Amendment's call for freedom from governmental interference, the social responsibility theory challenges the press to employ those freedoms toward the promotion of the public good. Peterson concurred with his predecessors about the influence of technology, homogenous media output through concentrated ownership, potential influences of advertisers, and citizens' frequent lack of motivation to discover the truth. Flourishes of the Hutchins report also were read anew in the 1968 National Advisory Commission on Civil Disorders Report, although not referred to by name. The Kerner Commission devoted a chapter to media responsibility in failing race relations, chastising mainstream "white press" for acting on its implicit biases. "A society that values and relies on a free press as intensely as ours is entitled to demand in return responsibility from the press and conscientious attention by the press to its own deficiencies," the report concluded (p. 203).

Fred Blevins' (1997) hindsight assessment a half-century hence shows how news media slowly infused some Commission ideology, including a broader array of op-eds and columns, hiring ombudsmen to address public concerns, and taking professionalism seriously through codes, training, autonomy, and public service orientation. Some Commission insights morphed into public journalism, a 1990s call – by academics – for news media to once again assess their obligations to cultivate public conversations that tackle societal ills through sound democratic principles, reengage with diverse publics, and promote transparency, even to the point of revealing how the sausage is made. But most media dismissed it as idealistic and akin to boosterism.

Some innovations withstood the test of time; others sputtered, including the now-defunct National News Council (1973–1984) and Newseum (1997–2019), both designed to encourage public understanding and increase public trust in media. Foremost news outlets (e.g., *The New York Times, The Washington Post, NPR*) touted contributions of ombuds/reader representatives but eventually tossed them aside, citing technology innovations that enabled reporters direct access to consumers through online article comments and social media. Although peer critiques flourish, most tear down competitors without improving the profession or citizens' access to public discourse.

21st-Century Relevance

In the 75 years since the Hutchins Commission report was released, what, if anything, has changed? We still face global uncertainty, and fears of a fragile democracy and flawed news outlets parallel those the Commission identified. Even with "vigorous mutual criticism," experimentation, associations, need for diverse perspectives, professionalism, research, and education, we have yet to solve the knotty dilemmas of balancing media's freedom with responsibility (Commission, 1947, p. 94). But is that really a bad thing?

Many current journalists believe, like the Commission,

> journalism in the public interest is as valuable and necessary as any public good, and … an ecosystem of local media sources – newsrooms, libraries, public access TV and radio stations, and other information hubs – can help communities determine their own futures.
>
> *(Holliday, 2021, para. 7)*

New insights continue to emerge: Less access to meaningful local news about their communities results in lower voter turnout and increased polarization. Conversely, government officials behave better and citizens are more likely to vote in areas with active local news outlets. An applied research hub recently revisited how to measure media trust by focusing on cross-cultural values in tandem with journalistic values. Results cut across political party lines; stories that underscored certain cultural values appealed to a broader audience – Democrats, Independents, and Republicans (Media Insight Project, 2021). These findings point to the role each person's perspectives, shaped by experiences and status, play in creating their standpoint; that is, how they view the world (Bajracharya, 2018). Standpoint theory can be another tool in the social responsibility toolkit. Reporters and citizens who first explore their own standpoint are better equipped to refocus their lens beyond their own perspectives to better understand the lives of others unlike themselves.

Also similar to the Commission's findings, today's new technology is a double-edged sword. We are inundated with instantaneous information, not all of which is true or valuable. The old gatekeeping role compelling journalists to collect, vet, and validate what is newsworthy competes with influencers who, not subject to professional standards, post directly to followers, often without verification. Still, social media users can be citizen journalists or "untrained accidental witnesses," a moniker Walter Lippman assigned to early 1900s reporters. At times, these witnesses have played significant roles documenting societal injustices – a 2021 cellphone video by teen Darnella Frazier helped convict Minneapolis officer Derek Chauvin for murdering George Floyd. Thirty years earlier, plumber George Holliday used his new camcorder to tape four Los Angeles policemen beating Rodney King during a traffic stop. Violence erupted when criminal charges didn't stick, but King won a multimillion-dollar lawsuit against the city. Since 2012, activist Logan Smith has called out white supremacists on his @YesYoureRacist Twitter account and exposed offenders' identities after a careful vetting process.

There is relevance to the cliché, "the more things change, the more they stay the same." Seventy-five years have passed and, like commissioners before us, we still lack all-encompassing solutions. Still, the aspirational Hutchins Commission report set foundations for subsequent generations to explore the media's freedom–responsibility conundrum within the contexts of their time.

References

Bajracharya, S. (2018, Jan. 6). Standpoint theory. *Businesstopia*. https://www.businesstopia. net/mass-communication/standpoint-theory

Bates, S. (2018). Is this the best philosophy can do? Henry R. Luce and a free and responsible press. *Journalism and Mass Communication Quarterly, 95*(3), 811–834. https://doi.org/10.1177/1077699017719873

Blevins, F. (1997). *The Hutchins Commission turns 50: Recurring themes in today's public and civic journalism*. Paper presented at the third annual Conference on Intellectual Freedom. Montana State University-Northern, Havre, Montana.

Commission on Freedom of the Press. (1947). *A free and responsible press. A general report on mass communication· Newspapers, radio, motion pictures, magazines, and books*. University of Chicago Press.

Holliday, D. (2021, December 15). Journalism is a public good. Let the public make it. *Columbia Journalism Review*. https://www.cjr.org/special_report/journalism-power-public-good-community-infrastructure.php

Media Insight Project. (2021, April 14). *How we studied moral values to understand trust in the news media*. American Press Institute. https://www.americanpressinstitute.org/publications/reports/survey-research/how-we-studied-moral-values/

Peterson, T. (1962). The social responsibility of the press. In F. S. Siebert, T. Peterson, & W. Schramm (Eds.)· *Four theories of the press* (pp. 73–103). Illini Books.

Press reaction to free press report. (1947, July). *Nieman Reports, 1*(3), 14–20.

Report of the National Advisory Commission on Civil Disorders. (1968). US Government Printing Office.

The Importance of Journalism Today

Dane S. Claussen

I should tell you first how I define journalism. It is reporting and research based, primarily or solely for the purposes of informing and not only persuading or entertaining, and intended to tell an audience information (including opinions and ideas) that most or all of them don't already know. It is done by a professional or an amateur, and it is for an audience broader than the communicator's relatives, neighbors, friends, and/or co-workers. It is, or is potentially, of importance and/or intellectual interest to many. It almost always is disseminated by a mass medium (broadly defined) or a social medium. So communications that rarely are journalism include, but are not limited to, conversations, text messages, emails, letters, church sermons, political speeches, classroom lectures, talk show interviews, and other TV interviews whose main goals are ratings and/or making political points. Editorial writers and columnists who report/research their work are doing journalism, while those who don't, well, aren't – anyone can rattle on with opinions not based on facts.

Journalism is therefore a genre of nonfiction, along with all nonfiction books, scientific and social scientific journal articles and papers, history journal articles, government reports, judges' opinions, museum exhibit labels, among other things. Real journalism is important for all reasons that all nonfiction is important.

A recent *Harvard Business Review* article, "The Case for Reading Fiction," by Professor Christine Seifert (2020), reports, "Warren Buffett, CEO of Berkshire Hathaway, spends most of his day reading and recommends reading 500 pages a day. Entrepreneur Mark Cuban says he reads more than three hours a day. Elon Musk, CEO of SpaceX, says he learned to build rockets by reading books. But business visionaries who extol the virtues of reading almost always recommend nonfiction. Buffet recommended 19 books in 2019; not one of the titles is fiction. Of the 94 books Bill Gates recommended over a seven-year period, only nine of them are fiction" (para. 3).

DOI: 10.4324/978 003315605-5

Seifert's claim is that nonfiction is good "only" for "knowledge," while reading fiction increases "social acuity" and a "sharper ability to comprehend other people's motivations" (para. 4) – in other words, developing one's emotional IQ. But her examples don't work at all or are not unique to fiction; her case is weak. She mentions a business's employees approaching their own difficult situation by discussing a fictional story… set in another culture/country. She claims that fiction always presents multiple viewpoints while nonfiction presents only two, neither of which is true in my experience other than journalists settling for only two sides ("both") more often than they should. Seifert claims that people who read and discuss fiction are "more willing to tackle tough questions" and fiction forces people to "keep an open mind while processing information" (citing one study on the virtues of short stories vs. "essays") while presenting no evidence that this is any more true for fiction than nonfiction (paras. 7–8).

Claims that fiction uniquely helps us understand multiple points of view and different people's motivations ignore not only the breadth and depth of modern history and current social science (psychology, anyone?), but also the past 50 years' changes in US journalism, now routinely criticized for focusing too much, not too little, on the psychologies, motivations, emotions, relationships, etc., of presidents, CEOs, movie stars, and NFL champions. In short, one can obtain everything from nonfiction that one can from fiction – with the added virtue that nonfiction is, well, true. I don't even grant that fiction is generally more entertaining; I think most fiction is not especially entertaining (intentionally or not) and I knew Mark Twain's line, "Truth is stranger than fiction" even before it was proved to me through journalism, history, sciences, social science, and other nonfiction. So journalism is important because it's a form of nonfiction, journalism even being called "the first draft of history."

What makes journalism special among nonfiction, which collectively can open our minds to the entire world and universe? Some say that it makes available information that must be reported, such as city council meetings, regardless of public interest. But this can be said about vast amounts of government data and reports, science, and social science. So can ideals of independence and objectivity. But several "Elements of Journalism" from Bill Kovach and Tom Rosenstiel (2001) are on point. They say journalists must strive to keep news "comprehensive and proportional" (p. xxvii). Newspapers (the most ubiquitous media geographically – and, until recently, always the most fully staffed) and news services (e.g., Associated Press) generally have succeeded at this for more than 100 years, in a way that television, radio, the internet, politicians, and individual news consumers (e.g., you and me) have not. Journalists engage in the gatekeeping and agenda-setting of huge amounts of news, and newspapers publish and post as much of it as they can, while TV and radio broadcast and post a small fraction.

The Elements include providing a "forum" for "public criticism and compromise," not just within news stories, but also via print-based media's editorials, regular columns, guest "op-eds," and letters to the editor. No other nonfiction does this every day or even regularly. The Elements state that journalism is a "monitor of power." No other nonfiction does this regularly or comprehensively (granted, news media need to do better – but there aren't enough journalists, and many we have do not have necessary combinations of courage and knowledge). Finally, the elements say journalism's "first loyalty is to citizens" (or at least that it should be; para. xvii). This also would ideally be true of, among others, academics, nonacademic scientists, government employees, and even businesses, but that loyalty is easiest to demand and assess, and is urgent (along with politicians), from journalists.

The late communications scholar James W. Carey equated journalism with democracy: one literally cannot have one without the other. He knew that non-democratic countries have journalism, but not good journalism. But like the Founding Fathers, Carey knew that the freest press and speech overall both supports, and results from, the best/most democracy. And today, like always, fiction and other nonfiction can't do that.

References

Kovach, B., & Rosenstiel, T. (2001). *The elements of journalism: What newspeople should know and the public should expect*. Crown.

Seifert, C. (2020, March 6). The case for reading fiction. *Harvard Business Review*. https://hbr.org/2020/03/the-case-for-reading-fiction

PART II

Rethinking Journalistic Objectivity and Ethics

Like all mass media, journalism is rapidly transforming, and adjusting not just to constantly evolving technologies, but also to shifts in public preferences and expectations. With these changes, new questions are being raised regarding what ethical and socially responsible journalism should look like in the modern world. Among these many new ethical concerns are questions addressing what journalism involves in a digital environment, and also considering whether or not the concept of journalistic objectivity should be reconsidered.

With digital journalistic ethics, one particularly salient question involves where the line should be drawn between news coverage that documents reality, and that which verges on voyeurism or exploitation. In the modern world, in which cameras have become ubiquitous, this dilemma is especially relevant regarding visual news coverage and photojournalism.

Additionally, the long-held concept of journalistic objectivity has recently come under renewed scrutiny. While many people today accept the idea that objectivity is a fundamental ethical standard on which journalism is built, the reality is that such a concept would have been strange or even unwelcome throughout much of this nation's history. Before the 20th century, newspapers were generally unapologetic in their bias, and it was fully expected and understood that news was almost always presented through a political or otherwise partisan filter, or at least in a direction reflective of the publisher's views and perspectives. Slowly, however, during the first decades of the 20th century, the concept of the "impersonal reporter" started to catch on, and then continued to become increasingly formalized in the decades that were to follow. In time, the public came to expect that journalists should operate as neutral arbiters of truth.

But the objective journalism model was not without its faults, and as times have changed, society and the profession are once again starting to question the very notion of objectivity. In Part II, we begin to address issues of journalistic ethics in a digital age, and especially explore varied perspectives on the appropriateness of the objectivity norm in the modern world.

DOI: 10.4324/9781003315605-6

4

JOURNALISM ETHICS

Dilemmas and Decisions

Maggie Jones Patterson

Their young bodies were so torn apart by the devastating force of an AR-15-style assault rifle that they could only be identified through their parents' DNA.

None of us wants to see photographs of that devastation. No one would want to put parents through the agony of viewing the destroyed bodies of their children.

Nevertheless, after the 2022 mass shooting at Robb Elementary School in Uvalde, Texas, responsible journalists weighed whether police or autopsy photographs of the bodies of some of the 19 children and two teachers murdered should be published. Advocates argued that the public needed to see the excruciating damage such automatic weapons and their owners cause. Withholding such images amounted to cover-up, they argued.

Certainly, viewing such "tremendously traumatic images" would haunt people long after seeing them, admitted Ed Wasserman, who teaches journalism and is former dean at the University of California at Berkeley (PBS, 2022). Appearing on the PBS News Hour six weeks after the May 24 Uvalde shooting, he said publishing photographs of the children's bodies would show disrespect for the people who mourn them. Putting these images into circulation would come at a great cost, Wasserman said.

Yet, he was arguing that authorities should release such photographs and news outlets should publish them.

Why? We are a visual culture, Wasserman said, but the images commonly used of families and communities grieving and praying after such mass shootings do the public a disservice. Viewers see nothing of the butchery. Consequently, they respond largely with sympathy instead of the anger and disgust that the situation deserves. Not showing the actual carnage borders on concealment, Wasserman argued. It panders to a level of public denial.

Offering counterpoint on the PBS broadcast, Sandy Phillips, whose daughter was shot six times and killed in the massacre at the Aurora, Colorado, movie theater in 2012, said making such violent photographs public is "a horrible idea."

DOI: 10.4324/9781003315605-7

At the trial for the Aurora shooter, the medical examiner wept on the stand describing the wounds suffered by Phillips' 24-year-old daughter, Jessi Redfield Ghawi. The press and public were also crying, and the judge called a recess. Forcing parents to relive that agony is a burden they should not be asked to carry, Phillips said.

Journalists are often forced to decide between two wrongs. Harm and damage may result no matter whether they publish or withhold deeply disturbing images or story details. They may be accused of sensationalizing the news on the one hand or censoring important information on the other. No response will be entirely right or entirely wrong, yet they must decide.

Those advocating for publication can cite the beneficial effects on society of earlier cases. Iconic but highly disturbing photographs have often been winners of journalism's most treasured prize, the Pulitzer. They are also often credited with changing the course of history.

For example, in the summer of 1955, 14-year-old Emmett Louis Till of Chicago was visiting his grandmother in Money, Mississippi. Unfamiliar with the unspoken code of behavior for Black males in the Jim Crow South, Emmett spoke to a grocery store proprietor named Carolyn Bryant, a 21-year-old, married, white woman. Although it is unclear just what transpired in the store, Emmett was accused of flirting with, touching, or whistling at Bryant. Later, Bryant's husband, Roy, and his half-brother, abducted, beat, and tortured Emmett before shooting him in the head. They weighed down his body with a fan blade stolen from a cotton gin and dumped it into the Tallahatchie River. When the body was found, it was so disfigured and bloated that his great uncle could only identify Emmett by the initialed ring he was wearing. Bryant and his brother were indicted for murder but acquitted. They later admitted their guilt.

Emmett's mother, Mamie Till, insisted on a public funeral back in Chicago and an open casket. As a result, photographs of Emmett's mutilated body, taken by *Jet* magazine and the *Chicago Defender* newspaper, both Black publications, were soon picked up and widely circulated by mainstream media. Public reaction to the story and the images was strong. Mamie Till's decision to make public the graphic image of what had happened to her son is widely credited with spurring the somewhat somnolent US civil rights movement into action. Almost 70 years later, media's widespread circulation of a bystander's disturbing phone video of George Floyd's suffocation under the knee of a Minneapolis police officer gave rise to Black Lives Matter.

"Can a photograph help end a war?" Nick Ut asked in a *Washington Post* editorial (2022, para. 1), published for the fiftieth anniversary of his Pulitzer-winning photo that is widely credited with doing just that. In June 1972, Ut pointed his camera at agonized children fleeing a small Vietnamese village where an aerial attack had dropped napalm bombs, meant to fall on a Viet Cong hiding place. At the center of the image, which would soon travel around the globe on the Associated Press wire, 9-year-old Kim Phuc ran naked with arms outstretched, crying as the napalm seared the flesh on her arms and shoulders. Ut drove the girl to the nearest hospital, and they have remained friends.

Although President Richard Nixon at first wondered if this photo had been staged, the public was moved by it. "Truth continues to be necessary," Ut (2022, para. 25) wrote as he paid tribute to the photographers covering the more recent war in Ukraine. "If a single photo can make a difference, maybe even help end a war, then the work that we do is as vital now as it has ever been." Aid rushed to Ukrainians after viewers reacted with a visceral mix of anger and empathy to Ukrainians' suffering after Russia invaded.

This way of thinking about ethical issues is called utilitarianism or consequential reasoning because it judges the rightness or wrongness of an action by its outcome. Did the decision minimize harm and benefit the largest number of people when compared with other possible actions? Would, for example, showing the torn bodies of the children shot at Uvalde awaken a public stupefied by images of teddy bears and flowers piled up at the site of the shootings, as advocates argued it would? Does the harm done by concealment outweigh that done by exposure? Can journalism be accused of paternalism when it holds back news that citizens need?

Photojournalism and stories often reveal the human costs of racism, catastrophic foreign policy, authoritarian rule, and war. For many, the ends precipitated by the publication of such images and stories justify whatever harm they caused.

But Sandy Phillips, mother of the Aurora, Colorado, shooting victim, pointed to one weakness of this way of thinking. Any claim that the photos of mass shooting victims "might" make a difference is no excuse for asking families to bear such trauma, she argued (PBS, 2022). Journalists have no crystal ball that will predict with certainty that any benefit will be forthcoming. They cannot be sure that the public will not simply wince with disgust and move on. In that case, whatever pain was inflicted would be for naught, according to the utilitarian way of thinking.

One example of unforeseen consequences is a famous photograph from 1975 that still appears in journalism ethics texts. Stanley Forman, staff photographer for the *Boston Herald*, was covering a fire in an older Victorian apartment building. He circled around the back of the burning building, where fire fighters were calling for a ladder truck to rescue tenants trapped on a fire escape. With a motorized camera focused on a young woman and a toddler standing on a fifth-floor balcony, he shot a series of photos of what he thought was going to be a routine rescue. But just as the fire fighter, with one arm around the pair, grabbed the ladder to rescue them, the balcony collapsed. The firefighter hung on to the ladder, grabbing only air where the woman and child had been. The camera followed their fall: the 19-year-old woman, who died when she hit the ground, and her 2-year-old niece and goddaughter who survived, in part because her fall was cushioned when she landed on her aunt's body. The dramatic photo of the two in mid-air won both the Pulitzer Prize for Spot News in 1976 and the World Press Photo of the Year. The *Herald* took criticism for invading privacy and pandering to sensationalism. At the same time, the photo prompted officials in Boston and other cities to upgrade fire escape safety laws. Neither Foreman nor his editors likely foresaw that beneficial outcome when they ran the photo. Does the consequential reform justify their decision? Would that same decision be unethical if reform had not resulted? Do journalists' motives matter or should their actions be judged only by the outcomes of their decisions?

Such questions prompt a different way of thinking about the issue.

Are affected families entitled to bear their agonizing losses privately no matter what public benefit might result? The law might say that their involvement in a news event makes them public figures and, thereby, limits their legal claims to privacy. However, the respectful ethical response to privacy concerns is more complex. If judging a decision by its consequences seems inadequate by itself, is there a principle that might provide additional guidance? Philosopher Immanuel Kant believes persons faced with ethical decisions should seek to perform a fundamental duty and to obey an important principle. Media codes of ethics strive to identify those kinds of duties and principles for journalists (Society of Professional Journalists, 2014).

The tragic events behind the photographs and stories described here happened to private citizens, but they took place in a public realm. They speak to the need for public action or show the human effects of current policies. Journalism often bridges the gap between private and public life in America. Storytelling is the vehicle used to cross that bridge. With pictures and words, journalism helps diverse Americans define who they are as a people. It serves as a major means of society's self-definition. Ideally in a democracy, audiences view these stories, not just as private individuals or consumers, but as citizens.

In the late 1990s, as new technologies began changing journalism, Bill Kovach and Tom Rosenstiel, both experienced journalists, studied what journalists and the public believed journalism should be and the role it should play in the democratic process. The book that resulted in 2001, *The Elements of Journalism: What News People Should Know and the Public Should Expect*, soon became something of a bible to the profession, and a work that has been revised several times.

Journalism, Kovach and Rosenstiel found, has consistently defined its mission in terms of a public service or a public trust. "[T]he purpose of journalism is to provide people with the information they need to be free and self-governing," they wrote, drawing on their findings (2021, p. 7). This obligation separates journalism from other forms of communication, and it is widely professed by journalism institutions. The American Society of Newspaper Editors (ASNE), for example, states as one of its goals: "fostering the public discourse essential to democracy" (American Society of Newspaper Editors, 2002). The first article of ASNE's Statement of Principles begins: "The primary purpose of gathering and distributing news and opinion is to serve the general welfare by informing the people and enabling them to make judgments on the issues of the time." Every newspaper mission statement the ASNE has on file advances a similar end. The News Leaders Association, which was formed from a merger of the American Society of Newspaper Editors and the Associated Press Media Editors, states its first purpose is to: "Advocate for the values of a free press and free speech, and engage local communities on the value of credible news" (News Leaders Association, n.d., Article 3.2a).

Kovach and Rosenstiel (2021), as well as the journalists and members of the public who participated in their study, worried that journalism was failing to observe its mission and instead was damaging public trust. The two authors emerged from their work with nine key elements they believed define good journalism and that should be followed no matter what technology delivered it. The first two of these principles are: Journalism's first obligation is to the truth and its first loyalty is to citizens.

Journalism's end purpose is not to bring about particular policies nor to stimulate citizens to an end the journalist finds desirable. Therefore, justifying decisions about what to publish by what outcome results – or could result – is risky business. Journalism's job is to place that outcome in the hands of citizens, to provide them the means to figure out the best path forward. To go beyond that purpose by striving to bring about some particular action, therefore, can be seen as overreach. It could be judged as either paternalistic or arrogant. Journalism's job is to trust the public, not to take it by the hand and guide it toward some preferred action.

On the other hand, journalists can present and weigh possibilities. It should not, for example, simply show audiences a violent image and leave them with a sense of despair or cynicism. "The ethical thing to do, as a news outlet, is to make darn sure that you're providing [audiences] with the information that they would need as democratic voting citizens to go out there and create change," Lauren Kogen, who teaches at the Klein College of Media and Communication at Temple University, told *The Journalist's Resource*. "[T]o leave your news audience feeling powerless, to feel like there aren't any solutions, then you are getting into the realm of being sensationalist" (as cited in Merrefield, 2022, para. 71).

The kind of guidance Kogen means is often to be found in follow-up stories. As William Coté and Roger Simpson wrote (2000), tragic stories can unfold like a play in two or three "acts" (pp. 113–120). Immediately after the event, Act I stories supply the traditional 5-Ws – who, what, where, when, and why. Act II stories can be told days, months, or even years after the initial event, following the ongoing effect of the trauma on the victims, their families, and communities. Act III stories can place "specific traumatic events within broader sociological, historical, or even economic contexts" (p. 120). Putting events within such a broader context allows audiences to discern causes and become better equipped to evaluate proposed means of addressing them. Tight economic resources at news outlets have limited journalism's ability to provide this deeper coverage, but it can be essential to the mission of treating audiences as citizens and not just voyeurs.

The concept of mission-driven decision-making goes back to the time of Aristotle, who used a Greek word *entelechy*, which has no direct English translation but literally means to have an end within itself or the realization of potential. The definition may be best understood through a metaphor: An acorn's *entelechy* is to become a magnificent oak tree. Although that may be its potential, few will find the optimal conditions to reach that height. Instead, most will become food for squirrels or fertilizer for the soil. Similarly, human institutions can and should be measured against their missions, their statements of their own intention and potential, and these institutions should strive to minimize their failures.

The mission of public trust is journalism's guiding light, which illuminates its duties to truth and loyalty to citizens. If that light grows dim, other less noble motives crawl in from the shadows. The mission, the *entelechy*, of journalism should be kept alive in newsrooms and story conferences where decisions are made. Human beings, Walter Fisher (1989) said, seek coherence in a guiding narrative or mission. They measure its coherence or fidelity against their lived experience. If the mission's words lose their meaning in action, it will be replaced other tempting narratives, such as attracting more clicks, pushing a political agenda, or acting for the sake of career advancement. While such goals have their own value, they are secondary. If they take the lead in decision-making, those who follow them will eventually head down a wrong and potentially destructive path. Management's expectations and the organizational culture found at news outlets can mold the identities of journalists about their profession and affect what criteria they use to make decisions. If editors and reporters lose sight of journalism's main mission, they lose their true purpose.

While keeping sight of their primary duty to citizens, reporters can still draw upon one of the most important tenets of utilitarianism: They can minimize harm by showing sensitivity to victims and families. The Dart Center for Journalism and Trauma, a project of the Columbia University journalism program, provides a wide range of resources. In the summer of 2022, for example, their website included a special section for those covering the Uvalde shootings, including articles about interviewing traumatized children. From Dart and other sources, reporters can brief themselves on the ways to exercise care. What victims object to in news coverage might surprise reporters. In conversations with victims and family members, William Coté found they were most deeply troubled by factual errors in reports – misspelled names, incorrect ages and addresses, twisted time lines – as well as simplified and hurtful characterizations. They wanted their story told accurately and in a manner that allowed them to feel a part of their community (Coté & Simpson, 2000).

When lives descend into violence and chaos, reporters can help victims and families regain some modicum of control by showing them the care of getting their stories right. Newsrooms have shrunk, and harried reporters are sometimes tempted to simply weave shooting victims' stories from their pictures and posts on social media. For good reasons, reporters may dread approaching victimized families, but many find survivors welcome the chance to tell their loved ones' stories and choose the photographs that will represent them to the community. In advising reporters about how to be sensitive to victims, Bonnie Bucqueroux (2004), former coordinator of the Victims and the Media Program at Michigan State University, warned against shoehorning story subjects into preordained storylines, like that of the purely innocent victim and villainous perpetrator. Life is usually more complicated than that. All reporters bring preconceived notions to the job, and they cannot simply set bias aside. Instead, journalists must be aware of their automatic thinking patterns and counteract them as much as possible.

Obtaining permission to photograph is not always possible in the midst of a major news event but making the gesture of asking helps to win public trust. While journalists' first loyalty is to the citizens in their audience, showing respect for their news subjects need not subtract from that obligation. Surely no responsible news enterprise would consider using images of the children shot in the Robb Elementary School in Uvalde without parents' consent. Mamie Till chose to show her son Emmett's mutilated body to world. No journalist should unnecessarily wrest that control from a grieving parent.

In the United States, where press freedom is protected by the First Amendment, journalism mission statements and codes of ethics should guide journalism decision-making. With freedom comes responsibility. Each story and photograph demands fresh thinking. But the main principles should remain in the foreground of that thinking. "Members of the Society of Professional Journalists [SPJ] believe that public enlightenment is the forerunner of justice and the foundation of democracy," reads the first sentence of the SPJ code of ethics (2014, para. 1). It is followed by an elaboration on four main tenets: seek truth and report it, minimize harm, act independently, be accountable and transparent.

Press freedoms in the United States place a heavy burden of ethical decision-making on journalists' shoulders. New technologies and market pressures have only added to that burden. The stories and photos discussed in this chapter are the kind that rivet public attention. They describe crises in which journalism has played a pivotal role in shaping how the public adjusted and responded to social and material upheaval. The storytelling choices journalists make can spread panic and disillusionment or encourage reconciliation and adaptation. By keeping its sights on its main mission, journalism can open community conversations that stimulate democratic processes that push toward progress.

References

American Society of Newspaper Editors. (2002). Handout #6: American Society of Newspaper Editors code of ethics. https://www.pbs.org/newshour/classroom/app/uploads/2014/03/mediaethics_handout6.pdf

Bucqueroux, B. (2004, October 15). *Tips on interviewing victims: The anniversary story.* Self-published pamphlet distributed at the Covering Violence: Crime Victims & the Media conference, *Pennsylvania Communication Association 65th Annual Conference in Sewickley, PA.*

Coté, W., & Simpson, R. (2000). *Covering violence: A guide to ethical reporting about victims & trauma.* Columbia University Press.

Fisher, W. R. (1989). *Human communication as narration: Toward a philosophy of reason, value, and action.* University of South Carolina Press.

Kovach, B., & Rosenstiel, T. (2021). *The elements of journalism: What news people should know and the public should expect* (4th ed.). Crown.

Merrefield, C. (2022, June 28). Should news outlets show graphic images of mass shooting victims. researchers and other experts weigh in. *The Journalist's Resource.* https://journalistsresource.org/media/graphic-images-mass-shooting-victims/

News Leaders Association. (n.d.). NLA bylaws. https://www.newsleaders.org/bylaws

PBS News Hour. (2022, July 11). Calls to release more graphic images meet opposition. https://www.pos.org/newshour/show/calls-to-release-more-graphic-images-of-deadly-attacks-meet-opposition

Society of Professional Journalists. (2014). SPJ code of ethics. https://www.spj.org/ethics code.asp

Ut, N. (2022, June 2) Opinion: A single photo can change the world. I know, because I took one that did. *The Washington Post.* https://www.washingtonpost.com/opinions/2022/06/02/nick-ut-vietnam-war-photo-kim-phuc/

5

JOURNALISTIC OBJECTIVITY

A Gold Standard or Myth?

E. S. McIntyre

Over the spring and summer of 2021, a longstanding tension in American journalism was brought yet again to the forefront of the public imagination as Arkansas newspaper heir Walter Hussman Jr. pitted his own journalistic values against those he assigned to Pulitzer-prize-winning *New York Times* journalist and University of North Carolina alumna Nikole Hannah-Jones, whom the school was trying to hire.

The situation brought to light issues regarding journalistic objectivity that had simmered for decades. "If every dispute about the history of race in America, every right-wing culture war and every debate over journalistic objectivity could be settled on a single battlefield," wrote media columnist Margaret Sullivan, former public editor of *The New York Times*, "the location might be Chapel Hill, N.C. And the time might be Wednesday afternoon" (Sullivan, 2021, para. 1).

As the "battle" unfolded, Americans followed the events via continuing media coverage, pitting their politics against one another while finding a new reason to distrust both "the media" and those who train young reporters. The saga played out in real time as journalism professors, local reporters, and national press tried to figure out what had happened.

The journalism school, renamed in Hussman Jr.'s honor in 2019 following his $25 million donation, had decided to hire Hannah-Jones, a 2003 Master's graduate whose reporting and commentary had earned her some of the industry's top awards: a MacArthur Fellowship, a Pulitzer, a Polk award. The school's dean had courted Hannah-Jones for years, hoping she would accept a prestigious position as Knight Chair in Race and Investigative Journalism. Previous journalists appointed to Knight Chair positions were granted tenure. However, in what many academics and the press called a "striking departure from precedent," Hannah-Jones initially wasn't. Hussman Jr. played a role. When the school's namesake donor learned of

DOI: 10.4324/9781003315605-8

the pending appointment, he began reaching out to the university, emailing his concerns to a variety of recipients including top UNC leadership.

Hussman Jr. is "an evangelist of old-school objectivity," noted reporter John Drescher of North Carolina's *The Assembly*, and one of his concerns related to the issue. Hussman Jr. wasn't sure, he told AP reporter Skip Foreman, if his and Hannah Jones' "journalistic philosophies aligned," according to an email sent by the AP to UNC Media Relations (Drescher, 2021, para. 2).

To the donor, such alignment deeply mattered. A condition of Hussman Jr.'s $25 million donation was that the school have his "core values" chiseled into the wall of its lobby, in granite. Every day, Hussman Jr. also required his chain of newspapers to print a nearly identical values statement. "The statement refers to 'impartiality' five times in seven brief paragraphs," noted Rick Edmonds on Poynter.org. "It reads as a manifesto for objectivity without using the word" (Edmonds, 2021, para. 23).

And although Hannah-Jones' nearly two-decade career of reportorial accomplishments boasted more accolades than the majority of other American journalists, Hussman Jr. focused his concerns on one piece in her prolific body of work: the 1619 project.

Conceptualized by Hannah-Jones, the ongoing initiative from *The New York Times* aimed "to reframe the country's history by placing the consequences of slavery and the contributions of Black Americans at the very center of our national narrative." The 1619 project is an example of journalism that prioritizes and values truth and accuracy over blind objectivity or faulty "balance."

Yet Hussman Jr. was critical, and, as revealed in a cache of public records and emails later obtained via Freedom of Information Act requests, he clearly insinuated that any intentional manipulation of fact should be a fireable offense in the news business. Hussman Jr. aired doubts about whether or not having her on the faculty would "distract from teaching the school's core values" (Drescher, 2021, para. 7) – which many interpreted as the same values Hussman Jr. had articulated as a condition of his donation.

Hussman Jr.'s pressure appeared to have an impact. The school's top officials froze the hiring process, and the university's Board of Trustees declined to vote on tenure for Hannah-Jones, effectively downgrading the job offer and simultaneously thrusting the case into the national spotlight.

The Background of the Objectivity Model for Journalism

Objectivity doesn't exist and is not possible to attain; yet, for decades, young reporters have been told to aim high and purify themselves and their work from any subjectivity. The handwringing is nothing new, but from time to time, the discussion ignites anew.

At the same time, it's an ongoing source of confusion. Part of the reason why is because of how the idea has been interpreted and applied to journalistic practice over time. When the concept began to take root in the 1920s, Tom Rosenstiel,

Executive Director of the American Press Institute, noted that it wasn't intended to denote that reporters were without bias. Instead, he says,

> The idea was that journalists needed to employ objective, observable, repeatable methods of verification in their reporting–precisely because they could never be personally objective. That meaning is so misunderstood by journalists it has almost been turned on its head.

As journalism professionalized in the years after World War I, the term "objectivity" was sometimes used as a cover under which political manipulation could be branded news. For instance, in the US, the majority of white Southern newspapers "declared their allegiance to the new norms of objectivity and impartiality," media scholar Sid Bedingfield wrote in an essay in *The Washington Post*. "But while they claimed not to push an agenda, they continued the battle on behalf of white-supremacist rule and anti-Black racism" (Bedingfield, 2021, para. 13).

Throughout the 1940s and 1950s, news was reported with little analysis. Readers struggled to eke out meaning on their own. That began changing in the 1960s, and analysis became a more central part of a reporter's job to help audiences understand how and why events transpired, and how they related to society and daily life.

Yet the lens through which analysis was done belonged to those responsible for creating news content. Even after the passage of the Civil Right Act of 1964, the majority of American newsrooms were segregated. The "mainstream" press was almost entirely comprised of white men.

Discussions about the advantages and drawbacks of reaching for an objective ideal continued to plague and frustrate these mainstream newsrooms through the 1970s, 1980s, and 1990s. In tandem, so did segregation. And despite the passage of anti-discrimination policies over a half-century ago, newsrooms today still remained highly divided by race.

A national reckoning around racism in America didn't start to inspire continuous coverage in the mainstream or white press until recently. It happened due to the work of Black reporters like Nikole Hannah-Jones, who wrote about equity in mainstream majority-white outlets like ProPublica and *The New York Times*. And while Hannah-Jones' work on education in the US was widely lauded, like her 2014 "Segregation Now" project examining apartheid schools, it didn't raise questions about objectivity. Yet when she subsequently drilled down to examine the root causes of social inequity – slavery, as analyzed in the 1619 project – some, including Hussman Jr., voiced discontent.

The Misguided Goal of Objectivity

In an analysis of the evolution of journalistic objectivity published in *Time* magazine, academic Matthew Pressman (2018) wrote that editors and executives at top news organizations generally hope that the coverage they produce appears centrist in order to appeal to the broadest possible audience. He wrote: "Objectivity certainly has its pitfalls – and just because a news outlet has a viewpoint, that doesn't make its coverage inferior. But those who see objectivity as a barrier to truth-telling are misunderstanding its requirements" (para. 17).

At the same time, Pressman noted that "while journalists continued to debate the pros and cons of objectivity in the decades after 1970, there was little doubt that it would remain the profession's guiding principle – that is, until recently" (para. 13). That's because that this "guiding principle" is still defined by power: it changes depending on who gets to define it, how it's wielded and applied, and why.

In an essay published by *The New York Times*, award-winning former *Washington Post* reporter Wesley Lowery (2020) broke it down, highlighting the disparate experiences of journalists in newsrooms nationwide and why they mattered when it came to Pressman's "guiding principle." Across the country, Lowery said, the "views and inclinations of whiteness are accepted as the objective neutral" (Lowery, 2020, para. 7). He continued:

> Since American journalism's pivot many decades ago from an openly partisan press to a model of professed objectivity, the mainstream has allowed what it considers objective truth to be decided almost exclusively by white reporters and their mostly white bosses…
>
> No journalistic process is objective. And no individual journalist is objective, because no human being is.
>
> *(para. 14)*

Worse, while it's true that white people are still dramatically over-represented in American newsrooms, even obtaining hard data on how desegregation has and has not worked is difficult. That's because researchers attempting to assess just how segregated the industry remains have been met with a continual lack of will toward participation by the very organizations they're trying to study. While reporting work is created in workplaces so hostile to integration that simple demographic research is viewed as threatening, American news outlets that don't represent the public they are tasked with serving cannot claim "objectivity" as a value or even a possible ideal guiding in their work.

Editors, reporters, newsroom leaders, and journalism instructors can, however, still focus on improvement of coverage while also improving their company demographics. In place of traditional "objectivity," author and scholar Tom Rosentiel suggests an updated focus on "transparency of method" and a "discipline of verification" (Rosentiel, 2020). Bringing a more rigorous approach to journalistic methodology can not only improve accuracy, but also potentially help rebuild trust and thwart the further erosion of public faith in the media.

Objectivity, "Bothsidesism," and False Equivalencies

At the center of the argument is the idea that "objective" reporting can lead to the creation of false equivalencies. To define false equivalency, the News Literacy

Project uses a simple example, noting it represents "a qualitative difference" in which two acts are compared as if they're equivalent: "Mr. Smith is a serial embezzler, but Mr. Jones once littered in the park. Both are criminals!"

Related to this are the concepts of "bothsidesing" or "bothsidesism," both of which have been defined by Merriam-Webster (n.d.):

> Bothsidesing is a critique leveled at the media and public personas referring to the practice of finding a second angle on a story in an attempt at appearing "fair" to each side, which can often be seen as lending credibility to a side or objectionable idea that has none. Bothsidesing and its related noun bothsidesism turn up in critiques of the news media when a journalist or pundit seems to give extra credence to a cause, action, or idea that on the surface seems objectionable, thereby establishing a sort of moral equivalence that allows said cause, action, or idea to be weighed seriously. By giving credence to the other side, the media gives an impression of being fair to its subject, but in doing so often provides credibility to an idea that most might view as unmerited.
>
> (paras. 5–6)

Such practices can have seriously negative implications. For instance, southern journalism historian and researcher Kathy Roberts Forde says notions of impartiality and objectivity in journalism have long served as a cover for white normativity and to normalize the continuation of presenting white perspectives as objective truth. That includes in decisions regarding what kinds of issues and topics are covered in the news, how they're covered, and who gets to cover them.

To Hussman Jr., however, journalism schools "need to adopt similar statement[s] of core journalistic values" like his own, which involves adhering to objective reporting even if doing so obscures or hides the truth. And, as Hussman Jr. (2019) wrote in a *Wall Street Journal* op-ed, it means rejecting the views of those who agree with Hannah-Jones that her job as a journalist involves "determining the truth, then sharing it with her audience" (para. 3).

As suggested by *Washington Post* columnist Margaret Sullivan, the brand of objectivity and bothsidesism Hussman Jr. promoted smacked of hypocrisy. "Hussman calls himself an ardent supporter of traditional objectivity – the endlessly debated idea that journalism should give essentially equal weight to both sides of political conflicts even if the two sides aren't equally valid, and that reporters shouldn't express their views," she wrote. "But … that's not necessarily the way he's run his newspapers in Arkansas" (Sullivan, 2021, para. 18).

In closing, she noted that Hussman Jr.'s newspaper was among the Southern newspapers "that spent decades declaring their allegiance to objectivity" (Sullivan, 2021, para. 19) while actually continuing what Sid Bedingfield, an academic who researches journalism in the Jim Crow era, called a "battle on behalf of white-supremacist rule and anti-Black racism" (Bedingfield, 2021, para. 13).

Eventually, the University of North Carolina leadership bowed to public pressure. Under glittering chandeliers inside a ballroom at the Carolina Inn, after months of uproar over the hiring of Hannah-Jones, the board of trustees of the University of North Carolina finally took a vote on to whether or not offer tenure to the potential new hire. The decision was yes.

But it was too late.

Hannah Jones declined. In a live television announcement a few days later, the investigative journalist said she'd be accepting a position elsewhere, in large part due to Hussman Jr. and his "values."

Media scholar Bedingfield summarized the underlying themes in a *Washington Post* column, branding the situation, including the value of journalistic objectivity, as ironic. He Wrote:

> "[African American journalists] have often carried out their campaigns in the shadow of a much larger White press that was fighting for just the opposite," he wrote. And as Hannah-Jones has shown in her reporting, the success of those White journalists decades ago has ramifications today, as the legacy of Jim Crow continues to shape fundamental inequalities in American society. Ironically, then, the history of newspapers eventually owned by the Hussman family explains why Hannah-Jones has an agenda today, and why she is carrying on the rich tradition of the Black press.
>
> *(Bedingfield, 2021, para. 15)*

Implications for the Future: Less Rhetoric, More Facts

Moving forward, the rhetoric of objectivity must be examined as the useful tool it often can be to those who wield it as a way of exerting power. In terms of actual craft, when teaching and conducting reporting, a focus on accuracy, context, and methodology needs to be prioritized. That type of craft can be applied to situations in which powerful people or institutions use the rhetoric of objectivity to achieve their own personal goals.

The saga of what happened at the University of North Carolina between Walter Hussman Jr., the faculty, and the failed attempted hiring of Nikole Hannah-Jones provides a powerful teaching moment about such rhetoric and journalistic skills. It also raised awareness around basic questions of equity that plague institutions of journalism and higher education alike.

Can institutions of higher education, and especially public universities, objectively be said to fulfill their mission of serving and educating the next generation if they don't represent those they serve and instead continue to perpetrate segregation?

According to data from the National Center for Education Statistics, out of the 622 professors with tenure at the University of North Carolina during the 2019–2020 school, only eight were Black women. That's about 1% of the full-time professors with tenure at the school. The journalism school granted tenure to one Black woman, Trevy McDonald, in 2018 – but only after an initial rejection led her to hire a lawyer. Today, she remains the only tenured Black woman at the school (Anderson & Heim, 2021).

Can the media – journalists and news leaders – of the United States be objectively said to fulfill their mission of serving and informing the public if they don't represent those they serve and instead continue to perpetrate segregation?

The News Leaders Association and American Society of News Editors' most recent report, released in 2019, found that people of color comprised 21.9% of salaried employees reported by the newsrooms surveyed ("How Diverse Are US Newsrooms," 2018). At the same time, people of color make up around 40% of the population of the United States (United States Census Bureau, 2020). Some media organizations – like the Arkansas outlets owned by Hussman Jr. – do not even participate in the survey.

Such questions – and their answers – deserve media coverage and in-depth reporting. As demonstrated by what Hannah-Jones described as the "national scandal" involving her time at the University of North Carolina (CBS, 2021), it is only by drawing attention to details and context that many issues and stories can really be understood.

Thankfully, in Hannah-Jones' case, some media outlets did dig deeper and provided wider context, linking the University of North Carolina's treatment of Hannah-Jones to other recent events such as the university's decision in the preceding years to pay $2.5 million to a Confederate group to maintain a statue of a white supremacist. Others drew connections to the university's struggle to hire and retain faculty of color.

Similarly, a small handful of journalists drew attention to Hussman Jr.'s background and motives. Notably, independent journalist Jeremy Borden (2021) took a stab at reframing the conversation on his blog, questioning whether debate over the idea of objectivity in journalism was "a more digestible conversation than the one it veils: grappling with the legacy of generational power and white supremacy." Drawing attention to this background and context was important to understanding the issues surrounding Hannah-Jones' situation. Similar reporting is needed on other issues as well.

Looking forward, there is no question about what journalism's role should be. As a public service and integral part of a democratic society, holding the powerful to account is the industry's top priority, even when doing so involves stepping away from a veil of objectivity. There's no room for the press to behave as anyone's lapdog – or for any institution training future journalists to behave as such – when the future of American democracy depends in large part on the work of watchdog journalism.

References

Anderson, N., & Heim, J. (2021, June 8) Black female professors voice solidarity with journalist Nikole Hannah-Jones in UNC tenure showdown. *The Washington Post*. https://www. washingtonpost.com/education/2021/06/08/unc-black-professors-hannah-jones-tenure/

Bedingfield, S. (2021, June 24). The irony of complaints about Nikole Hannah-Jones's advocacy journalism. *The Washington Post*. https://www.washingtonpost.com/outlook/2021/06/24/ irony-complaints-about-nikole-hannah-joness-advocacy-journalism/

Borden, J. (2021, June 2). Walter Hussman's views should end the debate over objectivity. *UntoldStory Substack*. https://untoldstory.substack.com/p/walter-hussmans-views-should-end?s=r

CBS [CBS Mornings]. (2021, July 6). *Journalist Nikole Hannah-Jones on turning down UNC role following tenure controversy* [Video]. YouTube. https://www.youtube.com/watch?v=RRRs6iEyBHY

Drescher, J. (2021, May 30). Nikole Hannah-Jones, a mega-donor, and the future of journalism. *The Assembly*. https://www.theassemblync.com/long-form/nikole-hannah-jones-a-mega-donor-and-the-future-of-journalism/

Edmonds, R. (2021, November 9). After the Nikole Hannah-Jones blowup, UNC's journalism school is healing, but slowly. *Poynter.org*. https://www.poynter.org/ethics-trust/2021/unc-hussman-nikole-hannah-jones-update/

"How Diverse Are US Newsrooms?". (2018). American Society of News Editors. https://googletrends.github.io/asne/

Hussman, W. Jr. (2019, September 10). Impartiality is the source of a newspaper's credibility. *The Wall Street Journal*. http://libproxy.lib.unc.edu/login?url=https://www.proquest.com/newspapers/impartiality-is-source-newspapers-credibility/docview/2287308748/se-2?accountid=14244

Lowery, W. (2020, June 23). A reckoning over objectivity, led by black journalists. *The New York Times*. https://www.nytimes.com/2020/06/23/opinion/objectivity-black-journalists-coronavirus.html

Merriam-Webster. (n.d.). Words we're watching: Looking at 'bothsiding'. https://www.merriam-webster.com/words-at-play/bothsidesing-bothsidesism-new-words-were-watching

Pressman, M. (2018, November 5). Journalistic objectivity evolved the way it did for a reason. *Time*. https://time.com/5443351/journalism-objectivity-history/

Rosentiel, T. (2020, June 24). *Twitter thread*. https://twitter.com/TomRosenstiel/status/1275773988053102592

Sullivan, M. (2021, June 29). "Why it's so important that UNC trustees give Nikole Hannah-Jones the tenure she deserves." *The Washington Post*. https://www.washingtonpost.com/lifestyle/media/unc-nikole-hannah-jones-tenure/2021/06/28/cb51a03e-d82a-11eb-bb9e-70fda8c37057_story.html

United States Census Bureau. (2020). *QuickFacts*. https://www.census.gov/quickfacts/fact/table/US/PST045221

6

HOW JOURNALISTIC OBJECTIVITY TURNS MATTERS OF SCIENCE INTO MATTERS OF POLITICS

A Closer Look at Climate Change and COVID-19 Reporting

Jason Turcotte and Nicolas Hernandez Florez

Dating back to the days of *The Sun* and the penny press, the news media evolved to prioritize objectivity in the news-gathering process – a priority that has largely endured through today's media landscape. This shift toward the norm of objectivity, an economic norm rooted in attracting mass audiences, established one of the prevailing conventions of contemporary journalism: that both sides of an issue deserve equal footing in news content. Although this news routine has helped to ensure fairness in coverage of some matters, particularly in regards to politics, the objectivity norm is a detriment to the reporting of serious scientific issues and threatens public health and safety. The paramount goal of a free press is truth-seeking and to advance truth. When it comes to matters of science, objectivity obfuscates truth. When the journalistic quest for truth is replaced by a quest for objectivity, public health and safety suffer. Providing equal footing to climate change deniers and COVID-19 skeptics may offer a diversity of views, but also amplifies perspectives consistently refuted by scientific inquiry and, consequently, muddles truth.

From amplification of climate change deniers and bogus evidence from the Oregon Petition to misleading and non-contextualized coverage regarding COVID-19, this chapter explores the tension between truth and objectivity in the context of science, more specifically within the context of climate change and the global pandemic. As legacy news outlets are increasingly sensitive to allegations of bias and as misinformation and fringe beliefs spread at a rapid rate on social media platforms, news gatekeepers have allowed a blind loyalty to objectivity misguide audiences, politicize science, and threaten public health. Objectivity should be abandoned once issues reach a level of scientific consensus. When it comes to matters of science, the news norm of objectivity is often an obstacle to truth seeking, not a pathway to it.

DOI: 10.4324/9781003315605-9

Casting a Wider Net: The Economics of Objectivity

Scholars and historians identify news routines as a theoretical foundation for understanding the news business, and in particular news-gathering and production processes. Warren Breed (1955) explained that similar conventions are adopted across newsrooms, resulting in some degree of uniformity in news values, and how information is gathered and communicated to news audiences. He notes that these routines are not necessarily directives or ultimatums, but a process of tacit indoctrination learned through staff meetings, editorials, the editing process, and how journalists are rewarded within a newsroom's culture. In other words, patterns and routines are learned through a socialization process. The hierarchical structure of a newsroom works to standardize and maintain news norms; consequently, conventions become embedded in journalistic practice. Among these "patterns of identifiable behavior" is the pursuit of objectivity.

The earliest newspapers in the United States paid little mind to objectivity. At that time, the news business embraced a partisan slant and catered to smaller elite audiences that consisted of businessmen, landowners, political elites, and religious leaders, while excluding women, racial minorities, and the working class. The partisan slant was a profitable model for the news business until the steam-powered printing press helped to democratize news and information. With the greater ease of mass production, newsprint was reconceptualized as a product, a good, a commodity. But, in order to warrant the cost of mass-producing news, news organizations would need to expand their reach and audience. Therefore, to appeal to mass audiences and maximize profit, the news business underwent a seismic shift in journalistic routines, perhaps the most notable and most enduring being the departure from partisan bias to a relentless quest for objectivity.

Objectivity as a Tool for Expanding Audiences and Boosting Bottom Lines

In prioritizing objectivity as a news convention, it is tempting to assume that the shift from the partisan bias of the press to impartiality was an ideological, philosophical, or moral one; however, the adoption of objectivity norms was rooted in economics more than anything else. With the rise of the penny press, politically slanted news organizations had to shed ideological bias to attract a wider audience, expand reach, and increase news sales and bottom lines. The news business, following the efficiency of the steam-powered printing press, became a competitive industry with news organizations jostling for market share.

Since that time, the norms, like objectivity, and routines of news professionals have become increasingly market-driven. Some scholars and historians have noted that contemporary news routines serve a dual purpose – improving journalistic professionalism and credibility as well as maximizing profit – but in fact, as John McManus (1994) argues, market interests often supersede journalistic logic. Essentially, the news industry as the public knows it today has less to do with creating a public good and more to do with packaging news as a commodity. Despite some successful cable news organizations, news websites, and blogs with a partisan slant, most mainstream newsrooms continue to cling to objectivity as a news norm. In today's environment of media abundance and declining public trust in news, objectivity has persisted among journalistic practices.

Objectivity as a Contemporary News Norm and Routine

Dominant newsroom routines and the objectivity norm also meant more reliance on official sources and greater emphasis on the news value of conflict. In a two-party system, public affairs reporting that emphasizes objectivity above all else often quotes competing and opposed official sources. Oftentimes, objectivity can exaggerate the level of conflict of a topic when diametrically opposed official sources dominate the perspectives in news – an exaggeration of conflict that could pose problems for science reporting. As Gaye Tuchman (1973) once argued, objectivity exonerates the journalist from seeking truth and, rather, implores the news audience to decide what is and is not truthful.

It is important to note that aspiring for objectivity does not imply that journalists actively try to obfuscate truth; often the desired outcome of objectivity is a defense of the profession and defense of a reporters' credibility, and the routine of objective reporting can serve as a defense from allegations of media bias. Such a defensive strategy makes sense in today's contentious media and political environments. Allegations of media bias have always been a prevailing narrative in the discourse surrounding the news business, but there is some indication that the perception of bias has only grown in today's environment of media abundance. This accelerating decline in trust emerged in the 1990s, after the introduction of high household adoption rates for cable, and, later, the internet's emergence as a source for news and information. Allegations of news bias are even louder on social media platforms, particularly as algorithms prioritize like-minded views and ideologically charged content. It seems today's media landscape encourages journalists to continue the tradition of objective reporting, despite the routine's limitations to truth-seeking.

Oversimplification and False Duality: The Limitations of Objectivity

Objectivity can do wonders for ensuring more equitable political coverage, but even in this context, there are limitations. First, objectivity often results in journalists treating all issues as binary issues, suggesting that every issue has two sides, two truths. In reality, though, even political issues can come with a range of perspectives and rich nuance that can be lost in coverage that adheres to norms of objectivity. Such a point and counterpoint presentation can limit public discourse and understanding. Moreover, it shirks the truth-seeking responsibilities of the press, replacing it with a model of news production that essentially lets audiences determine their own truth and creates a false sense of debate. This underscores another routine of journalism: an emphasis on conflict-driven news.

Focusing on conflict as a news value not only encourages more readers and clicks but allows the continuation of objectivity as a prevailing norm. Conflict coverage is evident in two main areas of political coverage: elections and policymaking. In these respective contexts, journalists adopt framing devices that advance conflict as a news value ahead of other points of emphasis which may be more substantive. In election coverage, for example, news outlets have been observed to predominantly adopt "horse race" framing, referring to reporting on which candidate is ahead in the election by emphasizing polling results rather than policy platforms. As Larry Bartels (1988) describes, horse race framing highlights "competition for competition's sake" (p. 31). The enduring predominance of the horse race frame in election coverage can be attributed to the cyclical incentives on both sides of the reporting. For reporters, covering the political horse race is both easier than more substantial policy-related coverage, and attracts audience attention. Therefore, on both the supply and demand side, the horse race is incentivized and conforms nicely to objectivity routines by underscoring the competitive aspects of the two-party political system.

Like horse race coverage during elections, political reporters frequently employ game framing when covering policymaking. Like the horse race, this kind of reporting detracts emphasis from policy proposals in and of themselves, and instead reports on policy as components in a game among political actors. For instance, an analysis on coverage of the Affordable Care Act (ACA) found that even local news elected to cover the political strategy surrounding the ACA more than specific provisions in the law (Gollust et al., 2017). Additionally, when covering the ACA in 2013 and 2014, news outlets were much more likely to use politicians in the executive and legislative branches as sources than they were to use sources like application counselors, insurance representatives, or researchers. Even more recent commentary on policy coverage has critiqued the news media's tendency to report on the failure of Congress to pass legislation strengthening voting rights as a loss for Democrats rather than as a threat to Americans' right to vote.

This emphasis on strategic implications of policy for both political parties, and the "both sides" sourcing of Washington's establishment also aligns nicely with the objectivity model of news production, allowing elites from both sides of the aisle to weigh in.

Whether in the context of elections or policymaking, numerous researchers have highlighted the shortcomings of political reporting's overuse of binary strategic frames as opposed to substantive coverage, and the overreliance on official and elite sources to create the appearance of fairness and objectivity. The temptation to frame issues from a "both sides" standpoint can be attributed to market demands, relative ease, and the adherence to objectivity norms. This kind of coverage can lead to oversimplification of nuanced topics, a result that can cause a disservice to consumers of political news. When employing this same kind of coverage to scientific coverage, it can arguably cause even greater harm.

Scientific issues are a poor fit for the objectivity model of news reporting because objectivity is not always synonymous with truth-seeking. Reaching out to sources for "the other side" forces a binary narrative that may create a false duality within an issue, threaten public understanding, and contribute to misleading narratives or misinformation. Nowhere is this more prevalent than in news coverage of climate change and COVID-19.

Objectivity in the Context of Climate Change

At the turn of the 21st century scientific understanding of climate change, human causation, and the consequences for the environment and public health gained considerable clarity and scientific consensus. Nonetheless, public certainty of climate change was beginning to erode, with steady and significant declines in the extent to which people believed that global warming was a serious problem and that there was "solid evidence" showing the Earth's warming. In other words, the greater the scientific certainty, the more doubt Americans had about the science behind climate change. It is evident that the journalistic quest for objectivity played some role in diminishing public understanding of climate change.

In a sourcing analysis, researchers found that climate change contrarians were sourced slightly more often than credible, scientific sources (Petersen, Vincent, & Westerling, 2019), creating what researchers concluded was a "false balance" in mainstream news reporting on climate change. Equally troubling, the contrarians considerably outpaced scientific expert sources in stories found on emerging, new media websites.

One of the most notorious examples in which objectivity norms amplified views outside the scientific establishment involved 2007's Oregon Petition. Signed and aggressively circulated by a group of non-experts and rogue scientists, the petition of approximately 30,000 names – a motley crew of celebrities, nonscientists, free market lobbyists, and those without advanced degrees – claimed that the science behind climate change was bogus. The petition attracted considerable attention from the news media. Despite the National Academy of Sciences publicly denouncing the merits of the Oregon Petition, sources from the Heartland Institute, the American Enterprise Institute, and other partisan elites such as Christopher Monckton (who, along with most of the names listed in the Oregon petition, does not hold a degree in science) were elevated to elite source status when it came to news coverage of climate change. The amplification of non-believers of climate science, regardless of whether they held any degrees or expertise in climate science, created a "false balance" and facilitated a misguided public.

Additionally, in prioritizing objectivity above all else, journalists may engage in self-censorship and avoid reporting on climate change with substantive context or solutions for fear that they will be perceived as biased or practicing advocacy journalism. Yet, better models for reporting do exist. For instance, while recognizing that adopting an advocacy model can amplify claims of liberal bias, Declan Fahy (2017) suggests that instead of sourcing and supplying all sides with a megaphone, journalists should emphasize transparency and consensus within the scientific community. This reconceptualizing of traditional news norms, particularly objectivity, could be supported by a reliance on more data-driven journalism (Robbins & Wheatley, 2021).

Problems of creating a false balance or allowing misinformation to influence public opinion also exist in other science-related topics, and one can draw several parallels between the flawed objectivity routines of reporting climate change with the ways in which objectivity limits and threatens public understanding of the COVID-19 pandemic.

Objectivity in the Context of COVID-19 Coverage

The longstanding norm of objectivity in journalism is ill-equipped to guide news coverage when scientific phenomena become important and urgent. Rather than serve to promote public health or scientific knowledge, the news media's preoccupation with appearing objective can lead to confusion and skepticism among the public at a time when factual understanding can save lives. Early news coverage of the COVID-19 pandemic illustrates the issues that may arise with a press more focused on objectivity and equal treatment of "both sides" than on factual, scientific-based reporting.

In an informal survey of *New York Times* articles in the US section from January–March, 2020, one trend observed was the saturation of COVID-19 coverage through the lens of politics. Of all articles which referred the COVID-19 pandemic in the headline or lead of the article, 56.2% were framed primarily through an emphasis on politics, with headlines like "Trump Moves to Calm Fears as First US Death From Coronavirus Is Reported." By comparison, just 9.9% of early *New York Times* US COVID-19 coverage focused primarily on science/public health.

Politics is an area in which the United States' two-party system facilitates "two-sides" coverage. However, rather than covering policy disagreements or differences of opinion among political groups or figures, covering a pandemic with the intent of truth-seeking and saving lives requires direct, fact-based information and greater emphasis on scientific sources over political elites.

An example of an instance in which "two-sides" coverage created a sense of medical and scientific uncertainty can be seen in a March 15, 2020 headline which reads: "Nunes Encourages People to Dine Out as Experts Urge Them to Stay Home." Devin Nunes, referenced in the headline, was a former US representative and one of former President Donald Trump's most loyal supporters in Congress. This headline presents a partisan political figure and the consensus of health experts as equals and implies that isolation in the face of a deadly pathogen was a matter of policy debate rather than a matter of public health. The article's first paragraph once again frames Nunes' encouragement and the advice of public health experts as two sides of a debate, and it is not until the seventh and eleventh paragraphs that the advice of public health experts is referenced again. During a time when respondents that identify as Republicans are less likely to say that the scientific method generally produces accurate conclusions and more likely to view scientists as biased, the equal footing of Republican politicians and scientific experts as credible sources in COVID-19 coverage is irresponsible.

These examples and trends from the early stages of the pandemic reveal the limitations of news organizations' reliance on objectivity in science-based news coverage. Whether sheltering in the comfort of political reporting where "two-sides" framing is expected or spotlighting contrarians for no other reason than to report on an opposing view, the objectivity norm continues to guide news organizations to the detriment of clear communication from the most knowledgeable sources.

Moving Forward

If contemporary journalism is to prioritize its truth-seeking role, news professionals must rethink objectivity, particularly relating to issues with strong scientific consensus. The objectivity norms practiced for political and public policy reporting may be somewhat effective in minimizing journalistic bias and ensuring perspectives from multiple stakeholders are represented. But, such objectivity does little to advance truth-seeking when applied, without reflection, to scientific matters. Emerging scientific discovery and theory may call for a range of perspectives, in order to provide context, but a focus on truth-seeking means that those perspectives should come from credible, scientific sources. And issues with consensus from the scientific community, particularly those that directly impact public health and public safety, must be reported sans forced "bothsidesism."

Doing so may require not only a rethinking of objectivity's applications, but also a level of bravery. News professionals will always be the target of accusations of bias; the perception of bias is not going away with *more* objective reporting. Rather, the accusations of bias have always been a part of the tension between news organizations and their audiences. Such accusations cannot derail journalistic pursuit of truth under any circumstances, especially when the consequences of inaccurate reporting can be a matter of life or death for people and for the planet.

References

Bartels, L. M. (1988). *Presidential primaries and the dynamics of public choice*. Princeton University Press.

Breed, W. (1955). Social control in the newsroom: A functional analysis. *Social Forces, 33*, 326–335.

Fahy, D. (2017). Objectivity, false balance, and advocacy in news coverage of climate change. *Oxford Research Encyclopedia of Climate Science*. https://doi.org/10.1093/acrefore/9780190228620.013.345

Gollust, S. E., Baum, L. M., Niederdeppe, J., Barry, C. L., & Fowler, E. F. (2017). Local television news coverage of the Affordable Care Act: Emphasizing politics over consumer information. *American Journal of Public Health, 107*(5), 687–693.

McManus, J. H. (1994). *Market-driven journalism: Let the citizens beware?* Sage Publications.

Petersen, A. M., Vincent, E. M., & Westerling, A. L. (2019). Discrepancy in scientific authority and media visibility of climate change scientists and contrarians. *Nature Communications*, *10*. https://doi.crg/10.1038/s41467-019-09959-4

Robbins, D., & Wheatley, D. (2021). Complexity, objectivity, and shifting roles: Environmental correspondents march to a changing beat. *Journalism Practice*, *15*(9), 1289–1306.

Tuchman, G. (1973). Objectivity as strategic ritual: An examination of newsmen's notions of objectivity. *American Journal of Sociology*, 77(4), 660–679.

When Objectivity Isn't Enough

A Case Study on Feminicidios, Violence Against Women, and Anti-Violence Activism

Leandra H. Hernández

Over the past several years, news reports, scholars, activists, and communities alike have lamented the violence that has plagued several Latin American countries. Mexico, Colombia, Argentina, and Venezuela, to name just a few, have experienced political turmoil and unrest resulting from the intersection of politics, religion, government structures, and cultural forces; indeed, Venezuela has been described as the most dangerous country currently in Latin America. Research has generated in-depth explorations of such violence, highlighting how violence – and gendered violence in particular – proliferates throughout several countries across Latin America. Violence against women – particularly feminicidios –has become a global public health epidemic that plagues women throughout Latin America.

In this essay, I address whether journalists should operate primarily as either objective reporters or moral witnesses as demonstrated through a consideration of how news organizations frame violence against women in US and Latin American contexts. I problematize journalistic news values associated with objectivity and advocate on behalf of journalists serving as moral witnesses in trauma-informed journalism contexts that focus on feminicidios.

Feminicidios and Violence against Women

Violence against women is a global public health epidemic and also a significant human rights issue. According to recent studies conducted by the World Health Organization (2013), globally, "38% of all women who were murdered were murdered by their intimate partners, and 42% of women who have experienced physical or sexual violence at the hands of a partner had experienced injuries as a result" (para. 6). Located within the larger umbrella term of gender violence against women are the interrelated terms femicide and feminicide (or feminicidio).

DOI: 10.4324/9781003315605-10

Femicide is defined as the misogynistic killing of women by men, or the killing of women by men *because* they are women (Hernández and De Los Santos Upton, 2018; Radford & Russell, 1992). Femicide focuses upon violence against women in the context of unequal gender relations and through the lens of patriarchal power and domination. In other words, gender is of utmost importance as it forms the main, material cause of the act of violence. Building upon the term femicide, the term fem*in*icide (or feminicidio in Spanish) more thoroughly encompasses and articulates the relationships between and among sex, gender, and violence in Latin American contexts with particular attention paid to the ways in which feminicidios manifest themselves in different state and nation contexts (Hernández & De Los Santos Upton, 2018). Feminicide, a term coined by Mexican feminists Julia Monárrez and Marcela Lagarde, centralizes the experiences of Mexican (and also Latin American) women and expands femicide, a gender-specific word for homicide, to include the killing of women based on their social or biological gender, and also the characteristics attributed to that gender.

Of the 25 countries with the highest rates of feminicide in the world, 14 countries are to be found in Latin America and the Caribbean. Several factors have contributed to disproportionately increasing rates of feminicide throughout Latin America. In Mexico, in particular, spikes in femicides made national and international headlines in the 1990s when several women who worked at maquiladoras were murdered in Ciudad Juárez. Later, Ciudad Juárez was ranked as the most violent city in the world outside of a war zone from 2009 to 2011. According to recent reports, between 1985 and 2014, some 47,178 women were killed in Mexico due to their gender; moreover, statistics on the number of femicides that occur in Mexico and throughout Latin America continue to increase with each passing year (Gamboa et al., 2020).

News Coverage of Violence Against Women

Scholars have long illustrated the ways in which the news as a cultural institution supports the beliefs, values, and norms of the ruling elite that wields social, economic, and political power within a hierarchy of social formations. As a cultural force that powerfully disseminates information about "reality" and shapes audiences' perceptions of various cultural groups, it is commonly believed that the news must appear ideologically neutral, fair, and unbalanced. Disguising its ideological roots, the news purports to portray everyday occurrences in a neutral or objective manner. In practice, though, this supposed "'neutrality' is won through the delimiting of arguments so that truly oppositional positions are never presented as legitimate considerations, and the framing of stories so that they appear not to be ideological at all, but instead seem natural and grounded in everyday reality" (Meyers, 2004, p. 96). When these strategies are utilized, journalists and news outlets illustrate that news coverage of people of color – particularly women of color – is actually not ideologically neutral at all. Additionally, through framing, news media have the power to proliferate certain views and repress others, emphasizing particular victims while ignoring others, and thus "disseminating powerful messages concerning who matters most in society" (Richards et al., 2014, p. 27).

As I mentioned earlier in the essay, violence against women is a global public health epidemic and worldwide concern. Moreover, media coverage of violence against women supports the interests of the state, with the news rarely covering violence against women unless it is an unusual or highly sensationalized topic. Given the heightened status of concerns surrounding gendered violence against women, the role of the mass media – particularly journalism – in disseminating information about violence against women becomes more pressing than ever. When news media choose to cover issues of violence against women by relying on distorted narratives about domestic violence (as one example of femicide), they perpetuate dangerous myths that minimize the seriousness of this violence. At the same time, however, when reporting accurately, news media can play an important role in shaping public opinion and mobilizing community support. Gender, race, and class intersect in powerful ways to shape how contemporary news covers and frames victims, perpetrators, and acts of violence.

From a feminicidio context, the scant literature that analyzes feminicidios of women throughout Latin America highlights problematic themes related to misinterpretation, culpability, spectacle, and dehumanization. As Héctor Domínguez-Ruvalcaba and Ignacio Corona (2010) illustrate, the news media play a significant, instrumental role in shaping the dissemination of and reception of information about gender violence against women. News discourses can misinterpret news information and events, neutralize events, impact perceptions of blame and culpability, and serve to incite fear amongst community members and those detached from geopolitical locations of violence. In Latin American contexts, for example, Guatemalan news outlets can feature up to 15 articles about feminicidios daily, which feeds the fear of local residents with sensationalized, gory details about the murdering of women throughout the country without any resolution or call to action (Godoy-Paiz, 2012). In this context, the peculiarities of feminicide news coverage discourses hypersensationalize the gore and violence, which is similar to broader news coverage of general feminicides in Mexico. Thus, given such themes present in news coverage of feminicidios – victims blamed for the violence they experience, victims lying about their violences, the erasure of all voices other than "credible white men," and the use of violence journalism to frame violence against women – I problematize news values associated with objectivity and advocate on behalf of journalists serving as moral witnesses in this context when necessary.

Moral Witnessing & News Coverage of Feminicidios

As I have noted thus far, news coverage of violence against women highlights several themes that problematize traditional news values and mores pertaining to objectivity. When journalistic concepts and dynamics such as credibility, spectacle, gore, and dehumanization lie at the center of news coverage of violence against women, other concepts such as objectivity, emotional distance, and emotional neutrality must be problematized and critiqued. Although outside the confines of this essay, I provide two questions that I hope will contribute to larger, continuing conversations about media ethics and news coverage of violence against women.

The first asks how *should* the news cover reproductive violence against women? What are ethically sensitive strategies that can be used to not further exacerbate and perpetuate problematic news themes and stereotypes? On the one hand, if the news purportedly strives to provide fair and balanced news coverage, it is sensible to focus mostly on the factual details of the case. However, one of the limitations of this news coverage strategy is that it can lead to reader detachment from and numbness to 1) the violence at hand and 2) the larger systematic factors that undergird and sustain violence against women. On the other hand, and at the other end of the spectrum, news coverage that sensationalizes violence against women and the gory details could potentially influence viewers to think that violence against women in a particular location is more exaggerated than is in fact the case. This exaggeration could lead to oversimplified, stereotypical perceptions of violence in the larger national imaginary, particularly when such coverage does not provide resolutions or calls to action for local and national justice systems to address such violence.

The second issue related to news coverage of violence against women concerns news values that privilege objectivity. In response to such privileging, we advocate on behalf of moral witnessing as one alternative to "traditional" journalism paradigms. As Marvi Pantti (2019) notes, when journalists serve as witnesses, they turn first-hand testimonials from witnesses into narratives and serve an important communicative function when they perform active moral engagement in violent, tragic events. As opposed to traditional journalistic reporting steeped within values of detachment and objectivity, bearing witness involves an attempt to elicit an affective experience that invites audience action. As Pantti (2019) describes, bearing witness is driven by a moral purpose and does not simply transmit information about the event or news story. Bearing witness is distinguished from traditional journalistic reporting because its morality is bound to the recognition of another's suffering. Put simply, bearing witness transmits moral responsibility.

Another consideration that arises in conversations of bearing witness is the extent to which journalists are trained in trauma-informed and culturally competent journalism approaches. I am not arguing that having Latin American journalists covering these stories is necessary from an authenticity perspective; however, having a person of color sensitive to the unique cultural, historical, and political nuances of the location or cultural group at the heart of the story can enhance the ways in which the news coverage is framed. For example, Frida Guerrera, a Mexican journalist with a column in *Vice*, is a reporter on the ground with intimate knowledge of Mexican culture and the systematic factors that promote and facilitate violence against women. She is a strong proponent of interviewing families, friends, and local activists in her news coverage of violence against women, rather than just male police officials. Moreover, her activist background and experiential knowledge as a domestic violence survivor – her embodied knowledge – informs the ways in which she frames violence against women in her news stories. Guerrera's journalistic approach to news coverage of violence against women is inspiring and highlights important implications about the transformative nature of her journalistic strategies.

Can this kind of news coverage – coverage that does not blame the victim, privilege male sources of information, or sensationalize gore – transform the ways in which violence against women is framed in the news? As a transformative mode of journalism that bears witness and is guided by a moral sense of action, this approach could humanize victims, expose problematic cultural institutions such as hyper-machismo and the government, and inspire readers to respond to this coverage in humanizing, activistic ways. Thus, trauma news contexts, such as feminicidios and violence against women, necessitate a critical interrogation of objectivity and detachment and can be handled more sensitively, effectively, and ethically when journalists bear witness communicatively and relationally.

Ultimately, the lessons learned in this case study about objectivity, moral witnessing, and the humanization of trauma can be applied to the field of journalism more broadly, not simply trauma journalism or violence journalism. Considering the role of the "myth" of objectivity, two fundamental questions arise: Whose interests does objectivity serve, and what are the implications of how seemingly objective reports may be (and are often) infused with ideological underpinnings (Brewin, 2013). This case study on news coverage of feminicides illustrates how objectivity can be detrimental to news coverage of several topics, particularly when it is not critiqued or its use is not problematized. Moreover, scholars and journalists could shift from "attacking" the concept of objectivity, as Mark Brewin (2013) describes, and instead consider the *performance* of objectivity instead. Such an approach, as Sandrine Boudana (2011) describes, highlights that objectivity is not a synonym for neutrality or detachment. Rather, a performance of objectivity places the concept within its appropriate moral and ethical considerations, views it as an evolving practice, and stresses the notion of "response-ability" that acknowledges the power journalists hold and their responsibility in responding to criticisms of their work. Such a reworking of objectivity could benefit the field of journalism more broadly and news coverage of violence against women more specifically, particularly in efforts to witness, strengthen relationality, and honor those covered.

References

Boudana, S. (2011). A definition of journalistic objectivity as a performance. *Media, Culture & Society*, *33*(3), 385–398.

Brewin, M. W. (2013). A short history of the history of objectivity. *The Communication Review*, *16*(4), 211–229.

Domínguez-Ruvalcaba, H., & Corona, I. (2010). (Eds.). *Gender violence at the US–Mexico border: Media representation and public response*. University of Arizona Press.

Gamboa, S., Shen-Berro, J., Flores Guzmán, K., & Abdelkader, R. (2020, January 24). Shooting death of young woman activist returns spotlight to 'femicides' in Juarez and Mexico. *NBC News*. https://www.nbcnews.com/news/latino/shooting-death-young-woman-activist-returns-spotlight-femicides-juarez-mexico-n1120811/

Hernández, L. H., & De Los Santos Upton, S. (2018). *Challenging reproductive control and gendered violence in the Américas: Intersectionality, power, and struggles for rights*. Lexington Books.

Godoy-Paiz, P. (2012). Not just "another woman": Femicide and representation in Guatemala. *The Journal of Latin American and Caribbean Anthropology*, *17*(1), 88–109.

Meyers, M. (2004). African American women and violence: Gender, race, and class in the news. *Critical Studies in Media Communication*, *21*(2), 95–118.

Pantti, M. K. (2019). Journalism and witnessing. In Wahl-Jorgensen, K., & Hanitzsch, T. (Eds.), *The handbook of journalism studies* (pp. 151–164). Routledge.

Radford, J., & Russell, D. (1992). (Eds.) *Femicide: The politics of woman killing*. Woodbridge, Twayne.

Richards, T. N., Gillespie, L. K., & Smith, M. D. (2014). An examination of the media portrayal of femicide–suicides: An exploratory frame analysis. *Feminist Criminology*, *9*(1), 24–44.

World Health Organization. (2013). Violence against women: A 'global health problem of epidemic proportions.' https://www.who.int/mediacentre/news/releases/2013/violence_against_women_20130620/en/

PART III

Diversity and Representation in Journalism

Like so many fields, journalism has traditionally been predominated by white men. This isn't a new problem. More than half a century ago, the Kerner Commission identified the issue; established by President Lyndon B. Johnson, the commission found that the press "has too long basked in a white world looking out of it, if at all, with white men's eyes and white perspective." The industry responded very slowly. Eventually, in 1979, the American Society of News Editors committed itself to address the issue, and promised to take steps so that by the turn of the century newsrooms would have racial and ethnic minority representation that matched the country overall. But that commitment was never carried out. Today, people from minority backgrounds make up more than 40% of the population and 35% of the workforce, but just around 20% of newsroom staff. The situation is even more bleak in managerial positions.

This fact has had a significant impact in a variety of ways. First, it has led to limited professional opportunities and promotions for people from diverse and historically marginalized communities, and a toxic work environment that pushes frustrated journalists to leave the field. Additionally, it has had a profound effect on the topics that are covered, and the tone of such coverage. When diversity is lacking, perspectives and viewpoints are similarly limited, and a non-inclusive workforce can lead to non-inclusive content that is culturally insensitive or which reinforces stereotypes.

This situation has broad implications. Because of the impact that news media have on the public agenda, problems within the field of journalism spill over and affect a range of cultural and social views, perspectives, and norms. Accordingly, Part III addresses several important dimensions related to diversity in journalism, and renews calls to recognize and improve coverage and representation today.

DOI: 10.4324/9781003315605-11

7

AFRICAN AMERICAN NEWSPAPERS

The Voice of the Community

Masudul Biswas

Historically, African American newspapers, also known as the Black Press, advanced the Black community's voice against slavery, racial segregation, and the deprivation of civil rights, such as voting rights. Additionally, the Black press countered negative stereotypes about African American identity in mainstream media. In recent years, these ethnic news outlets have also been vocal on the issues that matter most to the Black community, including racial injustice, police brutality, disparities in healthcare, and the disproportionate effects of the COVID-19 pandemic (Biswas, Sipes, & Brost, 2021).

Since an ethnic media outlet primarily serves a particular ethnic, lingual, or cultural minority group and is often, *not always*, owned by members of a community, newspapers that are geared toward the Black community are considered ethnic news outlets. African American newspapers, print or digital, also function as a type of community journalism by serving the African American community (Biswas & Kim, 2020). According to the National Newspaper Publishers Association (2022), there are more than 200 African American-owned community newspapers, and, according to the Pew Research Center (2021), there are 195 Black-oriented newspapers, which may not all be owned by African Americans but which publish content geared toward the African American community.

Defining the Black Press

As news publications become digitized, scholars and professionals struggle to come to a consensus regarding what constitutes African American newspapers or Black media. Traditionally, African American newspapers, also known as the Black press, are ethnic news outlets typically owned and produced by African Americans to serve the Black community in the US. Additionally, activism has also been cited

DOI: 10.4324/9781003315605-12

as an attribute of the Black press, as these news outlets historically have a mission to advance community members' rights (Wolseley, 1990). However, there are also non-Black-owned digital publications, such as *The Root* and *HuffPost Black Voices*, that are geared toward Black audiences. Accordingly, Miya Williams Fayne (2020) argues that "the definition of the Black press that was constructed based on traditional print Black press outlets is no longer comprehensive" (p. 716). It is also argued that a revision of a print media-driven definition of the Black press is necessary because of the growth of digital-first or digital-only Black media that are not Black-owned but are directed toward the African American community.

Therefore, though some would still prefer to stick to an old definition of the Black press, many Black journalists have begun to accept "one universal criterion:" the print/digital Black press includes any outlet "that targets an African American audience" (Williams Fayne, 2020, p. 716). Such a shift represents the argument that even if an outlet is not Black-owned, it can largely be Black-managed, and can contain more content about Black issues. This broader definition encompasses new and growing Black media spaces such as "Black Twitter," and other media that are increasingly important today. In summation, today the growing consensus is that the African American press can publish in either print or digital formats, does not necessarily need to be Black-owned, but should play an advocacy role.

Historical Roles of African American Newspapers

African American newspapers are the oldest ethnic media in the US; in 2027, the Black press will observe 200 years of its journey. Historically, starting with the publication of *Freedom's Journal* in 1827, ethnic news media in the US have played three major roles – political, social, and cultural (Biswas, 2011). While contemporary mainstream media may now cover Black issues more than in the past, African American newspapers still serve a critical "dual role" by informing the Black community about issues important to its members and taking a stance against acts of inequality in society. Further, Catherine Squires (2002) argues that by highlighting political ideology and community interests, these newspapers helped to form a group identity for the African American community.

The political role of the Black press has been well documented, especially in the context of racial segregation and the Civil Rights movement. In those eras, mainstream news media rarely covered racial discrimination against Blacks. For example, mainstream newspaper coverage ignored the issue of voting rights for Blacks in the state of Mississippi during the post-reconstruction period in the late 19th century. However, this issue was widely covered by Black newspapers. Additionally, mainstream newspapers throughout this period, including for example *The New York Enquirer*, promoted negative stereotypes about African Americans, particularly in association with crime. Black newspapers, like *Freedom's Journal*, however, combated such skewed coverage of *Enquirer*-type mainstream newspapers, avoiding criticism of Black people for even undesirable behaviors, highlighting crimes committed by whites, and linking whiteness with criminality in a manner similar to how crimes committed by Blacks were overrepresented in mainstream newspapers. Journalists working for *Freedom's Journal* used to gather and republish white crime stories from other newspapers to create an awareness that it is not Black people who are always involved with criminal activities. Additionally, this first Black news outlet highlighted safety concerns related to kidnapping and "white lawlessness" in the urban North where "free" (i.e. freed from slavery) African Americans lived (Baaki, 2019, p. 129).

Issues of racial segregation and discrimination certainly continued into the 20th century, during which time the Black press coverage generally emphasized civil rights issues and institutional discrimination that affect the African American community. While reporting on World War II, the Black press also covered issues of race relations and discrimination in Army units. Besides addressing consciousness about civic rights, the Black press also facilitated community empowerment through its coverage which highlighted the heroic and patriotic roles of Black Americans during a time of racism and systemic bias. By offering such coverage, these newspapers created awareness about the community's rights. Hence, African American newspapers became influential in terms of mobilization around issues in the Black community.

Mainstream newspapers not only ignored the issue of racial discrimination, but also provided negative coverage of Blacks. Whenever a Black person committed a crime or was allegedly associated with a crime, they became a subject of a news story in general-audience newspapers. This trend continued even long after formal policies of legally mandated segregation ended. For example, in its coverage of the Central Park Five case of 1989, many newspapers unfairly and inappropriately condemned the five Black youths who were alleged (later proven innocent) to have committed murder, while overlooking the miscarriage of justice that led to their unlawful conviction. In contrast, an African American newspaper, the *New York Amsterdam News*, reflected its advocacy mission of protecting the civil rights of the Black community by offering an alternative narrative to that seen in the mainstream press. In the *Amsterdam News'* counternarrative, the primary victims were five Black male youths who – as investigations years later uncovered – had been framed for the crime. Further, the *New York Amsterdam News* also placed emphasis on "racism, injustice, and hypocrisy on the plight of the youths involved in the case" (Beardsley & Teresa, 2017, p. 175). Similar to what *Freedom's Journal* did about 160 years earlier, the *New York Amsterdam News* advanced a counternarrative to what was offered in the mainstream newspapers' coverage.

The African American newspaper industry grew in reaction to the skewed and exclusionary role of the white press that ignored issues of concerns to Black minorities. To combat mainstream white media's negligence and prevailing racial injustice against the Black community, African American newspapers played advocacy roles since the early 19th century, contributing to many historical achievements, such as the abolition of slavery and legal reform around civil rights. For many of these publications, including acclaimed African American newspapers like *The Washington Bee*, the *Chicago Defender*, the *Cleveland Gazette*, the *Afro-American* in Baltimore, and the *Savannah Tribune*, all of which began publication in the late 19th or early 20th centuries, there was one common mission: to build pride, uplift the community, and encourage the fight for civil rights (Teresa, 2015). Consequently, the Black community found reading Black newspapers in lieu of mainstream newspapers to be both a symbol of protest and solidarity in the fight against racial discrimination.

During the Civil Rights Movement in the 1960s, smaller, independent Black publications, such as the *Black Panther*, *Muhammad Speaks*, *The Voice*, *Crusader* and *Negro Worlds*, offered more activist-style reporting than the commercial Black press, such as *Afro*, *The Philadelphia Tribune* and *The Chicago Tribune*. Commercial Black newspapers did not always agree with the viewpoints of smaller alternative outlets, often for fear of losing advertising revenue. Fred Carroll (2017) argues that such courageous coverage by alternative Black publications "forced the major news media outlets to acknowledge that no broadcast network or newspaper organization could provide complete coverage without including African Americans" (p. 161).

Along with monitoring and standing up against racial injustice, Stephen Lacy, James Stephens, and Stan Soffin (1991) observe that African American newspapers also played a non-political function by preserving the culture and heritage of African Americans in the US. For instance, while African American celebrities were often either ignored or harshly criticized in mainstream newspapers, these celebrities received important coverage in the Black press. Such instances demonstrate the broad cultural importance of the Black press and counters the notion that African American newspapers will only survive as long as there is anti-Black racism in society.

Contemporary Roles of African American Newspapers

Similar to the roles they played in the 19th and 20th centuries, African American newspapers have continued to serve as a voice for justice for the Black community in the 21st century, while also serving informational and cultural functions. In this new century, the scope of African American newspapers has expanded to digital news outlets, such as online versions of the *Houston Defender*, *The Philadelphia Tribune* and the *Chicago Defender*, or digital-only outlets such as *The Root*, *Blavity* and *Atlanta Black Star*. Keeping with the tradition of the Black press, these newspapers' coverage has continued to differ, in terms of tone and perspectives, from the general-audience news media in covering contemporary issues such as the Black Lives Matter movement, police brutality against the Black community, voting rights or voter suppression, access to healthcare, and the disproportionate effects of the COVID-19 pandemic among African Americans. Simultaneously, the Black community has found a new space for activism and civic engagement when their rights are restricted and when members of their community are treated unfairly by law enforcement and other institutions because of their race.

Killing of George Floyd and the Black Lives Matter Movement

The Black Lives Matter movement was launched with a social media hashtag in 2012 in the wake of Trayvon Martin's death and the controversial acquittal of George Zimmerman, and went on to shape Black Americans' civic engagement on social media platforms in the years that followed. Notably, a study by the Pew Research Center found that the #BlackLivesMatter hashtag was used about 30 million times from July 2013 through May 2018 (Auxier, 2020). This movement picked up momentum in 2014 after the deaths of Michael Brown in Missouri and Eric Garner in New York at the hands of police officers. Further, the summer of 2020 is regarded as a critical point in US history. Nationwide protests in response to George Floyd's killing transcended borders and spread to other nations, and reminded Americans that more work had to be done to address deeply ingrained racial inequalities and injustice. In the days immediately following the killing of Floyd, more than 8 million tweets were sent containing the hashtag #BlackLivesMatter (Auxier, 2020).

The protest movement was impossible to ignore, and both general-audience media and African American media covered the Black Lives Matter movement. But there was a difference between these two types of media in terms of the extent of coverage and community perspectives. Despite the continuation of police brutality directed towards the Black community, mainstream media's coverage of these incidents fell between 2015 and the killing of Floyd in May, 2020 (Mehta, 2020). Further, Danielle Brown (2020) argues that mainstream media outlets did not highlight the messages of all social protests fairly, focusing excessive attention on instances of violence and looting when covering protests against racism and police brutality, while focusing much more attention on positive aspects of women's rights marches and anti-Trump protests.

In contrast, African American newspapers reflected community voices in their coverage of Floyd's killing at the hand of a white police officer. The *Chicago Defender* ran a story with a headline, "Stop Killing Us," which is a slogan from the St. Sabina Church's demonstration in Chicago. Additionally, to educate community members on how to record an incident of racism and injustice with their smartphones, the *Chicago Defender* published a "how-to" article prominently on their website's homepage. In contrast, this type of content was not typically found or prominently displayed in general-audience news outlets (Biswas, 2020).

African American newspapers' coverage of Floyd's killing also offered context to readers. By addressing lingering frustrations with the incidents of racial injustice and ephemeral solutions to institutional racism, Black newspapers helped readers understand the significance of the large-scale protests. For example, *The Philadelphia Tribune*, which has been serving the Black community for over 160 years, ran an article on historical racial disparities in the US to educate readers, particularly those of the younger generations. The coverage around the Floyd killing also raised other, even bigger issues and concerns for the Black community, such as the disproportionate number of African Americans in correctional centers, and disparities in household income and career opportunities between comparably qualified Black and white people.

Additionally, in contrast to those mainstream media outlets that highlighted destruction caused by some protestors, African American newspapers focused on the positive steps taken by the Black community in response to incidences of violence and looting, such as cleaning up the streets and repairing stores and establishments in the affected neighborhoods. Additionally, African American newspapers also drew attention to way in which some white supremacist groups infiltrated Black Lives Matter rallies in order to sabotage protests (Biswas, 2020), and drew attention to the way in which police responded differently to white and Black protests. Notably, *Blavity*, a digital-only Black news publication, compared police inaction against gun-bearing lockdown protesters in Michigan, to the aggressive police response to anti-Black racism protesters.

Voting Rights

By early 2022, 19 US states had passed at least 34 laws restricting or regulating voting rights (Brennan Center for Justice, 2022a). For example, in September 2021, Texas passed a law that limits voting access by tightening mail-in ballot requirements, introducing measures to protect partisan poll watchers, and reducing options for ballot drop boxes and drive-thru voting. Texas was not alone, and other states also passed measures that limited days during which voting can occur, and that imposed stricter voter ID requirements. Such measures, as documented by the Brennan Center for Justice (2022b), disproportionately disadvantage and disenfranchise communities of color and increase the racial gap in voter turnout.

Such restrictions are especially concerning to the African American community, which has long struggled for voting rights. While the Fourteenth Amendment, approved in 1868, affirmed citizenship for African Americans, many states soon thereafter passed laws imposing new restrictions and burdensome requirements for voting. Requirements such as literacy tests and poll taxes limited the Black community's ability to vote freely for the next century. Enactment of the Voting Rights Act in 1965 improved the situation, but many people today still remain understandably concerned about any new measures that similarly restrict the vote. In such a context, African American newspapers, along with liberal mainstream media outlets, covered perspectives and information on how restrictive voting laws will affect communities of color, including the Black community. For example, *The Root* ran 89 stories from mid-2020 through early 2022 on voting rights. Even more dramatically, *Afro* ran about 226 stories on voting rights from early 2021 to early 2022, including a story in March, 2022, on Black voters' legal challenge to Louisiana's new redistricting map that did not accurately reflect African American demographics in the state. *The Root* also highlighted the roles of Black leaders in their fight to overturn restrictive laws and racialized redistricting of a congressional district, and ran a story about US Representative Terri Sewell's commitment to re-introduce the Freedom to Vote Act. A number of news and commentary articles published in *Afro* conveyed a sentiment that recent restrictions on voting gutted the Voting Rights Act and urged President Joe Biden to issue an executive order on expanding voting rights. When multiple states were introducing voter restriction laws in 2021, *Afro* ran an editorial, "Our Communities Need Citizenship for All," and published a commentary with the headline, "Citizens punished for voting fair and square in Georgia."

Healthcare

For a long time, African Americans have been one of the top uninsured groups in the US, and have suffered from racial disparities in healthcare and wide-ranging social inequities. Hence, racial disparities for Black Americans in healthcare has been another major news item in African American newspapers. For example, research has found that one-third of Black newspaper coverage of cancer utilized a health disparity frame. In such coverage, Black newspaper editors and writers drew on first-hand knowledge of and experience with the negative health outcomes caused by racial disparities in healthcare (Cohen et al., 2008). While mainstream newspapers also covered societal causes of racial disparities in healthcare, Amy Rasmussen (2014) observed that mainstream newspaper coverage was not as comprehensive as news coverage by African American newspapers. Moreover, compared to mainstream newspaper coverage, African American newspapers ran more stories regarding the impact of healthcare policy in their communities. Further, unlike African American newspapers, mainstream news media usually fails to blame politicians and policymakers who create and maintain policies that perpetuate health care disparities.

The Affordable Care Act (ACA, also known as Obamacare) became law in 2010, and, when it was fully implemented in 2014, began to help reduce the rate of uninsured African Americans. Though the ACA brought down the number of uninsured African Americans from 19% in 2013 to 11% in 2016 (Artiga, Orgera, & Damino, 2019), it did not fully address racial disparities in the US healthcare system. When President Donald Trump and Republicans in Congress made efforts to repeal and replace the ACA, African American newspapers focused on the political maneuvering and reflected the community's concerns. Notably, an examination of coverage of the 2017 policy debates about repealing and replacing the ACA in the online versions of three Black newspapers – *The Philadelphia Tribune, Afro,* and the *Atlanta Black Star* – shows that coverage overwhelmingly focused on conflict and consequence frames. While the conflict frame reflects ideological division and political maneuverings between Democrats and Republicans, the consequence frame largely highlights the potential impacts of an end to the ACA among the Black community (Biswas & Kim, 2020). These three Black newspapers also addressed the solution frame, and pointed out both the weaknesses and strengths in the ACA. Simultaneously, these stories promoted the idea of Medicare for All as a way to reduce healthcare costs for many who were not fully covered by the ACA.

COVID-19 Pandemic

The African American community was disproportionately affected by the COVID-19 pandemic (Johns Hopkins Medicine, 2020), largely due to the prevalence of pre-existing health conditions caused by high numbers of uninsured African Americans.

This issue, too, received significant attention in the Black press. Analysis of this coverage, during the first wave of the pandemic, showed that compared to general-audience newspaper coverage, Black news sites' coverage focused more often on the action frame, which included stories about safety guidelines and testing information, creating a task force on racial disparities in COVID-19 victims, tracking of COVID-19 cases and deaths by race, and mobilizing support for the worst-hit Black community members. Other stories that were framed similarly included articles about fundraising events to help African American victims of the COVID-19 pandemic, Black doctors' initiatives to expand COVID-19 tests in the African American community, and financial support for minority-owned businesses. Such articles also included headlines that demanded action, such as was the case with an article published in the *Michigan Chronicle*, "Save Black Lives from COVID-19." In contrast, general-audience newspapers – *The New York Times, The Washington Post*, the *Detroit Free Press and The Baltimore Sun* – used societal cause/responsibility and consequence frames significantly more often (Biswas, Sipes, & Brost, 2021).

African American newspapers also addressed the pandemic's impact on the community, and such content was frequently seen in the Black press, including publications like *Afro*, the *Michigan Chronicle, News One* and the *Atlanta Black Star*. Historically, African American newspapers have been vocal against racial disparities in health and other sectors, and have worked to bring attention to and how such disparities affect their communities. Reporting on societal causes of a problem and its consequences is an important function of African American newspapers, and sometimes these newspapers reminded readers of past or continued discrimination by running headlines like, "The Coronavirus Recession Is Economic History Repeating Itself for Black Folks."

Conclusion

A common role that African American newspapers played both historically and today involves speaking out against racial injustice directed toward the Black community. As an ethnic as well as a community media, African American newspapers, either print or digital, have a commitment to advance the perspectives and concerns of the Black community. Therefore, disparities against Black Americans in the criminal justice system, voting, and healthcare had been major topics for coverage. Additionally, there are other topics, not covered in this chapter, which also have received significant attention, including educational attainment, employment opportunities and disparities, and environmental concerns. Often, and especially compared to general-audience newspapers, African American newspapers address such issues directly, with headlines written as if a news story is speaking on behalf of a Black person directly: "Stop Killing Us," "Our Communities Need Citizenship for All," "Black Businesses are Bleeding," "Save Black Lives."

While advancing the community's perspectives around racial injustice, African American newspapers have also played an informational role in keeping the community aware of happenings in politics, the economy, and the society at large. By playing this dual role – both informing the community and advocating on its behalf – African American newspapers, and the Black press overall, stay relevant and competitive in a diverse media landscape where their community members have more options than ever for seeking news.

References

Artiga, S., Orgera, K., & Damino, A. (2019, February 13). Changes in health coverage by race and ethnicity since implementation of the ACA, 2013–2017. *Kaiser Family Foundation.* https://www.kff.org/disparities-policy/issue-brief/changes-inhealth-coverage-by-race-and-ethnicity-since-implementation-of-the-aca-2013-2017/

Auxier, B. (2020). *Social media continue to be important political outlets for Black Americans.* Pew Research Center. https://www.pewresearch.org/fact-tank/2020/12/11/social-media-continue-to-be-important-political-outlets-for-black-americans/

Baaki, B. (2019). White crime and the early African American press: Elements of reprinting and reporting in New York's Freedom's Journal. *American Periodicals, 29*(2): 121–134.

Beardsley, K., & Teresa, C. (2017). The journey from "just us" to some "justice": Ideology and advocacy, the New York Amsterdam News, and the central park jogger story. *American Periodicals, 27*(2): 165–179.

Biswas, M. (2020). Roundup: Ethnic media's coverage of protests around the death of George Floyd in police custody. *Media Diversity Forum.* https://www.mediadiversityforum.lsu.edu/ethnic-media-coverage-of-george-floyd-death.html

Biswas, M. (2011) *Ethnic online newspapers vs. mainstream online newspapers: A comparison of the news coverage of the 2010 health care reform debate.* (Publication No. etd-05192011-113732). [Doctoral dissertation, Louisiana State University]. https://digitalcommons.lsu.edu/gradschool_dissertations/4025

Biswas, M., & Kim, N. Y. (2020). African American online newspapers' coverage of policy debate on the Affordable Care Act in 2017. *Newspaper Research Journal, 41*(3), 349–367. https://doi.org/10.1177/0739532920950046

Biswas, M., Sipes, C., & Brost, L. (2021). An analysis of general-audience and Black news sites' coverage of African American issues during the COVID-19 pandemic. *Newspaper Research Journal, 42*(3), 397–415. https://doi.org/10.1177/07395329211030625

Brennan Center for Justice. (2022a). Voting laws roundup: December 2021. https://www.brennancenter.org/our-work/research-reports/voting-laws-roundup-december-2021

Brennan Center for Justice. (2022b). The impact of voter suppression on communities of color. https://www.brennancenter.org/our-work/research-reports/impact-voter-suppression-communities-color

Brown, D. (2020, May 29). Riot or resistance? How media frames unrest in Minneapolis will shape public's view of protest. *The Conversation.* https://theconversation.com/riot-or-resistance-how-media-frames-unrest-in-minneapolis-will-shape-publics-view-of-protest-139713

Carroll, F. (2017). *Race news: Black journalists and the fight for racial justice in the twentieth century.* University of Illinois Press.

Cohen, E., Caburnay, C. A., Luke, D. A., Rodgers, S., Cameron, G. T., & Kreuter, M. W. (2008). Cancer coverage in general-audience and Black newspapers. *Health Communication*, *23*, 427–435.

Johns Hopkins Medicine. (2020, April 20). Coronavirus in African Americans and other people of *color*. https://www.hopkinsmedicine.org/health/conditions-and-diseases/corona virus/covid19-racial-disparities

Lacy, S., Stephens, J. M., & Soffin, S. (1991). The future of the African-American press. *Newspaper Research Journal*, *12*(3), 8–19.

Mehta, D. (2020, June 11). National media coverage of black lives matter had fallen during the Trump era — Until now. *FiveThirtyEight*. https://fivethirtyeight.com/features/national-media-coverage-of-black-lives-matter-had-fallen-during-the-trump-era-until-now/

National Newspaper Publishers Association (2022). The Black press of America is more relevant than *ever*. https://nnpa.org

Pew Research Center (2021). Hispanic and Black news media fact sheet. https://www.pewresearch.org/journalism/fact-sheet/hispanic-and-black-news-media/

Rasmussen, A. C. (2014). Causes and solutions: Mainstream and black press framing of racial and ethnic health disparities. *Howard Journal of Communications*, *25*(3), 257–280.

Squires, C. R. (2002). Rethinking the Black public sphere: An alternative vocabulary for multiple public spheres, *Communication Theory*, *12*(4), 446–468. https://doi.org/10.1111/j.1468-2885.2002.tb00278.x

Teresa, C. (2015). We needed a Booker T. Washington … and certainly a Jack Johnson: The Black Press, Johnson, and issues of representation, 1909–1915. *American Journalism*, *32*(1), 23–40.

Williams Fayne, M. (2020). The great digital migration: Exploring what constitutes the Black Press online. *Journalism & Mass Communication Quarterly*, *97*(3), 704–720. https://doi.org/10.1177/1077699020906492

Wolseley, R. E. (1990). *The black press, USA*. Iowa State Press.

8

IT'S EVERYBODY'S PROBLEM

Why Journalism's Macho Culture Persists and How to Help Make it End

Meg Heckman

In most US journalism schools, female students outnumber their male peers, so it might be a surprise to learn that the opposite is true in many news organizations. Although women have been involved in the production of news since before the Revolutionary War, the field of journalism remains dominated and defined by men. As a result, news coverage often reinforces damaging gender stereotypes, and women seeking careers in journalism face sexist barriers when it comes to pay, promotion, and other forms of professional recognition. This is true despite more than a century of feminist activism aimed at improving gender equity in both newsrooms and news content. Journalism certainly isn't the only field struggling with deep-seated sexism, but, as this chapter will explore, the lack of gender equity in news creates barriers to women's ability to participate fully in civic life.

But first, let's define some terms. The words *sex* and *gender* are sometimes used interchangeably, but they mean different things. *Sex* is defined by a person's genitalia, chromosomes, and other biological or physical characteristics. A person's sex is generally assigned at birth based on these factors. *Gender*, meanwhile, is a social construct based on how we expect a man, woman or nonbinary person to look and behave. Those expectations are often based on stereotypes that can be harmful and limiting. (For a primer on gender-related terminology, see genderbread. org.) Stereotypes like these contribute to *sexism*, which is discrimination based on a person's sex or gender. This can manifest in many ways, including pay disparities, harassment, gender-based violence, and a lack of access to certain resources. People who work to end sexism are often called *feminists*. While the history and contours of feminist social movements are complex, a simple definition crafted by scholar and activist bell hooks is useful to keep in mind for this chapter: "Feminism is a movement to end sexism, sexist exploitation, and oppression" (hooks, 2000, p. xx). It's also important to note that sex and gender are just part of a person's identity. Other factors, such as race, ethnicity, religion, sexual orientation, ability,

DOI: 10.4324/9781003315605-13

socioeconomic class and geography, all play a role in how a person is perceived. When a person identifies with more than one of these historically marginalized groups, that person may face especially complex challenges – a concept legal scholar Kimberlé Crenshaw defined using the term *intersectionality*.

So what does all of this have to do with journalism? A lot, actually. News organizations have tremendous power to influence the way audiences perceive the world. They do this by deciding what stories get covered, which sources get quoted, and how various current events are framed. As we'll explore below, those decisions are often heavily influenced by sexist stereotypes that overemphasize the accomplishments, needs, and lived experiences of white men. That leads to what feminist media scholars call "symbolic annihilation" – a phenomenon in which girls and women are omitted, trivialized, or condemned in news, popular culture, and other forms of mass media (Tuchman, 1978). This can lead to skewed perceptions of women and may make it harder for them to advance in certain spheres or decrease the likelihood that issues more likely to impact them – reproductive health, caregiving support, sexual misconduct, etc. – are taken seriously by policymakers. This has serious consequences for society, which is why it's important for everyone to work for gender equity in news.

Historical Context

To trace the history of women in journalism is to ponder the very definition of journalism itself. Traditional press histories tend to focus on the men who built what trailblazing feminist media historian Maurine Beasley (2001) calls "media empires." She argues that, because these empires excluded women from prestigious roles, it's necessary to judge the contributions of female journalists differently than those of their male counterparts:

> All women who have made use of journalistic techniques – gathering new information of current value and presenting it in various popular formats – have a claim to be studied as journalists, regardless of whether their primary mission has been to advocate, report, comment or entertain.
>
> *(p. 217)*

As a result, a full accounting of women's contributions to journalism means examining the careers of those who worked inside major mainstream news organizations as well as the efforts of women journalists who, because of structural barriers related to gender, race or both, did not have access to such institutions.

Women have been involved in American journalism as reporters, columnists, and even publishers since the colonial era. The list of notable early women journalists is long and continues to grow thanks to the efforts of feminist media historians scouring archives for overlooked women. Here are some examples that give a sense of the ways women shaped media during the colonial period and the early decades of the United States: Elizabeth Timothy became the first female editor and publisher in America (and likely one of the world's first women journalists) when she took over the *South Carolina Gazette* from her late husband in 1739. Roughly a century later Maria Stewart wrote a regular column that argued against slavery and in favor of women's equality for the *Liberator*, a Boston-based abolitionist newspaper. Stewart was one of many women who used journalism to advocate for the end of slavery and the enfranchisement of women. Many of them created publications of their own to advance these causes and make space for women's voices in news media.

Despite notable contributions such as these, women were, until the last few decades, largely absent from formal histories of American journalism. The seminal *History of American Journalism*, for instance, opens with portraits of nine men. One of the first people to attempt to give female journalists their historical due was Ishbel Ross, a reporter for the *New York Tribune* who covered a number of high-profile stories, including the Lindbergh baby kidnapping. In 1936, Ross published *Ladies of the Press*, a thick, quirky book that is often cited as the first formal history of women in the American media. Over the course of 600 pages, Ross manages to be both celebratory and misogynistic, praising various women journalists for meeting male professional standards while still having enough "time to buy their hats" and engage in other feminine pursuits. The women who cared to work into the night chasing front-page stories were, in Ross's eyes, "freaks" better suited to meeting deadlines than meeting the needs of a husband and children. Ross also failed to note the important journalism produced by women of color. Still, Ross provides a good snapshot of how quickly the ranks of women journalists grew around the start of the twentieth century, noting that the female workforce at the *Chicago Tribune* spiked from just 16 in 1896 to more than 400 by the mid-1930s. She also counted more than 300 female editors and publishers at small, mostly rural newspapers across the United States.

The number of women entering journalism continued to grow, although women were limited in terms of what they could report and how long they could stay on the job. But, at the same time newspaper executives were restricting women's access to newsroom jobs, they were working to attract female readers—a desirable audience for the lucrative department store ads that were an important part of newspapers' business model during much of the last century. A centerpiece of that effort was the creation of what became known as the "women's pages," a concept pioneered toward the end of the nineteenth century by Joseph Pulitzer at his New York *World*. These pages were packed with content about food, family, fashion, and other topics that might appeal to women. And, because these sections were often overlooked by many male editors, they also became arenas for topics that helped fuel the feminist movement of the 1960s by publishing stories about domestic violence, birth control and equal pay (Voss, 2018). At the same time, though, these pages turned newspapers into publications segregated by gender which prioritized the work of men by placing it on the front page and literally burying content featuring women in the middle of the newspaper. As discussed below, this false distinction between "hard" news topics such as politics and business and "soft" news topics such as fashion and family continues today and contributes to gender inequities in many newsrooms.

During the 1970s and 1980s, second-wave feminism launched women – most of them white, well-educated, and wealthy – into the workforce. Newsrooms across the country saw an influx of young women with degrees from prestigious liberal arts colleges or big-name journalism schools. They were ambitious but faced real challenges. The term "sexual harassment" was unheard of; gender-based pay disparities were commonplace; and, until 1978, it was legal to fire a woman for getting pregnant. This began to change as women in major newsrooms like those at *Newsweek* and *The New York Times* grew frustrated, began to organize and filed landmark sexual discrimination lawsuits.

News and Gender Today

These lawsuits helped clear the way for many talented, ambitious women journalists to rise through the newsroom ranks and into leadership roles at news organizations, both big and small. It's no longer legal to discriminate based on gender – although it does still happen, as discussed below – and women have made tremendous gains in society as a whole. These changes are, to a certain extent, reflected in a typical modern newsroom. The women's pages are gone (although some of their features endure in modern style and food verticals), and people of all genders now work as reporters, editors, photographers, designers, producers, data journalists, and more. It's routine for women to land front-page bylines, win Pulitzer Prizes and other major awards, debate the issues of the day on cable news and report live from the sidelines of professional sporting events.

During the final two decades of the twentieth century, it became increasingly common for women to hold top leadership positions at suburban and metropolitan newspapers. Women were also deeply involved in the creation of National Public Radio – so much so that NPR often refers to journalists Linda Wertheimer, Susan Stamberg, Nina Totenberg, and Cokie Roberts as its "founding mothers." Many early experiments in online journalism were also guided by women, although their contributes have, until fairly recently, been almost entirely overlooked (Heckman, 2014). But, as was the case in other professional fields, progress toward gender equity stalled and now appears to be sliding backwards.

Data on the demographics of today's newsrooms is scarce because far too few news organizations are willing to participate in an annual industry census. The count was first conducted in 1978, but participation in the survey has dwindled so much in recent years that, in 2022, it was shelved (Scire, 2022). This lack of transparency makes it difficult to monitor progress or lack thereof in diversity in journalism. It's also rather ironic given that news organizations are in the business of holding powerful institutions accountable. The last year of the census was 2018, and the response rate was so low that it's risky to draw too many conclusions from the data. The 239 newsrooms that did respond, however, reported that roughly 40% of their managers were women.

In television and radio, meanwhile, women are also struggling to advance into leadership roles. A 2018 survey by the Radio Television Digital News Association found that just 22% of radio station general managers nationwide are women. In television, women made up 34% of news directors and less than 20% of station general managers. Although it's common to see women as reporters on television, it remains rare for women to regularly anchor network newscasts. Some more recent numbers come from the Global Media Monitoring Project (GMMP), which has been tracking gender-related metrics in journalism since 1995. In its 2020 report, it found that women accounted for 43% of print journalists, 37% of radio journalists and 63% of TV journalists at the media outlets sampled. Raw numbers, of course, only tell part of the story. Women are more likely to face on-the-job harassment and threats of violence than their male peers and, in far too many newsrooms, are still struggling for equal pay and promotion. These challenges are all the more difficult for women of color and people who identify as queer. Some studies have shown that, as a result, women leave journalism for other communication fields at rates far greater than their male peers.

All of this is evidence of how the relationship between news organizations and women remains complicated. That's in part because, as feminist media scholar Bernadette Barker-Plummer (2010) notes, "professional socialization in news values is essentially an education (or re-education) in male socialization for many women journalists" (p. 160). As a result, many norms of news production – story selection and placement, sourcing, framing and more – reflect a male point of view. This can lead to lopsided power dynamics inside and outside the workplace and contribute to gender inequities in society.

In journalism, that gendering plays out in many ways, some of which echo the historical distinction between soft/feminine news and hard/masculine news. For instance, beats covering business, sports and politics are seen as "male" and often come with better pay, a higher profile and more chances for awards and promotions. "Soft" beats such as health, education and arts are more commonly associated with women and have historically not been valued by news organization leaders when it comes to pay and promotion and prestige, even though those beats are among some of the most popular among audiences. Gender representation in news content is also lopsided. This includes the topics covered, the people portrayed, and how stories are framed. In 1995, the first year the GMMP collected data, just 17% of news subjects (people interviewed about the news) were women. That number has improved somewhat, but the gender gap remains. The GMMP's 2020 report found the overall presence of women subjects in news in North America was 33% in print, radio, and television media and 37% in digital media. Women subjects were especially scarce in stories about science and politics.

There are a number of organizations working to improve representation of women in news media. One of these is the Women's Media Center. Its 2021 report catalogued many of the challenges described above, but it also included a few bright spots. Women are well represented in nonprofit newsrooms, with 69% of staffers identifying as female. This hints that it is possible to create more equitable news organizations.

Journalists at existing news organizations are working to improve the way their coverage portrays women, sometimes by creating specialized gender beats that cover sexual misconduct, reproduce health, caregiving, the impacts of structural sexism and other topics traditionally overlooked by newsrooms. Other journalists, meanwhile, are striking out on their own and launching news organizations explicitly focused on coverage that reflects gender equity. Examples include The 19th and The Fuller Project.

Navigating the Present… and Working for a Better Future

Just as women journalists throughout history have worked both inside and outside of major news organizations, efforts to bring lasting gender equity journalism will require efforts from multiple fronts. The long-term goal should, of course, be to change newsroom cultures and professional norms in ways that make journalism more inclusive. But any gender-conscious journalists entering the field today will also need some short-term coping mechanisms. The first step is to understand some of the power dynamics at work. The history covered in this chapter is a good place to start. Further, books written by public radio journalist Stacy Vanek Smith and lawyer and broadcast journalist Adrienne Lawrence may also be helpful. In those books, Smith and Lawrence provide clear, honest, and practical advice for negotiating fair pay, combatting sexual harassment, and other workplace challenges. Mentorship is also crucial, and journalism educators and professional organizations need to work to make sure early-career journalists from all backgrounds have access to mentors with shared lived experiences.

When it comes to news content, journalists of all genders should pay careful attention to who they're interviewing and seek to quote sources from a variety of backgrounds. For help, check out SheSource, an online database of women experts available for media interviews. Another resource is NPR's Diverse Sources Database. Some news organizations, including a number of local public radio stations, have taken this a step further by periodically auditing and publishing the demographics of their news sources. This is a good practice that more news organizations should adopt. It's also crucial for media companies to be transparent about their newsroom demographics by participating in the types of surveys discussed earlier in this chapter.

Finding a path to gender equity in newsrooms and news content is everybody's job. It's important for journalists – especially newsroom leaders – to embrace some of the tactics outlined above. But news consumers need to be smart, too, and everyone ought to educate themselves about gendered tropes and push back when they see them in the news. At the same time, we should all find ways to support news organizations that are led by women or cover gender well. Doing so will benefit not just women who are interested in seeking jobs in journalism but society as a whole by helping to demolish stereotypes that limit people of all genders.

References

Barker-Plummer, B. (2010). News and feminism: A historic dialog. *Journalism & Communication Monographs, 12.* https://doi.org/10.1177/152263791001200302

Beasley, M. (2001). Recent directions for the study of women's history in American journalism. *Journalism Studies, 2*(2), 207–220. https://doi.org/10.1080/1461670C117394

Heckman, M. (2014, March 24). *Women were digital media pioneers, but there's still a gender gap there.* Columbia Journalism Review. https://www.cjr.org/minority_reports/early_digital_women.php

hooks, bell. (2000). *Feminism is for everybody: Passionate politics.* South End Press.

Scire. (2022, April 12). Yet again, newsrooms aren't showing up to the industry's largest diversity survey. *Nieman Lab.* https://www.niemanlab.org/2022/04/crushing-resistance-yet-again-newsrooms-arent-showing-up-to-the-industrys-largest-diversity-survey/

Tuchman, G. (1978). The symbolic annihilation of women by the mass media. In Tuchman, G., Daniels, A. K., & Benet, J. W. (Eds.), *Hearth & home: Images of women in the mass media* (pp. 3–38). Oxford University Press.

Voss, K. W. (2018). *Re-evaluating women's page journalism in the post-World War II era: Celebrating soft news.* Palgrave Macmillan.

9

HEROES AND VILLAINS?

How US News Organizations are Shifting Their Representations of Protesters and Authorities

Jennifer Brannock Cox

Black teenager Trayvon Martin was walking through a gated community where his father's fiancée lived in Florida on February 26, 2012, when he was shot and killed by a neighbor who viewed him as "suspicious." Coverage of the shooting was sparse at first, relegated to local journalists for whom crime reporting was just part of the daily routine. But the story did not take long to become national news, largely due to the efforts of social-justice actors who publicized the issue, landing it on news networks' radars as an issue of significant public interest. News organizations covered the aftermath of the shooting and subsequent trial ad nauseum, using traditional pro-white/anti-Black frames that were all too familiar to the Black community, and portraying Black sources as villains and deviants and white sources as heroic protectors (Lane et al., 2020). Martin's shooter, George Zimmerman, was acquitted of second-degree murder due to the state's controversial "Stand Your Ground" law, which protects those who kill in self-defense when they feel they are "significantly threatened." Many blamed the decision on the media for legitimizing claims from Zimmerman – who is of mixed race – and vilifying Martin, who was unarmed.

In subsequent years, however, a different narrative has emerged, sparked by national outrage over the media's coverage of Martin's killing and the Black Lives Matter movement gaining support across the country. By the time another Black man, George Floyd, was killed by a police officer on May 25, 2020, the media coverage had shifted significantly toward overwhelming support of protesters and criticism of law enforcement officers, who were often associated with the term "brutality" in news stories.

The protest paradigm framing Black sources and protesters as villains and white elites as heroes dates back to the early days of US journalism. Yet, the frame appears to be dissolving in contemporary journalism. This chapter will explore the roots of the protest paradigm and examine recent events that have begun chipping away at the problematic frame.

DOI: 10.4324/9781003315605-14

Influences on News Reporting and Production

Journalists play a crucial role in society, gathering information and synthesizing it into easily understood mass media messages. Their status as information liaisons is not as passive as it seems, though. Although journalists are trained to report facts through objective, impartial reporting methods, their opinions – and the opinions of those around them – creep into their work.

Journalists select and present stories based on individual, organizational, and societal influences. In his seminal 1979 book, *Deciding What's News*, sociologist Herbert Gans found journalists' use of news routines affected the work they do. Reporters are constrained by the need to find news pegs that resonate with audiences, which can lead reporters to pursue stories that feature prominent people more frequently than those highlighting average citizens. Additionally, the strain of deadlines forces journalists to use sources that are easily accessible, which, again, leads to the exclusion of lesser-known sources.

Outside influences also factor into journalists' decisions about what should be considered "news" and what should be excluded. Reporters are more willing to deem a story newsworthy when the sources who pitch them exert influence in society and control over journalists' access to information. In essence, journalists are incentivized to placate those who might help them on future stories.

These constraints on journalists' news-making decisions lead to a reliance on official and elite sources and minimize the voices of those who are less known. Official sources are those who have authority and power in society, including elected officials, high-level government workers, and police officers. Their roles as lawmakers and law-enforcers command attention from all who operate in their communities. Their access to information and control over its distribution make officials ideal sources for journalists who need credible comments while working on deadline.

Elite sources include those whose power is rooted in their affluence. Wealthy elites, such as corporate executives and company representatives, exert influence over society based on their economic importance. Elite sources affect the development of laws and policies that impact the way the country functions, as well as those whose finances are influenced by corporate interests.

Official and elite sources are interested in maintaining the status quo in society because it preserves their positions of power. When journalists rely too heavily on these sources, opposing viewpoints from those who seek change are overshadowed and dismissed. Not much has changed since Gans' landmark work. Research indicates journalists still operate on "autopilot" when selecting sources (Barnoy & Reich, 2022). Reporters are quicker to trust officials and less likely to investigate the veracity of the information they give compared with unofficial and citizen sources. The result is the continued amplification of information from society's most powerful figures. This ensures that those figures continue setting the agenda for news audiences while diminishing the perspectives of those outside the sphere of influence.

The Protest Paradigm

The dominance of official and elite voices has traditionally led to the exclusion, and even vilification, of others who seek to challenge the status quo. During times of societal unrest, journalists tend to rely on official sources in their initial reporting. Such sources often deliver a narrative that dismisses activists and protesters as deviants and troublemakers. This coverage sets the tone for future stories that frame demonstrations as violent and criminal, while bolstering the actions and statements of officials and law enforcement officers as heroic and noble. This pattern of journalists demonizing demonstrators and championing those in power is known as the protest paradigm.

Douglas McLeod and James Hertog (1999) identified news frames, reliance on official sources, the invocation of public opinion, delegitimization, and demonization as characteristics of the protest paradigm.

News Frames

News routines compel journalists to look for efficient ways to tell a large number of stories while on deadline. Therefore, journalists employ news frames to tell stories quickly and consistently. These frames develop as reporters are educated, trained, and eventually employed in newsrooms. Educators and mentors demonstrate their storytelling "shorthand" to emerging journalists, who adopt the frames into their own work. As they become teachers themselves, they pass those frames along to new reporters, and the cycle continues.

When covering crime, journalists employ a traditional "good guy, bad guy" frame in their narratives. The alleged "criminals" are the bad guys, and the law enforcement officers who bring them to justice are the good guys. When a news event occurs that challenges this narrative, and there is a question as to who the good guys and bad guys are, journalists have a difficult time breaking from their traditional storytelling frames.

This "heroization" of law enforcement officers by the media spills over into protest coverage. Journalists have historically portrayed officers as peacekeepers, whereas demonstrators are depicted as anarchists who make life difficult for everyone else. In news stories covering protests, there is typically little focus on demonstrators' perspectives, and their voices are either silenced or diminished.

Reliance on Official Sources

As previously discussed, journalists rely on official sources for information due to their availability and suitability. Official sources are easier for journalists to locate and access quickly due to their involvement in bureaucratic activities. Their contact information is readily available, and they are typically used repeatedly as sources, so they are primed to speak concisely and knowledgably during news interviews.

Journalists also consider official sources to be "suitable" because their positions of power and authority lend credibility to news stories. On the surface, this makes sense. A journalist wouldn't immediately trust an average citizen who called in reports of suspicious or criminal activity to the newsroom; but if that information came from a police source, journalists would report it without hesitation.

The overreliance on official sources and belief that they are more credible than the average citizen leads reporters to value their information above others. However, officials are prone to framing the information they divulge in ways that advocate for their own self-interests and minimize challengers' views. In the case of crime stories and protests, officials are going to deliver a pro-police narrative, providing only their point of view for journalists, who, in turn, amplify that perspective in their stories and further undermine opposing positions.

Public Opinion

Public opinion is a factor in how journalists frame the news, but the ways in which they assess public opinion are not as inclusive as the term would imply. News organizations rarely use scientific methods for gauging peoples' opinions. Occasionally, larger media companies will conduct or sponsor surveys or polls on timely, mainstream topics, such as politics. More often, reporters simply quote sources – typically, official sources – who make generalizations about what the public thinks based on their own perceptions and interactions within communities.

The protest paradigm suggests journalists also estimate public opinion based on their observations of behavior. Most protests are comprised of a relatively small percentage of the general population, so one could *assume* that the issue is not that important to the general public. However, there are many reasons why people don't participate in protests, including fears of encountering resistance, lack of time and/or resources, or even knowledge that protests are occurring. Nevertheless, journalists continue to conflate lack of participation in protests with lack of interest, and portray demonstrators as societal outliers.

Delegitimization and Demonization

When news organizations rely on official accounts in their storytelling, nuanced explanations from opponents are left out of the coverage. With little to no information available about the meanings and messages behind protests, it can be difficult for news audiences to take them seriously. Journalists delegitimize demonstrators' points by ignoring them as sources and failing to represent them fairly in stories. Employing frames that feature officials' and law enforcement officers' comments as the "mainstream opinions" pushes others into a category of deviant or alternative opinions. News audiences have traditionally been reluctant to support efforts outside the mainstream, quashing protesters' efforts to evoke change.

However, journalists do not simply ignore protesters' views; they can go so far as to demonize those who act outside the bounds of mainstream behavior. The media need audiences to follow their coverage, so they spotlight deviant activities that will incite emotional opinions. Researchers have observed a correlation between how radical a protest or organization is and the amount of news coverage it gets (McLeod & Hertog, 1999). In essence, the more deviant a group's behavior is, the more media coverage it will receive.

That may seem advantageous for protesters who are desperate to spread their message, yet it is anything but. When radical outliers promote violence as their means toward resolution, peaceful protesters – who comprise the majority – are discredited as deviants as well by association. Thus, their cause is further delegitimized, and those involved are considered proponents of anarchy.

What's in a Word?

Journalists have traditionally vilified protesters using their most powerful weapon – words. In reporting on demonstrators, reporters have used negative words to frame them as aggressors and criminals. The most common approach to characterizing protesters who challenge the status quo is to label them as "rioters" and "looters." These terms suggest criminal activity and violence, which may not accurately portray the actions of most demonstrators. Even peaceful protests have been labeled "riots" if one person or a small number of participants act aggressively.

The term "rioting" is loosely applied in many scenarios – from in-fighting among group members, to violence against opponents, to damaging property. "Looting" is similarly broad, failing to distinguish between people scavenging for basic needs in times of crisis and stealing during more loaded acts of rebellion and chaos. Journalists may not use these terms to create bias consciously. They often use them to underscore conflict in news events, which attracts audiences to their content. However, the use of the terms "looting," "rioting, and "raiding" in news articles paints a polarizing picture for audiences that can minimize much-needed context in a story.

The Demonization of Black Men

Frames that vilify protesters are disproportionately applied to Black men in the media, who are referenced more frequently as criminals and aggressors than their white counterparts. Following the killing of Black teenager Trayvon Martin, news organizations applied classic anti-Black, pro-white frames in their reporting of the subsequent investigation and trial. Many news outlets looked for ways to demonize the unarmed teen and classify him as a hoodie-wearing "thug" who did not deserve sympathy. When defense lawyers for his killer, George Zimmerman, released images and texts from Martin's phone, which included texts and photos referencing guns and marijuana, the media took the bait. They portrayed the 17-year-old as a menacing and dangerous Black man. Testimony from those who knew Martin – including statements describing him a "good kid" – received far less coverage.

The portrayal of Black people as criminals extends beyond incidents of shootings. After Hurricane Katrina hit New Orleans in 2005, the Associated Press garnered criticism for captions written under two nearly identical pictures of residents wading through water with groceries. One caption accompanying a photo of two light-skinned subjects referred to them as residents who "found" bread and soda at a local grocery store. The caption from a similar photo of a dark-skinned subject referenced him as a young man who had looted a grocery store. The captions provided no context for the difference between those who "found food" and the man who "looted" it. The wire service claimed "stylistic differences" were to blame for the different captions (Mikkelson, 2005).

Not only are Black men routinely demonized in news coverage; white sources are often framed as saviors and virtuous protectors. This is particularly apparent in crime stories, where Black men are overrepresented as criminals and white sources – typically men – intervene as heroic police officers and concerned citizens. These frames have been used to draw focus away from issues of racial profiling and police violence toward Black Americans and to perpetuate a narrative of liberty for white men and justice against Black men.

Shifting Paradigms

Research has shown that the media will deviate from the protest paradigm when both public opinion *and* elite sources support demonstrators' causes (McLeod and Hertog, 1999). Issues that have public support but are largely ignored by powerful officials garner little attention, but those that can be used by political and affluent elites to enhance their status and further their platforms tend to receive more coverage and endorsement in the news. But this dynamic may be changing. The increased polarization in US politics in recent years and the dramatic rise of social media as a platform for average citizens to air their grievances and mobilize support for their movements have begun to shift the traditional protest paradigm and the ways in which journalists portray demonstrators.

George Floyd

The case that most disrupted the protest paradigm, undeniably shifting the pro-white/anti-Black narrative in most US news outlets, was the murder of George Floyd in 2020. Floyd was a 46-year-old Black man living in Minneapolis, Minnesota. A convenience store clerk alleged Floyd used a counterfeit $20 in his store on May 25, 2020, and called the police to investigate. Four officers arrived, and Floyd was killed during the encounter with them. Eyewitness videos showed white police officer Derek Chauvin pinning Floyd to the ground with his knee for eight minutes and 15 seconds while he screamed, "I can't breathe," before losing consciousness and dying at the scene. Chauvin was subsequently convicted of third-degree murder and second-degree manslaughter, and the other three officers at the scene were fired from the police department and found guilty of violating Floyd's civil rights.

Black Lives Matter Protests

Floyd's murder rejuvenated the Black Lives Matter protest group and turned their demonstrations into worldwide news. The group formed after Trayvon Martin's death in 2013 to advocate for justice for oppressed Black people in the US. The popularity of the movement ebbed and flowed in the years since its creation, gaining some popularity after incidents involving white people killing Black people but largely fading into the background shortly afterward. However, Floyd's murder sparked massive, worldwide protests calling for police reform and justice for Black citizens. Even at the height of the COVID-19 pandemic, Black Lives Matter protests spiked, with surveyors speculating about 15–26 million people in the US had demonstrated in related protests throughout June 2020.

News coverage of the Black Lives Matter protests was persistent throughout the summer of 2020. A study of the six most-popular US newspapers and television news channels – Fox News, MSNBC, CNN, *The New York Times*, *The Washington Post*, and *The Wall Street Journal* – during that period found the outlets posted a combined total of 286 stories on Facebook – an average of 3.12 per day – about the movement and protests (Cox, 2022). This coverage far exceeded that of any other incidents involving racial justice, indicating the media were certainly not ignoring the cause.

News audiences also turned to Facebook to demonstrate their interest in coverage of Black Lives Matter. Stories posted on the topic received an average of 15,312 reactions, 2,922 comments, and 4,081 shares per story (Cox, 2021). By comparison, previous research found the top-performing posts by news organizations averaged 6,400 "likes." The average number of "likes" on Black Lives Matter stories was about 24% higher throughout the summer of 2020, demonstrating the issue's resonance with audiences. Although the level of interest among the media and their audiences dipped after the initial month of coverage, the most-popular news organizations continued to turn out a steady stream of news stories on the movement and protests (an average of 2.38 stories per day), and audiences continued to engage with those stories (averaging 13,081.35 reactions per story).

A Changing Narrative

Sensing a shift in public opinion in favor of the Black Lives Matter movement, some media had already demonstrated their reluctance to apply the protest paradigm to the cause. When Black teenager Michael Brown was shot and killed by police in 2014, a handful of newspapers focused more of the coverage on the protesters and their messages and less on crimes associated with the demonstrations – a dramatic departure from past events (Elmasry & El-Nawawy, 2017). Stories in those publications applied positive frames, emphasizing the peacefulness of the demonstrations and minimizing language suggesting deviant behavior. This resistance to the protest paradigm was notable, given that many of the early demonstrations following Brown's death included incidents of violence and fighting between police and protesters, as well as looting that resulted in nightly curfews. However, sustained protest efforts were concentrated to the Ferguson, Missouri area where Brown was killed, and much of the coverage and audience interest in the story faded with the next news cycle.

The 2020 murder of George Floyd ushered in a new attitude among journalists, who overwhelmingly sympathized with protesters. During the summer protests, the six most-popular US news organizations portrayed the Black Lives Matter movement and protesters positively in more than three-quarters of their stories, calling their efforts "peaceful" and referring to participants as demonstrators seeking social justice (Cox, 2022). They largely abandoned terms with negative connotations, such as "looting" and "rioting," preferring the more neutral terms "protesting" and "demonstrating." The news outlets also relied more heavily on sources who supported the movement and its participants and minimized voices in opposition, bucking the conventional narrative aimed at maintaining the status quo.

Heroes and Villains?

News organizations did not just break the protest paradigm with their copious coverage of demonstrations and support for protesters. They also rearranged the traditional "good guy/bad guy" assignments, applying negative frames and language to *police* rather than protesters. In direct opposition to the normal narrative of police as protectors and heroes, stories about the Black Lives Matter movement following Floyd's death often-cited sources who referenced "police brutality" and argued for police reform.

The negative frames persisted across all topics related to Black Lives Matter, including crime, politics, governance, and culture. The coverage made one thing abundantly clear to news audiences: the classification of heroes and villains in news stories could no longer be reduced to black and white.

Why Now?

Unlike many previous instances of police violence against Black suspects, George Floyd's murder was captured live on camera and broadcast unedited across social media. The gruesome spectacle of Floyd begging for air while the officer knelt on his neck was too powerful for officials to spin in their favor. Outrage grew as views of the footage expanded and left little room for an alternative telling of the story that portrayed the police involved positively. Opponents attempted to use similar tactics employed in the Trayvon Martin case, painting Floyd as a criminal thug and suggesting that drugs played a role in his death rather than the officer's aggressive use of force. But if a picture is worth 1000 words, Floyd's video was worth millions, as it rallied protesters across the globe to mobilize and fight injustice toward Black citizens.

As previously noted, news organizations are inclined to flip the protest paradigm when public opinion favors demonstrators. During the summer of 2020, it was in their best interest to do so. News consumption has radically shifted from legacy products, such as newspapers and television broadcasts, to social media platforms during the past decade. Social media sites are also where news consumers go to express their opinions and share articles. Therefore, it made sense for journalists to approach a topic with as much impact and emotion as Floyd's murder and the subsequent protests with a similar tone expressed by their audiences.

Organizational Values

Social media has also prompted new expectations from news consumers regarding journalistic objectivity. Audiences that once demanded total objectivity from journalists now prefer the algorithms on social media that feed them news with which they already agree. News organizations have capitalized on this shift, and journalists have been coached to use news frames that are consistent with their organizations' values. Organizational heads look to their targeted audiences to determine news frames.

Most audiences of the popular news outlets CNN, MSNBC, *The New York Times*, and *The Washington Post* trend more liberal in their social and political beliefs and would most likely support the Black Lives Matter movement. Those news organizations needed only to scan the comments on Black Lives Matter stories to get a sense of their audiences' support of the movement and calls for police reform. Therefore, it made sense for these outlets to publish articles with frames that portrayed protesters positively and police negatively, as they did in the vast majority of their articles.

By contrast, Fox News audiences trend more conservative in their beliefs, and the stories published by the outlet largely reflected its audience's values. During the coverage of the Black Lives Matter movement and protests, Fox News was the only major outlet to employ the traditional protest paradigm, framing demonstrators negatively in more than two-thirds of stories and police positively in nearly half. Again, journalists for Fox News could easily gauge their audiences' preferences by looking at the comments and reactions to these stories on social media, and their stories appeared to reflect those beliefs.

These findings point toward a trend of polarization among news organizations and audiences that could have serious implications for the future. As social media news consumption continues to trend upward, more news organizations are likely to tailor their frames toward niche audiences who want their beliefs echoed back to them than to a general public seeking unbiased information.

What Now?

The shift away from the protest paradigm isn't the only apparent change in coverage of racial issues. Protests about other political, social, and economic issues have also gained media attention and validity in recent years. Protests related to immigrants' rights, women's issues, health, and the environment have received increased coverage and legitimacy in the media over time (Kilgo & Harlow, 2019). News organizations that once commented on women's appearances and questioned the need for feminist movements have since adopted frames favoring equality. Environmentalists who were once dismissed as fearmongers are now taken seriously as the realities of climate change and other threats to the environment have gained widespread acceptance.

It's unclear whether the overall shift away from the protest paradigm in race coverage will join these topics in becoming more permanent, but the evidence points in that direction. There has been a dramatic tonal change regarding coverage of race-related protests just in the past decade – from the negative framing of Trayvon Martin to sympathetic coverage of Michael Brown to outright support for George Floyd. Noting the growing encouragement for racial change in the US, it's likely news organizations will continue to mirror their audiences' attitudes toward these demonstrations in the future.

However, it's worth noting that the protest paradigm is not completely gone. While news organizations were less likely to use problematic terms, such as "looting" and "rioting" in their coverage of the George Floyd demonstrations, many of the stories were still framed as breaking news crime coverage rather than more in-depth enterprise features on a range of topics (Cox, 2022).

What is clear from the recent protest coverage is that media routines are changing to reflect audiences' views rather than defaulting to a traditional maintenance of the status quo. The media will continue to be tested, as advances in communication technology allow average citizens to better illuminate injustices around the world and broadcast their preferences openly. How journalists engage with audiences and incorporate their beliefs into the reporting process will be worth noting in the years to come.

References

Barnoy, A., & Reich, Z. (2022). Trusting others: A pareto distribution of source and message credibility among news reporters. *Communication Research*, *49*(2), 196–220. https://doi.org/10.1177/0093650220911814

Cox, J. B. (2022). Black lives matter to media (finally): A content analysis of news coverage during summer 2020. *Newspaper Research Journal*, *43*(2), 155–175. https://doi.org/10.1177/07395329221092719

Cox, J. B. (2021). Reacting to Black Lives Matter: Facebook engagement with news coverage during the summer 2020 protests. *Proceedings of the annual Association for Education in Journalism and Mass Communication national conference*. All Academic Digital Library.

Elmasry, M. H., & el-Nawawy, M. (2017). Do black lives matter? A content analysis of New York Times and St. Louis Post-Dispatch coverage of Michael Brown protests. *Journalism Practice*, *11*(7), 857–875. https://doi.org/10.1080/17512786.2016.1208058

Gans, H. J. (1979). *Deciding what's news: A study of CBS Evening News, NBC Nightly News, Newsweek and Time*. Northwestern University Press.

Kilgo, D. K., & Harlow, S. (2019). Protests, media coverage, and a hierarchy of social struggle. *The International Journal of Press/Politics*, *24*(4), 508–530. https://doi.org/10.1177/1940161219853517

Lane, K., Williams, Y., Hunt, A. N., & Paulk, A. (2020). The framing of race: Trayvon martin and the black lives matter movement. *Journal of Black Studies*, *51*(8), 790–812. https://doi.org/10.1177/0021934720946802

McLeod, D. M., & Hertog, J. K. (1999). Social control, social change and the mass media's role in the regulation of protest groups. In D. Demers & K. Viswanath (eds.), *Mass media, social control and social change: A macrosocial perspective* (pp. 305–330). Iowa State University Press.

Mikkelson, D. (2005, September 1). Were Hurricane Katrina "looting" photographs captioned differently based on race? *Snopes.* https://www.snopes.com/fact-check/hurricane-katrina-looters/

The Uneven History of Diversity in Journalism

Gwyneth Mellinger

Because representation is the media's stock in trade, the narratives and images circulated by media have structured and fragmented our nation since its founding. In telling America's story, journalism, with its claims to truth and objectivity and its stakes in the daily record and first draft of history, defined both the potential and the limits of our democratic aspirations. Of the political and social polarizations that strain American culture, none has deeper roots or greater consequence than the enduring divisions about social justice and race. Although journalism has often pointed the way forward from a past rooted in racial difference, the reckoning for its history may never be finished.

Gradually and over time, most journalists have assumed an ethical duty to portray news subjects of all races accurately and with sensitivity; however, the profession's acceptance of this social responsibility has at times been halting and contentious, often a reaction to public pressure and political exigency. Indeed, concern for diversity in journalism was an important legacy of activism before and after the 1954 *Brown v. Board of Education* decision. As the public began to examine the segregated institutions of American society, the US newspaper business was clearly among them, divided as it was into a white press and a Black press, each with its own professional standards and infrastructure – news services, leadership associations, and circulation auditing systems. For me as a white scholar, this democratic paradox has been my primary intellectual curiosity: How could this happen in America and why did generation after generation of white journalists, always attentive to their own freedoms, ignore such a stunning ethical and constitutional double standard?

Importantly, this injustice was not new information when reformers took up the cause in earnest in the 1960s and 1970s. White domination of the press was directly challenged when *Freedom's Journal*, the first Black newspaper on record, was first published in 1827 and its founders claimed their voice with the stirring

DOI: 10.4324/9781003315605-15

announcement that "too long have others spoken for us." Though their newspaper appeared in the early decades of the Republic, its publishers framed the complaint as a problem of longstanding created by exclusions of both diverse content and diverse personnel. Unfortunately, this inequity would persist and be taken for granted in a segregated journalism profession.

As a white scholar discussing diversity in journalism, I interrogate the language I use, not to be "politically correct" or "woke," terms I avoid because they can minimize the stakes of the social justice commitment. Rather, I choose my words carefully to enact the journalistic responsibility and values that affirm diversity as an ethical imperative. When we discuss diversity in journalism as a problem that historically had to be remedied by whites, we risk re-anchoring nonwhites at the margins of the profession.

In fact, just part of the profession historically was dominated and controlled by whites. Although the white press claimed the authority to define reality and was deeply exclusionary, the Black press and other ethnic presses have, throughout US history, circulated discourses of empowerment and critique, such as the counternarrative announced in the first issue of *Freedom's Journal*. In thinking about diversity, it is important to imagine the term "journalist," even and especially in a historical context, and before the civil rights movement of the mid-20th century, as describing news workers who were not necessarily white – and there were many. It is also important to foreground the work of nonwhite journalists in contributing to the profession as a whole, not solely for their advancement of diversity.

Importantly, the civil rights movement made racial inequity newsworthy and exposed the limitations of the white-centered worldview. During the 1960s, when racial unrest gripped US cities, white news staffs found themselves unable to cover tumult in the Black community, and Black journalists were suddenly needed to tell the story of the Black discontentment that had erupted as the promises of the civil rights movement went unfulfilled. Ironically, white editors, who had shunned Black Americans from so-called mainstream, daily journalism and relegated them to the weekly alternate press, now viewed their racial identity as part of a desirable skillset. Their superior qualification for this reporting was found in both access to the Black community and their authentic, firsthand perspective on life in the Black community.

Sadly, it would be several decades more before Black journalists were widely valued for their perspective on American society as a whole, but the unrest of 1960s was a turning point. A signal moment for newsroom diversity arrived in 1968, when a chapter of the Kerner Report (National Advisory Commission on Civil Disorders) documented the racial divide in news, specifically the white press's neglect of Black readers and the Black community, and Black journalists' exclusion from employment in white newsrooms. In coming decades, when Black journalists asserted their right to participate in mainstream news media, they found more opportunities in the newsrooms of daily, predominantly white newspapers, but they also met resistance.

The entrenched nature of racism, both societal and institutional, was partly to blame, but journalism was slow to articulate an ethical value that encompassed racial diversity. Subsequent generations of journalists, who referenced the 1996 ethics code of the Society of Professional Journalists (SPJ), would be advised to "avoid stereotyping" and "give voice to the voiceless," as components of seeking and reporting truth; however, such language was not found in the 1973 code. Importantly, that code was written by white journalists who had experienced the seismic shifts of the previous decade and yet the code did not formalize an official professional expectation for social justice until nearly thirty years after the Kerner Report.

Language in an ethics code has an impact on professional expectations and practices when newsroom employees revere and quote those standards, as they have the SPJ guidelines. As a white journalist working for daily newspapers during the 1980s and 1990s, I saw two employers hire their first Black reporters, even without an ethical prescription from the SPJ. The courage of the nonwhite employees who integrated previously all-white newsrooms still inspires me today.

For rank-and-file newsroom employees, both white and nonwhite, an ethical framework would have clarified the professional necessity of diversity and the moral repair that the moment initiated. Once the fallacy of the all-white newsroom was exposed, journalism that covered the community with a limited, monoracial perspective or covered just some of its residents could no longer be considered accurate and ethical. Editors in those newsrooms may have been personally motivated to integrate their workforce or may have been influenced by hiring initiatives of the Associated Press Managing Editors or American Society of Newspaper Editors. Or, ideally, they simply chose the best candidates for those jobs.

PART IV

War and Conflict Reporting in a Multidimensional World

It is a sad reality that war and armed conflicts have been constants throughout human history, and continue to occur with frequency and intensity. As such, reporting on armed conflicts of all types is necessary, and serves an important purpose in society. Because most people learn about and understand wars only through reports they see in news media – and not from first-hand experience – war and conflict reporting plays an outsized role in helping citizens understand both their own nation's military operations, as well as those of other nations globally.

Yet, while important, war and conflict reporting is particularly challenging; in addition to problems related to access, it is a uniquely dangerous specialization that requires reporters to, quite literally, put their lives on the line for a story. At the same time, war correspondents have long been widely criticized by governmental and military leaders, as well as the public, for being alternately too pro-war or too anti-war, too critical or too patriotic, and too graphic or too whitewashed. Part IV addresses these complexities, and considers the relationship between journalism and governments in the coverage of wars and armed conflicts, presenting a brief history of war reporting in the United States, and moving on to a consideration of contemporary challenges and opportunities.

DOI: 10.4324/9781003315605-16

10

THE COMPLICATED HISTORY OF WAR AND CONFLICT REPORTING IN THE UNITED STATES

Hans C. Schmidt

It was during the darkest days of the first world war that Philip Snowden, a British Member of Parliament, wrote that "truth is the first casualty of war" (1916, p. x). Snowden's phrasing may have been distinctly memorable, but his sentiment was of longstanding, and has been expressed in various ways since antiquity. Perhaps the earliest recorded reference to this idea came from Greek playwright Aeschylus in the fifth century BCE, who even suggested that such wartime lies are not only inevitable but divinely justified.

Clearly, it has long been understood that accurate accounts of war are rare. Nevertheless, warfare is among the most ancient of human events, and people have been making efforts to document wars, in some form, for as long as the means to do so have existed. Ancient civilizations etched records of battles in stone and clay, and oral histories of war date back even further. Later, in a more methodical fashion, Thucydides recorded exploits from the Peloponnesian War, as did many historians who followed him in the centuries to come. But, with few exceptions (like Thucydides), such reports were typically one-sided accounts, written after the fact by the victor, from afar, and by authors who had not witnessed the fighting.

Slowly, over the course of thousands of years, this war writing evolved, improved, became more formalized, and eventually came to be seen – not just as storytelling or historical documentation – but as a form of professional journalism. This idea – war reporting as news – started to enter the public imagination in the late 1700s, corresponding with the growth of newspaper publishing in Europe and North America.

In the soon-to-be United States, there were some isolated instances of first-hand reports of battles during the Revolutionary War (1775–1783), including Isaiah Thomas' printed account of the Battle of Lexington in 1775. In the following years, some American newspapers reported a handful of first-person accounts from the War of 1812 (1812–1815), and enterprising European papers began hiring writers

DOI: 10.4324/9781003315605-17

to send news reports of fighting from afar. Notably, the London *Times'* Henry Crabb Robinson wrote articles detailing second-person accounts of Napoleon's 1807 military campaign, and the Spanish Revolution of 1808. Later, there was the London *Morning Post's* Charles Lewis Gruneison who, while in Paris, wrote of the 1830 French Revolution, and later traveled with the British Legion and sent back articles about the Spanish Civil War of 1837–1838. Even during these early days, those endeavoring to report about war faced both mortal danger and opposition from the governments and militaries they wrote about.

The Mid-1800s: War Reporting Expands

While some early publishers and writers had already pioneered the idea of war reporting, it was during the Mexican–American War (1846–1848) that the first real war correspondents emerged in the US. Notably, George Wilkins Kendall, publisher of the *Picayune* in New Orleans, set up a satellite office near the fighting and hired correspondents. While innovative, Kendall was far from an impartial observer; he participated in the military campaign of General – later President – Zachary Taylor and earned the honorary rank of major. This was similarly the case with the correspondents he hired, most of whom held commissions in the Army and wrote dispatches as a second, part-time job.

The practice of war reporting continued into the Crimean War (1853–1856). Though not covered directly by any American correspondents, the war was well documented in the London press, and some reports were also reprinted in American newspapers. Among the most popular reports were those written by William Howard Russell, of the London *Times*, whose work on the Crimean Peninsula made him the first famous war correspondent. One of his dispatches – a report about the catastrophic charge of the Light Brigade of British cavalry – was the basis of Alfred Lord Tennyson's poem of the same name.

The Crimean War also saw the first war photography, and the first war photojournalist, Roger Fenton. Using a cumbersome wet-plate collodion process, Fenton took photographs that were sent back to London, where they were converted into woodblocks and printed in the *Illustrated London News*. The most renowned of these images, Valley of the Shadow of Death, depicts a post-battle cannonball-strewn valley. While the photo was actually staged – no battle had occurred there, the location pictured was certainly not the site of the Light Brigade's charge, and none of the dead bodies Fenton had witnessed were depicted – its stark nature nevertheless addressed the bleak reality of modern warfare.

Since Fenton's work avoided the depiction of any graphic details, it was tolerated by the authorities. But reporters such as Russell were an unwanted presence; military officials and governments were completely unfamiliar with the idea of having their campaigns chronicled by an observer who was not under their command or control, and the relationship between journalists and military authorities soon soured.

During the US Civil War (1861–1865) newspaper coverage was much more extensive, with up to 500 reporters following the Northern Union Army and about

100 covering the Southern Confederate Army (Knightley, 2004). The reporters varied widely in terms of their background and experience (Risley, 2012). Some worked for their newspaper on a full-time basis, while many were professional soldiers who sent dispatches back to their hometown newspaper, usually using a pseudonym, when they had free time. Much of the reporting was sloppy or propagandistic at best, and some reporters even fabricated news to satisfy eager readers back home.

The reporting on this war was unprecedently dramatic; articles were often based on first-hand accounts, and written in a narrative style. The use of photography further heightened the dramatic nature of this reporting. While photographs could not be printed directly in newspapers, they were still shared and distributed – often as traveling exhibits – and were considered to be news content and examples of early photojournalism. What the public saw in the images was a stark contrast to the mythology of battlefield heroism that had traditionally been depicted in artist renderings and paintings. With photography, the public could see – with their own eyes – the gruesome nature of war and its aftermath: the death, the destruction, and the grim nature of a soldier's life. And there was much gruesomeness to be seen in this conflict; the war claimed an estimated 750,000 lives at a time when the nation's population was just 31.4 million.

At first, reporters had a surprising level of freedom, at least officially. In the South, reporters were given a favored status, and they were commonly exempted from compulsory military service. Northern reporters were afforded no such courtesy, and were drafted like everyone else. But the Union Army and Navy did initially agree to allow the press access to the battlefront, and permission to both obtain and transmit military news. The Union government also began providing – by means of the Associated Press – regular war bulletins and announcements.

The free rein of reporters did not last, however. Union generals complained, and before long a new policy was adopted in which newspaper editors were legally barred from publishing anything "that might furnish aid or comfort to the enemy." In addition, government censors at telegraph offices began inspecting all news dispatches, suppressing news deemed inexpedient to the North, and sometimes even replacing reports with fake news items involving fictitious Union victories.

Those who evaded the censors and violated the orders faced the threat of imprisonment, and offending publications also ran the risk of being shut down. Within certain military units, though, punishment could be even more severe; for instance, General William Tecumseh Sherman, well known for his hatred of the press, warned that infractions of strict censorship codes would lead to punishment as a spy and execution.

In the South, Confederate leaders similarly established restrictions. From 1862 onward, reporters were denied access to the front lines, and all war-related reports began requiring approval from a military censor. Yet, because the South was perpetually crippled by limited resources, enforcement was less consistent than in the North.

In retrospect, it is clear that some of these efforts to restrict or control the press had entirely negative consequences. Yet the professional specialization was still in its infancy, and some regulations actually did help to nudge reporters toward greater accuracy and professionalism. For instance, in response to government pressure to increase accountability and reduce speculative and unverified reports, newspapers adopted the practice of adding a byline to stories.

The Late 19th Century: Boosterism and Hype

Press coverage continued in the wars that followed. For example, reporters traveled with Army units in the military campaigns against Native Americans in the later years of the 19th century. Among these was Mark Kellogg, of *The Bismarck Tribune*, who famously traveled – and died – with the US 7th Cavalry at the Battle of Little Bighorn in 1876, writing, "I go with Custer and will be at the death." Kellogg's allegiance to the unit he was covering was not uncommon among his contemporaries; at this time the distinction between military reporting – observation – and military participation – fighting or assisting – was blurry at best.

In the Spanish–American War (1898), war reporting assumed unprecedented proportions. Leading newspapers were far from impartial, and several played a key role in pushing the US towards war with Spain, sensationalizing the explosion on the USS *Maine*, promoting a faulty pretext for war, and whipping the public into a nationalistic fervor. William Randolph Hearst, through the pages of his *New York Journal*, was especially shameless in promoting and profiting from the war. Hearst – who at the time was engaged in a fierce circulation battle with Joseph Pulitzer and *The World* – understood that war news would be great for circulation, and he spared no expense in ensuring that war broke out. Notably, Hearst sent an illustrator to Havana in the runup to the war. Upon arrival in Cuba, however, the illustrator, Frederic Remington, realized that there was no story to cover, and cabled his boss, "Everything is quiet. There is no trouble here. There will be no war. I wish to return." Hearst, though, was having none of it; the reality didn't fit the narrative he was selling, and he famously responded with the words, "Please remain. You furnish the pictures. I'll furnish the war." Remington complied, and Hearst – true to his word – delivered as well.

War was declared, and Hearst was shockingly willing to admit his involvement in goading the nation into combat, even printing the headline "How Do You Like the Journal's War?" across the *Journal*'s front page (McLaughlin, 2016, p. 67).

The answer was all too apparent: the public did like the war, and there was a tremendous public thirst for war news. Hearst certainly liked "the *Journal*'s war" even more, and the *Journal*'s daily circulation increased by more than 430% between 1896 and 1898.

To keep the pages full of war news, no expense was spared. Reporting was plentiful. Reporters roamed freely throughout Cuba and faced minimal censorship. For the most part, reporters were far from objective, and their stories made heroes of military leaders, including Theodore Roosevelt who gained national fame for his exploits leading the 1st Volunteer Cavalry, known widely as the Rough Riders.

The Dawn of the 20th Century: Restrictions Increase

This cozy relationship between the press and the military was not to last, however, and the government's approach toward war reporting started to shift in the decades to come. When the US sent troops to occupy Veracruz (1914) during the Mexican Civil War, General Fred Funston issued press credentials to only a handful of publications, and limited reporter access. Additionally, all journalists' reports were reviewed by a censor, and reporters were required to post a bond that would be refunded only if they avoided any violations of the policies. This set the tone for the relationship that would develop in the coming years.

At the onset of the First World War (1914–1918), American newspapers sent reporters overseas almost immediately. This was not to say, however, that reporters had much access. Initially, the British, French, and Belgians denied any press accreditation, and even prohibited reporters from entering the entire war zone. Eventually though – as the war continued and it became apparent that this was not to be the short weeks-long campaign that the public had initially been promised – it became obvious that preventing any press attention was no longer feasible, and governments began developing systems to allow very limited, and tightly controlled, reporting.

In Great Britain, just a handful of reporters (five British and one American) were given accreditation, and were inducted into the Army with the honorary rank of captain. Additionally, the Defense of the Realm Act imposed strict censorship, and made it illegal to do so little as "spread reports likely to cause disaffection or alarm..." (Defense of the Realm Act, 1914; Dubbs, 2017). Further, as constrained as the press was by the British military, other countries adopted even more restrictive policies; the French, for instance, prevented the publication of almost all combat-related news. Photography was censored even more tightly by the allies; publishing an image considered to be helpful to the enemy would result in a twenty-year prison sentence, and in the war's early period, any reporter who took photos at the front was subject to the death penalty (McLaughlin. 2016). Such broad mandates had a chilling effect on the press.

Not all journalists were willing to play by the rules; a handful of reporters flaunted the regulations and operated on their own. In this regard, American correspondents – foreigners who had no allegiance to Great Britain or its allies and were from a nation that, until 1917, was neutral – were especially effective. Some of these reporters provided the public with the first accurate descriptions of the war's horrors, such as grueling trench warfare, mechanized fighting, Germany's use of chemical weapons, and the spread of disease among troops. Western governments did not view such reports favorably; they threatened the correspondents, and publicly discredited their reports.

When the US entered the war in 1917, it soon became apparent that the United States intended to adopt a similarly restrictive model. President Woodrow Wilson appointed a Committee on Public Information to distribute government war bulletins, censor independent publications, and encourage voluntary censorship. The Espionage Act, Sedition Act, and Trading with the Enemy Act all placed further limits on press freedoms. On top of these heavy restrictions, the military also instituted its own systems of censorship. Under General John J. Pershing, the American Expeditionary Forces instituted a system whereby credentialed reporters wore a military officer's uniform, were subject to military rules, and were typically prohibited from accessing the front lines. All dispatches written by journalists overseas were read and censored by members of the Army's Intelligence Department.

As the war continued, some additional access was granted. At the start, the US Army issued credentials to just 15 reporters, but eventually visiting correspondents from small-town newspapers were also granted limited access to specific Army units. Also, starting in May 1918, the American Expeditionary Forces began issuing daily military bulletins about enemy actions and movements. Unsurprisingly, while many reporters did try to report honestly and accurately, much of the reporting had a decidedly pro-government tone.

World War II and Korea: The Press Joins the War Effort

After World War I war ended, America retreated back into its policy of isolationism, as did much of the press corps. Some ambitious reporters did travel overseas to cover international conflicts, but by and large the American press was increasingly focused on news closer to home. After the onset of fighting in Europe in 1939 and the start of what would become World War II (1939–1945), however, it became clear that some level of American involvement was becoming increasingly likely, and the American press once again began to send reporters abroad. In turn, the government began making efforts to once again tighten its control over the nation's news media. To this end, the Espionage Act of 1917 was renewed, and the Smith Act of 1940 was passed, which mirrored the Sedition Acts of 1798 and 1917 and placed further restrictions on what could be legally printed or publicized.

When war came to the United States, suddenly, with the Japanese attack on Pearl Harbor in 1941, formal governmental systems of censorship were quickly developed. Systems were established in which reporting would be encouraged, but steps would be taken to ensure that the coverage was largely pro-war and nationalistic in tone. Domestic news reports would be reviewed by government censors before publication, and news reports for international audiences would be subject to particularly strict scrutiny. This process was administered by the aptly named Office of Censorship, which largely coordinated the spread of military-related reports, and the Office of War Information, which operated as a government public relations machine and coordinated and controlled the spread of domestic content.

Those reporting from overseas also had to contend with a bevy of additional restrictions put in place by each branch of the armed services. Correspondents were generally given front line access, but required accreditation, wore a military uniform, held the rank of captain, submitted their reports to military censors, and were very dependent on the military for transportation and access to the technologies needed to transmit stories back home.

But, even if these restrictions were not imposed, the reality was that most of the American news media had little interest in criticizing the government or military anyway. Most news services and publications were very supportive of the American war effort, voluntarily complied with requests to engage in self-censorship, and followed the guidelines articulated in the Code of Wartime Practices. Many news organizations willingly formed partnerships with the Office of War Information. The press saw itself, largely, as part of the war effort.

Clearly, much of the reporting lacked objectivity, but the war did receive extensive coverage in Allied nations, even when it was going poorly. More than 1600 war correspondents were accredited by the US military alone, and another 500 reporters worked overseas in some other capacity. These reporters faced significant danger, and many paid with their lives.

World War II also saw a number of new technologies employed on a large scale for the first time. Photography was not new, but images took on a new importance during the war, especially after technology improved and it became possible to transmit images from abroad via transoceanic telegraph cables. Film, too, had been used to a very limited extent in World War I, but its use became mainstream in the US during World War II. Primarily, this was in the form of newsreels: motion picture shorts about the news which were shown in movie theaters before the start of a feature film. While the newsreels offered some information to the moviegoing public, they were largely superficial, pro-war, and comprised of footage that was oftentimes presented out of context or fabricated to fit the narrative structure. Radio was also an important medium for the first time during World War II, and it played an important role in bringing the public timely reports.

The war also gave new opportunities to women; with so many men joining the military or being drafted, women had the opportunity to become involved in the news business; almost 100 (more than 6%) accredited war correspondents were women, including a handful who reported from the front lines (Bradley, 2005).

After the war, the government ended many of its censorship operations. The Office of War Information ceased operation soon after the war's conclusion in 1945, and the Office of Censorship closed later that year. But only a few years passed before the nation's next war, in Korea.

During the Korean War (1950–1953), General Douglas MacArthur at first planned to rely on correspondents to self-censor themselves, but soon – starting in December of 1950 – established a system of prior censorship. From this point on, all dispatches were screened by a military censor, and journalists were prohibited from any criticism of United Nations troops and commanders (Knightley, 2004). The military's restrictions were supplemented by a public that was generally in support of the war, and had little appetite for critical news reports. It was the era of McCarthyism, the House Un-American Activities Committee, and the nation's cold war anti-communist stance was at a peak. As a result, coverage in the American press was largely pro-war and much of the reporting also suffered in quality.

Vietnam: A Uniquely Independent Press

This trend toward sympathetic news media coverage, though, was about to change dramatically with America's next war, in Vietnam (1964–1975). Initially, at the onset of US military intervention, government officials generally anticipated that any news coverage would be sympathetic to the American point of view, just as it had been throughout earlier wars.

But, as the fighting expanded and US involvement became more dramatic – and especially after the draft was instituted – the fact that the war would be covered independently became apparent. Because war was never formally declared, the government lacked the legal apparatus to impose the same type of censorship that had been used in nearly all previous wars. Thus, while coverage was initially limited, it soon came to include hundreds of reporters. The military assigned public information officers to manage the press, but otherwise, journalists operated with an unprecedented level of freedom. Reporters were given the ability to interview any personnel – regardless of rank – and the military typically provided air, land, and sea transportation.

Some governmental guidelines regarding the content of news reports were established, but their enforcement was lax: try as they might, the American administration lacked a legal framework to institute strict censorship. As a result, to a large extent, the most the government could do was attempt to influence coverage by withholding information – such as casualty reports – or by providing misleading information, often through daily briefings known as the "Five O'Clock Follies."

As such, the relationship was hardly a harmonious one. But good journalism prevailed; reporters reported what they saw, namely, a rapidly deteriorating situation and ineffectual strategy. The visual coverage of the war was also unprecedented. Television news crews broadcasting from Asia made Vietnam the nation's first "living room war." Photography was also used extensively, leading to many photo spreads in magazines like *Life*. What the public saw was, often, shocking; TV camera crews jumped from helicopters to follow troops into action, filmed combat, and interviewed everyday soldiers, marines, airmen, and sailors. Photographers caught unforgettable images like the Buddhist monk, Quang Duc, immolating himself in protest, the aftermath of a napalm strike, or the summary execution of a Vietcong suspect.

Coverage of the war – and especially TV coverage – had a dramatic influence on public attitudes. Notably, many have argued that the true turning point in the public's perception of the war came when Walter Cronkite – the popular anchor of the *CBS Evening News* and a veteran war correspondent – traveled to Vietnam to report on the war's status. His summation of the intractable war had such a powerful impact on the public that President Lyndon Johnson is known to have stated, after viewing the report himself, "If I've lost Cronkite, I've lost middle America" (Cronkite, 2006, p. 258).

Many in positions of governmental and military authority came to blame news media, not just for affecting public perceptions, but for outright losing the war. In reality, though, years after the war's conclusion, Robert McNamara – Secretary

of Defense in the Kennedy and Johnson administrations and one of the key archi-
tects of the war – candidly set the matter straight, stating, "Many people today …
believe that, well, it was the press that lost the war, that if they'd just kept their
mouth shut, the people wouldn't have turned away from it and we'd have had
the American people behind it and we could have won. That is totally wrong ….
The problem was that we were in the wrong place with the wrong tactics"
(C-SPAN, 1995).

Nevertheless, in the years that followed Vietnam, the military began retooling its
policies in ways that would dramatically roll back Vietnam-era press freedoms and
change the relationship between the military, the press, and the public.

The Late 20th Century: A New Approach to Controlling the Narrative

New approaches to managing wartime news media were pioneered during minor
US military operations in Grenada (1986) and in Panama (1989). By the start of the
Gulf War (1991), it was clear that the era of nearly unfettered press access, such as
had been witnessed in Vietnam, had ended. Instead, the military reinstituted a pool
system, with the goal of encouraging media attention while also ensuring that such
coverage was carefully curated by the military. Formally, the Department of Defense
advocated openness, but in practice, this "openness" existed within very limited
parameters; while reporters would be granted extensive access, it would only be to
locations and information that the military wanted to be seen.

Nevertheless, news coverage was extensive. The war coincided with the advent
of 24/7 cable news and new satellite technologies. There was a strong public
demand for visuals, and efforts were made to ensure this desire was met. Yet, while
the extensive content created an illusion of transparency, the reality was that the
images seen by the viewing public had been heavily curated by military public
relations operations. Journalists, for instance, were allowed to watch and film military aircraft, missiles, tanks, Humvees, and other military hardware. all of which
made for exciting photos and video footage. But – unlike in previous wars – what
journalists could not do was accompany ground troops on the short-lived ground
assault. Nor could they access the locations of missile strikes or bombings.

In addition to limited access, reporters were subjected to heavy censorship and
had limited use of the technology needed to transmit stories or video content. As
a result, much of what the public saw was Pentagon-provided footage, and most
journalists – 1500 from the US alone (Fialka, 1992) – operated away from active
combat zones. Daily briefings were also held, but these too were tightly orches-
trated events with little detailed information, no enemy casualty estimates, and
plentiful video footage of photogenic American military hardware.

The military itself was pleased with the coverage it received. Secretary of Defense
Pete Williams stated that it was "the best war coverage we've ever had" (Williams,
1991, p. D1). There was, however, widespread backlash from the press. Yes, the war
had been tremendous for TV ratings – it made CNN into a world news leader – but

many serious journalists began questioning their professional integrity. The result was renewed tension between many war reporters and the military they covered.

Wars in Bosnia, Afghanistan, and Iraq: The Embedded Reporter

By the time of the next large-scale military engagement, namely, the UN and NATO intervention into the Bosnian war in the mid-1990s, it had become apparent that new technologies were changing the fundamental nature of reporting, and would require both the press and the government to again adapt their policies and practices. In an age of satellite television feeds and wireless digital technologies, it had become impractical to even attempt to embargo information. Gulf War-style media management was simply no longer feasible.

As such, a new strategy was developed that would dramatically change – both for better and for worse – the relationship between the American military and the press: embedded reporters. The system, initially devised by General William Nash, was quite different than that used during the Gulf War. Instead of pooling reporters at bases far from the action, reporters would travel with troops, thus allowing for greater transparency – or at least the appearance of it.

The system became more formalized during the runup to the US wars in Afghanistan and Iraq. Under the policy, there would be a dual system that would involve both embedding reporters – such as happened in Bosnia – as well as providing daily "Freedom Briefings"– such as happened in the Gulf War. Embedded reporters lived, worked, and traveled with a military unit. Rules were also set regarding what correspondents were allowed to include in their reports, and specific details about unit strength, size, or location, and various other things that could potentially "jeopardize operations or endanger lives" were off-limits (United States Department of Defense, 2015, p. C-1; McLaughlin, 2016).

Many journalists willingly participated in the system and briefings; it was both exciting work, and provided access to an important story. But many were also skeptical; it was clear that the system was set up to encourage favorable coverage. Because journalists spent all of their time living with the men and women of the units in which they were embedded, and relied on these individuals for food, transportation, and protection, developing personal relationships was nearly unavoidable. Over time, it was easy for reporters to begin feeling like they were part of the units they were covering, which could quickly lead to sympathetic coverage. Because of these factors, not all journalists agreed to participate in the embed system, and they instead operated as accredited "unilaterals" without military protection and with much less access.

In retrospect, there were many good aspects to the reporting from Iraq and Afghanistan. Coverage was extensive; at the start of the war in Iraq there were about 700 war correspondents on hand at Central Command. These reporters broke important news stories, and provided vital news to audiences back home. But the embed system was certainly not without its problems, and much reporting was one-sided, and, especially in the early years of both campaigns, extremely pro-war.

Conclusion

Overall, it can be seen that there is a longstanding friction between the people and institutions that report on wars, and the governments that wage them. This tension has appeared different at various times, as military and government perspectives alternated between seeing the press as something to be despised, tolerated, assimilated, controlled, managed, or partnered with.

Today, at least among Western democracies, governments typically see news media as a valuable tool to tell their story, and generally work to subtly shape news coverage by providing easy-to-use content, and relying on the patriotism and professional values of individual reporters. At times, journalists are willing participants. There is much to gain by partnering with military minders and presenting the story within the military's frame, and history is replete with examples of instances where this has occurred. Yet there are also many instances where journalists have operated independently, presented truth, and bravely risked both careers and personal safety to tell the world what is really happening within a war zone.

Finding a balance is unquestionably difficult. Journalists do not operate within a vacuum, and both the press and the military can be blamed when coverage is poor. But one thing is for certain: when truth is lost, the true loser is the public, and the average citizens who are called to fight and who, far too often, pay with their lives.

References

Bradley, P. (2005). *Women and the press: The struggle for equality*. Northwestern University Press.

Cronkite, W. (2006). *A reporter's life*. Knopf.

C-SPAN. (1995, April 19). Booknotes. https://www.c-span.org/video/?64642-1/in-retrospect-tragedy-lessons-vietnam

Defense of the Realm Act. (1914). https://www.nationalarchives.gov.uk/education/britain 1906to1918/transcript/g5cs1s1t.htm

Dubbs, C. (2017). *American journalists in the Great War: Rewriting the rules of reporting*. University of Nebraska Press.

Fialka, J. (1992). *Hotel warriors: Covering the Gulf War*. Woodrow Wilson Center Press.

Knightley, P. (2004). *The first casualty: The war correspondent as hero and myth-maker from the Crimea to Iraq*. The Johns Hopkins University Press.

McLaughlin, G. (2016). *The war correspondent*. Pluto Press.

Risley, F. (2012). *Civil war journalism*. ABC-CLIO.

Snowden, P. (1916). Introduction. In E. D. Morel (Ed.), *Truth and the war* (pp. xiii–xv). The National Labour Press.

United States Department of Defense. (2015). Joint Publication 3-61 Public Affairs. https://www.jcs.mil/Portals/36/Documents/Doctrine/pubs/jp-3_61.pdf

Williams, P. (1991, March 17). Let's face it. This was the best war coverage we've ever had. *The Washington Post*, D1.

11

MEDIA, WAR, AND THE PROPAGANDA OF PRETEXT

Oliver Boyd-Barrett

Articulating the idea of "media imperialism" in 1977, I argued that in place of one single theory of media imperialism, scholars should treat the many different, complex, and dialectical relationships, between phenomena widely described as "imperialism" and phenomena identified as "media" of communication.

My studies of the phenomenon have adopted two approaches. One considers media as enterprises that, through their accumulation of capital, collusion with all other major sources of societal power, geographical expansion, cooption of popular culture, and centrality to the operation of capitalism itself, may be described as imperialistic. There are many instances where powerful media, mainly situated in and closely identified with powerful nations, absorb, or subordinate the media of less powerful nations, with a view to commanding the attention and managing the perceptions of citizens.

A second approach addresses relations between powerful media and the imperialistic aggressions of the countries in which they are headquartered and with which they are closely identified. This involves territorial acquisition and/or other forms of economic, political, social, and cultural extension that diminish the autonomy of the targeted. The process typically demonstrates induction of media proprietors and managers in both cosmopolitan and local capitals into the political, military, and intelligence machineries of imperialistic nations and shapes how media represent topics and events of importance to the interests of the imperialists.

This second approach is the focus here, with reference to how "big media" (mis)represent official pretexts that imperial nations invoke in justification for their aggressions. Imperial pretexts problematically invoke notions of "freedom," "democracy," and "human rights" as weapons against threats that media ascribe to the alleged terrorism, drugs, crime, or weaponry of their own governments' official enemies. Influential audiences for such propaganda include the citizens of the imperialist states themselves, whose connivance with predatory foreign policies supplies legitimacy.

DOI: 10.4324/9781003315605-18

Imperialistic propaganda and warfare critically depend on the malleability of mainstream media. Media collusion with power is particularly evident in the largely uncritical and respectful attention they bestow on official reasons – the pretexts – cited for war.

Pretexts for War as Propaganda

The reasons officially given for state violence against another nation are rarely accurate or sufficient, customarily masquerading for agendas which would otherwise command little legitimacy. The lead-up to the great wars of the twentieth century featured "false-flag" events designed to lure, or to provide the excuse for, US participation in support of allied European powers, amid tectonic shifts of the international order. Pretexts for other twentieth-century conflicts included the "protection" of citizens and settlers of imperial powers from indigenous insurgency, and missionary "civilization" of natives through efficient administration, religion, and education. US Cold War aggressions were justified as saving the "free world" from Sino-Soviet forms of Communism even where – as in Iran in 1953, Guatemala in 1954, Brazil in 1964, Greece in 1964, Chile in 1973, or Argentina in 1976 – this entailed US support for authoritarian or militaristic regimes, which was presented as a "necessary evil" to preserve both their internal order and US international security from revolutionary destabilization. Post-Cold War pretexts appealed to such evils as the drug trade (as in Panama in 1979), threats against allies (as when Iraq invaded Kuwait in 1991, and Russia invaded Ukraine in 2022,) savaging of "democracy" by "dictators" (as in Iraq in 2003, Libya in 2011, Syria from 2011 onward), and facing down "terrorism" (pretext for US wars against Afghanistan, Iraq, Libya, and Syria).

Classic interventions on dubious pretext include the US invasion of Panama in 1989. Cited pretexts appealed to: protection of US citizens (yet there were few if any instances of Panamanian aggression against US citizens, and even these may have been provoked); restoration of "democracy" (yet there had been little democracy in Panama; the country itself was born in a US-instigated seizure of territory from Colombia for the purpose of constructing the canal); anti-dictatorship (yet the effective leader, Manuel Noriega, had been a CIA asset in the USA's "drug war"); and counter-narcotics (the CIA supported Noriega precisely because he was familiar with and participated in the drug trade, and supported US counter-insurgency operations in Central America). Real agendas, however, were various, and related to different US constituencies. Some wanted to crush the Panamanian army prior to an agreed return of control of the canal to Panama in 2000 and to install a weak, democratic, but pro-US government (Trent, 1992).

The 1991 US invasion of Iraq was justified as (1) expelling an Iraqi invasion force from Kuwait (an oil sheikdom once integral to Iraq but carved out by the British in the wake of Ottoman demise), (2) crippling the "dictator" of Iraq, Saddam Hussein (once a CIA asset whom the US had supported during his eight-year war with Iran), (3) reprisal for Hussein's use of chemical weapons (ingredients supplied by the US and western powers) and (4) a response to false allegations that Iraqi soldiers in Kuwait City had removed babies from incubators. Actual US agendas certainly included a desire to restore Kuwaiti sovereignty, but also extended to an interest in rebalancing power in the Middle East and diminishing Hussein in the interests of Israel. Aggression against Iraq continued long after the conflict had "ended," extending from 1991 to the 2003 US invasion, during which time at least half a million Iraqi children died because of Western-backed sanctions and continual air-strikes.

The principal pretext for the 2003 US invasion and occupation of Iraq has been extensively critiqued. Saddam Hussein's Iraq was said to have amassed weapons of mass destruction (WMD), even though UN inspectors had previously testified to the identification, securitization and/or destruction of WMD stocks. It was also claimed that Hussein could use WMD against Western powers with very little notice. It was far from clear why he would want to do this, but loud insinuations that Hussein was in some way involved in the attacks of 9/11 in 2001 (he wasn't) helped to fan public suspicion and fear. Subsequent investigation has shown that any evidence in support of these claims was fabricated or greatly exaggerated. The "real" motivations included a neoconservative agenda in the Bush–Cheney administration to overturn seven Muslim nations in five years, of which one was Iraq (whose vast oil reserves had been nationalized by Hussein). Further, the invasion was a bid to reshape the Middle East in favor of US interests, and to implement the 2002 "Bush doctrine" of US international and regional hegemony whereby challenges to US power would be crushed by any means, including preemptive warfare (Dolan 2017).

Comparable examples include the US role in the 2011 bombing and dismemberment of Libya on the false pretext that Libya's President Ghaddafi planned to massacre insurgents. Additionally, an alliance of the US and Arab monarchies – including Saudi Arabia, Qatar, and the UAE – instigated and financed an attempted regime change against Syria's President Bashar Assad between 2011-2020 under the pretext of restructuring the misleadingly described "dictatorship" of Assad as a western style democracy (Boyd-Barrett, 2022). The "real" purpose, however, was to destabilize an independent Arab state with positive ties to Russia, Iran, and Lebanon, that was not a neoliberal stooge and which set a limit to Israeli expansionist ambition.

A two decades' Western fiction that Iran, with no nuclear weapons but in competition with Saudi Arabia and Israel for the status of Middle East hegemon, constitutes a nuclear "threat" served as pretext for ruthless gutting of the Iranian economy. Of continuing relevance are Western color revolutions in Ukraine in 2004 and 2014 involving the USA's contribution to the 2014 "Euromaidan" *coup d'état* in the name of NATO expansion and the destabilization of the Russian Federation, a forerunner to the 2022 pre-nuclear crisis between Russia, on the one hand, and Ukraine, Europe, and the US, on the other (Boyd-Barrett, 2017).

Scholarly Approaches to Propaganda

What is the role of propaganda, (dis)information, or "hybrid" warfare in these events? A standard US university text on propaganda by Garth Jowett and Victoria

O'Donnell (2018) dedicated a chapter to psychological warfare and referenced seven "devices" of propaganda identified by the Institute for Propaganda Analysis (IPA) in 1937: name-calling; glittering generalities; transfer; testimonial; plain folks; card-stacking; and band wagoning. This list was amplified by later military applications such as the US military Chieu Hoi program, which targeted North Vietnamese soldiers with "fear of death" threats, appeals to the hardships endured by the Viet Cong, their presumed loss of faith in a communist victory, the common soldier's concern for family members and their hardships, and disillusionment with war.

Later analysts augmented the IPA list. Swiss Policy Research (2020) has identified standard gambits such as: the enemy is solely responsible for the war whereas we are innocent and peace-loving; the enemy has barbaric features; we fight for a good cause whereas the enemy fights for selfish ends; the enemy commits atrocities on purpose but, when we do it, it's an oversight; the enemy uses illegal weapons; our losses are small whereas those of our opponents are enormous; our cause is supported by artists and intellectuals; our mission is sacred; anyone who doubts our reporting is a traitor. In studying the three-way conflict between Ukraine, Russia, and the West following the US-backed 2014 *coup d'état* in Kiev, many media propaganda memes could be discerned, as in assessments of the legitimacy of elections, which resonated with the classic 1988 work of Edward Herman and Noam Chomsky on US media coverage of Central America:

Elections for independence that take place under the rule of authorities who do not enjoy the approval of Western powers will be considered less than legitimate by those powers and their media, especially when they occur in periods of conflict and unrest (as in Crimea). Elections for independence that take place under the rule of authorities that are approved by Western interests may not even be necessary (as in Kosovo) or, if held, are reassuring signs of democracy even in the most unpromising of circumstances (as in presidential elections in Ukraine that elected Poroshenko to the presidency, and the parliamentary elections that were held in August 2014) (Boyd-Barrett, 2017, p. 154).

Describing the 'Nayirah' incident during the prelude to the first Gulf War, Jowett and O'Donnell established a deeper perspective on propaganda as a conjuring of perception through coordinated communications from multiple sources and their respective "evidence," with a view to staging a fake reality. Jowett and O'Donnell also outlined a model of propaganda analysis and a companion case study revealed how, during Gulf War 2, television networks colluded with official war propaganda, hiring former military generals, briefed for the purpose by the Pentagon and sometimes employed by defense companies, whom they presented as independent "pundits" for news shows.

Beyond the "Message"

Construction of effective propaganda campaigns therefore involves numerous levels of deception, going well beyond the design and contents of a "message." These include the chiseling of public assessment of the sources of a message, the staging of reality to create "facts" available for incorporation into the message, and the arrangement of multiple streams of dissemination and repetition to ensure domination of the public sphere over rival understandings. Such strategies deceptively replicate the conditions under which large numbers of people among the targeted audience are usually inclined to believe any given narrative.

This approach to propaganda was foreshadowed by political philosopher Walter Lippmann, and in both the writing and practice of the godfather of public relations Edward Bernays, nephew of Sigmund Freud, the founder of psychoanalysis. Bernays substituted the term "public relations" for that of "propaganda." Working for "Big Tobacco" in the 1920s to overcome social taboos on women smoking, he staged a "news" event at which young women lit up cigarettes as "torches of freedom" during a New York Easter Day parade. Bernays instructed press photographers where and when to capture the moment. From this he crafted a template for staging regime-change operations, as in the 1954 US-backed overthrow of democratically elected president Jacobo Arbenz in Guatemala. The US banana company United Fruit owned swathes of Guatemalan land but felt threatened by a modest proposal that it should be remunerated for the redistribution of its unproductive land to peasants. However, the campaign portrayed the Guatemalan government as a threat, not to United Fruit, but to the US, on account of Guatemala's (non-existent) pro-Soviet, "communist" government. Disinformation suffused the campaign with the help of US newspapers and other subscribers to a regional news agency Bernays had established for the purpose. Bernays also hired "anti-government protestors." He wined and dined selected, naive New York journalists. He secured the active support of the secretary of state, Foster Dulles, and Foster's brother Allen, the then head of the CIA. These mobilized a counter-revolutionary militia from adjoining territory to oppose the Guatemalan army and flew CIA planes to bomb Guatemala City (Curtis, 2002).

The Propaganda Model

A theoretical model explaining the relationship between power and media representations was developed by Herman and Chomsky in *Manufacturing Consent* (1988). They identified five filters through which potential news stories had to jump.

First, stories should not undermine the media conglomerates themselves. Second, since advertising constituted their primary revenue stream, news stories should not undermine advertisers, or pour cold water on consumer-friendly media prattle. Third, stories should comply with news media's business model by prioritizing "authoritative" sources, and routine institutional sources, including public/press relations handouts and news agencies. Fourth, journalists should be obsequious in the face of sources with the power to punish them or their publications. Fifth, they should not question the ideological presumptions of powerful sources: anti-communism in the 1980s, which has today been substituted by a neo-liberal ideology of financial deregulation, "free" trade, and the exploitation of human rights pretexts for undermining the sovereignty of uncooperative nations.

This was a systemic model whose operation was the involuntary outcome of US military, economic and cultural global dominance. The authors conducted detailed case studies of media coverage of Vietnam and Central America. These showed, among other things, how in representing state violence in countries allied with the US, the media marginalized and depersonalized its victims. When blame was attributed to state actors in such cases, these would be low-level, rogue operators. In contrast, victims of state violence in countries not favored by Washington were humanized and lionized, and blame was attributed to even senior members of government. The resulting theory of "deserving" and "undeserving" victims has been amply confirmed.

The system emphasis of the propaganda model was contradicted by evidence of conscious journalistic agency and obvious biases of which media workers could scarcely be unaware. Nor did the model allow for evidence of news manipulation by intelligence agencies through (1) infiltration of news media; (2) suborning of journalists through flattery, bribery, or threat; and (3) disproportionate journalistic dependence on intelligence. To the role of intelligence agencies could be added public relations, lobbyists, and 'dark money' influences whose ability to shape news agendas go beyond whatever Herman and Chomsky inferred when discussing journalistic dependence on authoritative sources (Boyd-Barrett, 2010).

A Propagandist Focus

A different critique finds the Herman and Chomsky model "media-centric" and focused on highlighting the importance to propaganda of mass media while overlooking the role of propagandists. By contrast, a propagandist-focused model goes beyond the "linguistic" or "semiotic" realms of the "message" and examines "real-world" acts of incentivization and coercion (Bakir et al. 2018) that determine behavior. The focus on propagand*ists* is inclusive of all institutions within a contemporary promotional culture whose spin and deception create and circulate propaganda – state bureaucracies, corporations, NGOs, human rights organizations, think-tanks, and academia. The focus is more on the production of propaganda, and less on its publication. It considers the vast sums of money expended by states on "public diplomacy," and the creation and distribution of inaccurate or misleading information in support of imperial projects (e.g., "weapons of mass destruction" propaganda as the rationale for the illegal 2003 invasion of Iraq), often aligning with regime-change operations justified by "responsibility to protect" or anti-terrorism appeals.

Hardly limited to the cerebral production of messages, this approach is inclusive of concrete actions undertaken to generate desired meanings that might otherwise be improbable. War itself serves this purpose when the crushing of an opponent is secondary to the warning this directs to potential future opponents, or when conflict is extended without hope of clear-cut resolution merely to let others understand that they will pay dearly if they mess with the propagandist. Exhibitions of immense force and violence, as in the case of the Reichstag Fire, "shock and awe" bombing, or the destruction of the "twin towers" of the Center (as appropriated by

Washington for political purposes), have been cited as physical acts of propaganda whose purpose was radical subversion and reordering of political boundaries from the 1933 Nazi takeover of Germany, through the 1991 re-assertion of Western imperial hegemony in the Middle East, to the 2001 "war on terror" for the perpetuation of US global dominance.

Aspects of the real world to which a propaganda message refers sometimes require refinement so as to establish an evidentiary basis. The message has little value without a machinery for its overwhelmingly pervasive, apparently multi-sourced, repetitive, and constantly reformulated dissemination in both communicative and action-oriented, concrete form.

Pretexts for War against Afghanistan

The official pretext for the October 2001 invasion and the subsequent twenty-year occupation of the sovereign nation of Afghanistan was that Afghan's Taliban government had given harbor to Al Qaeda training camps, responsible, it was claimed, for attacks on the World Trade Center in New York and the Pentagon in Washington on September 11, 2001. Within days, US and international media consolidated a narrative around the official Washington designation of Osama Bin Laden and Al Qaeda as the culprits, enabled by the Taliban. Drawing on extensive media monitoring as well as internet and database searches, this author (2003) identified seven dimensions of media collusion with the official narrative, a narrative whose foundation in evidence was fragile, to say the least, and long before the results of any official investigations which might have provided legitimacy for invasion but which, when they appeared, were deemed inadequate by many experts, even by some who headed these committees.

The seven dimensions included, but were not limited to, the following:

(1) Mobilization of popular outrage, through the use of slogans and icons of national pride, and a vocabulary of "war" suffusing, as though on cue, a monopolized media sphere comparable, in its shrill adherence to one narrative, with later COVID coverage between 2020 and 2022, and representation of the 2014 and 2022 Ukraine crises.

(2) Unambiguous identification and vilification of a single culprit (Osama Bin Laden and his terrorist network). In this regard, the classic propaganda techniques of demonization and personalization – used to cultivate popular hatred of the enemy – were pursued in the absence of unambiguous evidence that either he or the Taliban who had "hosted" Al Qaeda under their governance, were responsible. Rather than being captured, interrogated, and tried, which would likely have been a revealing source of information relevant to the mainstream narrative, Osama Bin Laden, with whose family the Bush family had longstanding business ties, was conveniently murdered in a hideout known to, and probably under the protection of, Pakistan's intelligence service by a 2011 US Navy Seals operation. Doubts as to Bin Laden's role surfaced amidst

later suspicions that Al Qaeda was itself a convenient proxy for covert US foreign policy interests, and the fruit of earlier meddling in Afghanistan by the US, Saudi Arabia, and Pakistan in a terrorist operation designed to entrap the Soviet Union in a costly Afghan quagmire (1979–1989). Some accounts suggest that figures in US political, intelligence, and investment circles had foreknowledge of the attacks. That the principal person charged with the attacks, Khalid Sheikh Mohammed, subject at least 183 times to waterboarding in an offshore prison in Guantanamo, Cuba, has been in US custody for twenty years without trial, is a judicial and human rights atrocity of medieval proportion and anything but helpful to the credibility of the official narrative.

(3) Omission of investigation into other possible culprits (including Saudi Arabia – from which hailed all but one of the alleged hijackers, and at least two of whom were shielded ahead of 9/11 in the US by the FBI and CIA). Identification of the hijackers in a manner that unambiguously confirms their presence on the supposedly hijacked planes has eluded investigators to this day. Suspicion of the involvement of the intelligence community remains robust in view of doubts that the collapse of the World Trade Center Towers 1 and 2, and also of Building 7 – which no plane hit – was only the result of planes crashing into buildings.

(4) In the wake of 9/11, media fawned on an otherwise fumbling, frequently incoherent president who at times appeared secondary in real power to his vice-president, Dick Cheney. Momentarily eclipsed from view was his rabidly neo-conservative administration, which included members who, in the 1990s, had salivated for just such a pretext as 9/11 to reshape the world in the US image. This cabal had spearheaded the "Wolfowitz doctrine," father to the more formal "Bush doctrine," which promoted principles of regional and global US supremacy, to be accomplished, if necessary, by pre-emptive war. It employed 9/11 as a pretext for the invasion of Iraq (discussed by Cheney within hours of the attacks).

(5) Media convergence on the official narrative involved sustained ridicule and marginalization of dissident voices, and suppression of unprecedented controversies surrounding the 2000 Election that had previously undermined the legitimacy of President George Bush. Additionally, coverage avoided references to other 9/11 events or processes that, had they been foregrounded, might have undermined support for the war. These included the previous administration's support for the Taliban, in its pursuit of US-friendly oil and gas pipeline projects. These implicated, among others, the US oil company Unocal, and the notorious, soon-to-be-bankrupt Enron, both players in an industry in which many top administration officials had extensive ties. Nor was it publicized that US plans to topple the Taliban were drawn up and signed off on a day prior to 9/11.

(6) Abandonment of journalistic curiosity was illustrated by media torpor over such extraordinary revelations as the Wall Street "put operation," shenanigans that appear to have predicted the catastrophic consequences of the attacks for various sectors of the economy; uncritical acceptance of intelligence claims as

to its poor penetration of fundamentalist networks, despite having achieved precisely that in the 1980s; the long reluctance of the Bush administration to set up an Independent Commission, and its attempts to subvert its independence, first through proposing that it be chaired by the notoriously devious former Secretary of State Henry Kissinger and then through setting up back-channels to the White House.

(7) Strategies of direct punishment of media dissidents, censorship, self-censorship, and intimidation in the year following 9/11 merely consolidated suspicions as to the integrity of all parties associated with the administration's response to those events.

Conclusion

In this chapter I have briefly reviewed several instances of uncritical media endorsement of false pretexts for US war. Such endorsement is essential for the secure conduct of war principally because it generally appears to achieve broad popular consensus for war and therefore legitimizes the actions of those who promote war. Such consensus also typically extends through the media of US allies, and even further afield in countries that lack their own machineries of news gathering and dissemination. In concluding this overview of specific cases, I shall merely advocate for a language of media representation that critically interrogates the propaganda presumptions and frameworks of power, on the grounds that without critical dissection these grossly obstruct the potential for rational diplomacy and robust public analysis.

References

Bakir, V., Herring, E.. Miller, D., & Robinson, P. (2018). Organized persuasive communication: A new conceptual framework for research on public relations, propaganda, and promotional culture. *University of Bath.* https://researchportal.bath.ac.uk/en/publications/organized-persuasive-communication-a-new-conceptual-framework-for

Boyd-Barrett, O. (2003). Doubt foreclosed: US mainstream media and the attacks of 9/11. In N. Chitty, R. Rush, & M. Semati (Eds.), *Studies in terrorism* (pp. 35–54). Southbound Press.

Boyd-Barrett, O. (2010). Recovering agency for the propaganda model: The implications for war reporting of war and peace. In R. Keeble (Ed.), *Peace journalism, war and conflict resolution.* Peter Lang.

Boyd-Barrett, O. (2017). *Western mainstream media and the Ukraine crisis.* Routledge.

Boyd-Barrett, O. (2022). *Conflict propaganda in Syria: Narrative battles.* Routledge.

Curtis, A. (2002). *A century of the self.* BBC.

Dolan, C. (2017). *In war we trust: The bush doctrine and the pursuit of just war.* Routledge.

Herman, E. S., & Chomsky, N. (1988). *Manufacturing consent: The political economy of the mass media.* Pantheon Books.

Jowett, G., & O'Donnell, V. (2018). *Propaganda and persuasion.* Sage.

Swiss Policy Research. (2020). *The propaganda key.* https://swprs.org/the-propaganda-key/

Trent, B. (1992). *The Panama deception.* C-SPAN. https://www.c-span.org/video/?467566-1/the-panama-deception

12

CHALLENGES IN TERRORISM COVERAGE IN THE UNITED STATES

Yiyi Yang

Terrorism has been practiced throughout history and the meaning of the term "terrorism" has evolved over time. Contemporary scholarship highlights a few characteristics that help to define how terrorism is understood today: terrorism includes politically motivated threats or acts of violence that are not bound by established codes of war, and which are intended to have psychological effects on the public. Reflecting this understanding, the US Department of Homeland Security defines terrorism as "premeditated, politically motivated violence perpetrated against noncombatant targets by subnational groups or clandestine agents, usually intended to influence an audience" (Homeland Security Act, 2002, Section 2656f).

A more comprehensive definition is provided by Alex. P. Schmid, a United Nations officer, who synthesized a variety of definitions and generated the following definition:

> Terrorism is an anxiety inspiring method of repeated violent action, employed by (semi-) clandestine individual, group or state actors, for idiosyncratic, criminal or political reasons, whereby—in contrast to assassination—the direct targets of violence are not the main targets. The immediate human victims of violence are generally chosen randomly (targets of opportunity) or selectively (representative of symbolic targets) from a target population, and serve as message generators. Threat- and violence-based communication processes between terrorist (organization), (imperiled) victims, and main targets are used to manipulate the main target (audience[s]), turning it into a target of terror, a target of demands, or a target of attention depending on whether intimidation, coercion, or propaganda is primarily sought.
>
> *(1988, p. 28)*

DOI: 10.4324/9781003315605-19

Such a definition highlights the differences between terrorism and general crimes in terms of both their targets and objectives. It also highlights the role of communication in achieving psychological objectives and leads to a discussion regarding the important role journalists play in shaping the way people perceive and make sense of terrorist attacks. In the following sections, we will touch on a few prominent challenges journalists face when reporting the complex topic of terrorism, as well as some ways to improve the quality of terrorism coverage.

The Challenge of the Amount of Coverage

The dynamics between media and terrorism are complex. On one hand, the public relies on the news media for important, fundamental facts when acts of terrorism occur. Such reliance is well documented in scholarship. Yet, despite the reality that such reporting can powerfully influence the public's awareness and interpretations of those events, journalists reporting on recent terroristic acts may not have the time and the information resources to follow routine journalistic practice. For example, in the first five hours of breaking news coverage of the 9/11 attacks, and while events were still unfolding, analysis shows that news media reported rumors and unconfirmed reports, and relied on anonymous information sources (Reynolds & Barnett, 2003).

On the other hand, terrorists rely on the media to intimidate and threaten their target publics. For instance, in the aftermath of the 9/11 attacks, media attention to threats of violence caused a significant amount of fear and anxiety among the American public. While reporters may understand that such coverage can unwittingly help terrorists achieve their aims, the alternative – censoring or limiting media coverage of terrorism in order to reduce public anxiety – can also have negative consequences and involve unethically withholding vital information and acting in such a way as to damage journalistic credibility. Relatedly, scholars argue that declining media coverage of terrorism could explain, in part, why the 9/11 attacks were particularly surprising to the American public (Kern et al., 2003).

Such dilemmas have been recognized by scholars working to explain the media–terrorism relationship. For instance, Kevin Barnhurst (1991) suggested that news media can be seen as either a vulnerable victim of terrorism, or as culpable, because media coverage ignites more terrorism, triggering more media coverage and so on in a detrimental cycle.

The Challenge of Biases

In addition to news selection, the media influence how the public makes sense of attacks through news treatment, including if attacks are labeled as terrorism, as well as how they are framed. In the process, it often becomes the case that coverage is shaded by personal biases, and, unfortunately, numerous studies have found that news coverage of terrorism is not impartial.

For instance, research shows that both print and television news provide disproportionately more coverage of attacks perpetrated by Muslims (Dixon & Williams, 2015; Mitnik et al., 2020), and have been found to perpetuate a discourse of fear against Islam and Muslims (Trevino, Kanso, & Nelson, 2010). Additionally, not all terrorists are treated the same in news coverage: domestic terrorists are generally portrayed as intelligent but mentally unstable, whereas foreign terrorists are portrayed as more violent, and as part of some external hostile force, or, frequently Islamic conspiracy (Powell, 2011). Similarly, another study found that violent acts by Muslims are more likely to be labeled as "terrorism" than acts by non-Muslim actors, and Muslim perpetrators are more likely to be labelled in relation to their religion and ethnic identities (Kanji, 2018).

An example of this difference can be seen by comparing coverage of two similar terrorist attacks: the 2009 Fort Hood shooting and the 2013 Washington Navy Yard shooting. In this case, Aysel Morin (2016) found that only the Fort Hood shooter, a Muslim American named Nidal Malik Hasan, was framed as an extreme terrorist; by contrast, the Navy Yard shooter, Aaron Alexis, was described as an individual with mental health issues.

Another example could be the 2002 Washington DC sniper shooting, in which the shooters' veteran status, immigrant identity, and Muslim identity – intertwined with the uncategorizable nature of the crime – led to a confusing media representation regarding the meaning and the nature of the shooting. Similarly, media coverage of the 2010 Times Square bomber vacillated between focusing on the perpetrator's Muslim identity and his American citizenship, describing him as an outsider who used his insider identity to camouflage and actualize the attacks. Further, in coverage of the 2016 Orlando Pulse Nightclub shooting, two competing media frames – the Islamic terrorism frame and the homophobic hate crime frame – were found to define the nature of the attack (Walter et al., 2017).

The persistent link between terrorism and Islam in news coverage can be harmful in a number of different ways. For instance, this overly generalized media coverage can lead to resentment among Muslim audiences, and both cultivate and reinforce anti-Islam attitudes among the public, especially when the audience has limited experience with, or knowledge about, Islam and Muslims. The consequences can be very real, and damaging; according to the Pew Research Center, following the events of 9/11, the United States witnessed a surge of hate crimes against Muslims, Arabs, and those perceived to be of a Middle Eastern origin, with 93 reported incidents in 2001, compared with 12 reported in 2000 (Kishi, 2017). Since that time, such anti-Muslim violence has continued, with FBI records indicating between 100–150 such incidents each year thereafter.

Just recognizing that biases exist in reporting about terrorism and terrorists is, however, not sufficient. Steps also need to be taken to improve such coverage. In this regard, the concept of news differentiation offers some potential. First, journalists could focus on avoiding overt generalization, and instead draw a distinction between terrorists and the general Muslim population (von Sikorski et al., 2017). Further, more media coverage needs to focus on providing facts and context about the culture and religion of minority groups, and in this regard Western media might learn from Muslim reporting which more frequently engages in such differentiation (Matthes et al., 2020).

Second, it could also help if journalists provide a balanced view of an event by including different sources in news coverage. For instance, in terrorism coverage, it is more likely for Western media to use non-Muslim than Muslim sources for news stories (Matthes et al., 2020). Third, while it is common practice to contextualize a terrorist incident by referencing past events, care must be taken to avoid creating inaccurate comparisons and instead conduct rigorous research about a past event before using it as a comparison.

The Challenge of Political Instrumentation

In the wake of terrorist crises, constraints of time and resources can make it infeasible to verify information, comprehensively contextualize an event, or even understand if an event should be labeled as terrorism. As a result, journalists sometimes tend to over-rely on easy-to-access sources within political elites and governmental agencies to provide information or identify whether or not an act should be classified as terrorism. While such sources may be unavoidable, it is important for journalists to be mindful that information they obtain from such sources may be framed to advance a political agenda.

For instance, even the use of the term "terrorism" can be politically or ideologically charged, and could be used as a means to strategically marginalize and silence individuals and groups of people while also cultivating politics of fear and advancing political goals.

Examples could be drawn from the Obama and Trump administrations. While Barack Obama made an effort to avoid alienating US citizens who follow the Islamic faith (Diaz, 2016) and was sometimes reluctant to use the term "terrorism," Donald Trump ardently criticized Obama on this matter in his 2016 campaign, while also failing to call out domestic terror events, including those associated with the 2017 Unite the Right white supremacist rally in Charlottesville, Virginia.

As such, it's imperative for the media to uphold news independence, inform the public in an accurate and transparent manner, use multiple verified sources, and question governmental decisions and actions when necessary.

The Challenge of a Shifting Media Environment

The present-day media environment is more hybrid and competitive than ever. Modern communication technologies allow lower-cost and easier access to information, resulting in more competition across media platforms. Additionally, such changes and new communication technologies have made public participation – in both news distribution and interpretation – easier and more widespread than before. Aided by social media and other interactive online forums, ordinary citizens are increasingly capable of joining media institutions in constructing and sharing social narratives related to terrorism. Sharon Meraz and Zizi Papacharissi (2013) argued that, no longer silent actors, the public redistributes, builds, and evolves existing news frames through online participation and the process of networked framing. For example, when social media users share news articles from elite news media, they usually add additional information and include their own narratives that can either build on or alter existing frames.

Accordingly, as terrorism-related news stories are framed and reframed by both journalists and the public, entirely new narratives are constructed, and the public's ability to accurately understand and interpret events is affected. Entirely eliminating threats caused by today's interactive media landscape may be beyond the ability of any individual news organization; however, journalists can take steps to improve the situation and improve credibility by engaging in honest and ethical dialogues with their audience. Sometimes, this may involve admitting mistakes associated with both news reporting and interpretation. At other times, it may involve managing online comments, or filtering user-generated content that is offensive, violent, or inappropriate.

Conclusion

Reporting on terrorism is challenging, and covering terrorism can take an emotional and psychological toll on reporters. Further, journalists face a variety of obstacles associated with biases, political agendas, and interpretive framing. Therefore, in today's fast-evolving media environment, journalists need to be adaptive and be aware of larger, emerging socio-cultural media discourses. The changing power dynamics between emerging media, the public, and news institutions may further complexify the actual effects and journalistic practices surrounding terrorism. Today, algorithm-driven news facilitated by social media giants, such as Facebook and Twitter, have the power to redistribute content using algorithms and artificial intelligence technologies, meaning that journalists are no longer the sole players in shaping how the public understands or responses to terrorist events. In addition to all these challenges, journalists must also contend with the fact that terrorists themselves are also capable of co-opting the narrative by turning to social media, artificial intelligence, and other emerging technologies to advance their purposes. These challenges can also serve as opportunities for journalists to reflect and improve. Doing so involves finding ways to provide accurate information and representations, and meaningful interpretations and explanations.

References

Barnhurst, K. G. (1991). The literature of terrorism: Implications for visual communications. In A. O. Alali & K. K. Eke (Eds.), *Media coverage of terrorism: Methods of diffusion* (pp. 112–137). Sage.

Diaz, D. (2016). Obama: Why I won't say 'Islamic terrorism'. *CNN*. https://www.cnn.com/2016/09/28/politics/obama-radical-islamic-terrorism-cnn-town-hall/index.html

Dixon, T. L., & Williams, C. L. (2015). The changing misrepresentation of race and crime on network and cable news. *Journal of Communication, 65*(1), 24–39.

Homeland Security Act of 2002, 22 USC § 2656f [d]. (2002).

Kanji, A. (2018). Framing Muslims in the "war on terror": Representations of ideological violence by Muslim versus non-Muslim perpetrators in Canadian national news media. *Religions, 9*(9), 274–300.

Kern, M., Just, M., & Norris, P. (2003). *Framing terrorism: The news media, the government, and the public.* Routledge.

Kishi, K. (2017). Assaults against Muslims in US surpass 2001 level. *Pew Research Center.* https://www.pewresearch.org/fact-tank/2017/11/15/assaults-against-muslims-in-u-s-surpass-2001-level/

Matthes, J., Kaskeleviciute, R., Schmuck, D., von Sikorski, C., Klobasa, C., Knupfer, H., & Saumer, M. (2020). Who differentiates between Muslims and Islamist terrorists in terrorism news coverage An actor-based approach?. *Journalism Studies, 21*(15), 2135–2153.

Meraz, S., & Papacharissi, Z. (2013). Networked gatekeeping and networked framing on# Egypt. *The International Journal of Press/Politics, 18*(2), 138–166.

Mitnik, Z. S., Freilich, J. D., & Chermak, S. M. (2020). Post-9/11 coverage of terrorism in the New York Times. *Justice Quarterly, 37*(1), 161–185.

Morin, A. (2016). Framing terror: The strategies newspapers use to frame an act as terror or crime. *Journalism & Mass Communication Quarterly, 93*(4), 986–1005.

Powell, K. A. (2011). Framing Islam: An analysis of US media coverage of terrorism since 9/11. *Communication Studies, 62*(1), 90–112.

Reynolds, A., & Barnett, B. (2003). This just in… How national TV news handled the breaking "live" coverage of September 11. *Journalism & Mass Communication Quarterly, 80*(3), 689–703.

Schmid, A., & Jongman, A. J. (1988). *Political terrorism: A new guide to actors, authors, concepts, data bases, theories and literature.* (p. 28). Transaction Books.

Trevino, M., Kanso, A. M., & Nelson, R. A. (2010). Islam through editorial lenses: How American elite newspapers portrayed Muslims before and after September 11, 2001. *Journal of Arab & Muslim Media Research, 3*(1–2), 3–17.

Von Sikorski, C., Schmuck, D., Matthes, J., & Binder, A. (2017). "Muslims are not terrorists": Islamic State coverage, journalistic differentiation between terrorism and Islam, fear reactions, and attitudes toward Muslims. *Mass Communication and Society, 20*(6), 825–848.

Walter, N., Billard, T. J., & Murphy, S. T. (2017). On the boundaries of framing terrorism: Guilt, victimization, and the 2016 Orlando shooting. *Mass Communication and Society, 20*(6), 849–868.

ESSAY

War Coverage

Perspectives from the Academy to the Field

Sean Aday

In January 2009 I contracted with the US State Department to train local journalists in Mosul, Iraq in advance of important municipal elections. I would end up doing similar work on several trips to Afghanistan in the future, but this would be my first experience in an active war zone. Everything was new, exciting, and of course more than a little frightening as I tried to navigate the unfamiliar worlds of a war-torn country I had never visited, and a military community I relied on for daily protection that was almost equally foreign to me.

On my first day of work a convoy of heavily armored Humvees brought me to a fortified enclosure housing several local news organizations. They shared a common location for security purposes, as I learned when I asked my translator what the beautiful calligraphy on the wall outside the entrance to the compound said.

"It's from al Qaeda," he explained. "It says, 'The media are corpses. We have the gravediggers.'"

My task that morning was to teach a group of about 30 Iraqi journalists, many of whom had to go to work every morning greeted by this threatening message, the basics of covering elections and politics, and how to hold officials accountable. I had been briefed that I would be meeting with an energized group of capable, if raw, reporters who were eager and passionate to learn their craft and do their part to build a new, independent media in their country. But I was also told that because a free press hadn't existed in decades, if ever, I would need to start with the basics.

So I prepared a kind of "Journalism 101" lecture emphasizing some basics about lead writing and story construction, how to be a beat reporter, etc. Things seemed to be going pretty well, and the journalists seemed engaged and rapt. Then I turned to interviewing tips, and went into a relatively rote discussion of how to ask tough questions, draw out answers from a reluctant source, and basically be a bulldog reporter. I'll admit to a bit of hubris in putting the terrorist's graffiti out of my mind and thinking I was doing a great job on day one.

DOI: 10.4324/9781003315605-20

Then a hand went up.

> "Yes, but sir," asked a well-dressed man with an imploring look that made clear how much he wanted me to have a helpful answer, "when they get mad about my story they threaten to kill me. What do I do then?"

Needless to say, this had not come up in my freshman "Newswriting" class at Northwestern.

That first day of work provided several stark reminders of the challenges of trying to understand, relate to, and tell the stories of another culture, especially one ravaged by war. In fact, that same day I unwittingly committed a major cultural faux pas by illustrating the importance of verifying information with the old journalism maxim "If your mother tells you she loves you, check it out." My translator told me later that the silence in the room was because I had insulted mothers by implying they would lie. "Best to just not mention mothers at all," she advised.

It was a lesson in humility on a personal level, but also helped me better understand the strengths and limitations of war coverage, itself often an attempt to understand and explain dramatic and tragic events in another country. The experience also highlighted the importance of listening first in new environments rather than falling into the trap of seeing only through the prism of one's own experience and perspective.

Indeed, one of the most important and persistent findings in research on war reporting is that it tends to be ethnocentric. Despite the tremendous efforts many of these journalists put into developing local sources and understanding the societies they often are forced to parachute into, inevitably most still end up framing the news through the prism of their own country's values, priorities, and assumptions. We saw this in the early days of reporting on the Russian invasion of Ukraine, for example, when several journalists reflexively made statements that betrayed a belief that white European victims of aggression were somehow more deserving of pity and support than people of color in conflicts around the world.

Another way we see ethnocentric coverage is in the self-censorship many media organizations practice by rarely, if ever showing home country casualties. Although the US government banned images of dead or seriously wounded American military personnel throughout most of World War II and the Korean War, from Vietnam onward news media were free to show audiences as much or as little of war's brutality as they saw fit. Yet, as studies of wars from Vietnam through Afghanistan show, most Western media coverage has largely avoided these images (Aday 2005; Hallin 1986). This appears to be due to a combination of cultural norms and commercial imperatives (e.g., the concern that audiences will blame the messenger and turn the channel).

This ethnocentrism has been exacerbated in the past 40 years by drastic cutbacks in overseas reporting and bureaus, especially in the American press. This has made reporting about the world even more DC-based, and thus even more likely to reflect the frames of US foreign policy elites, especially in the White House.

This was always the case to some extent, and is true of most other countries, as well. But without significant resources to cover the world, the news becomes especially myopic and biased.

This makes news about war and conflict even more source-driven than is the case in other domains of coverage. An important way in which we see this is in what can be called a hard power, or militarism bias in news about international crises. This is not to say that war reporters are "pro-war," because, as they will testify, they detest it. Rather, it's to say that there is an underlying tendency to be more favorable to hard power solutions to crises, and, by extension, to be more skeptical – or to amplify skeptical critics – of diplomacy and soft power. This reflects the general tendency of the foreign policy establishment in many countries, especially the US, to be quick to endorse and justify hard power solutions.

This enhanced ability of US foreign policy elites to frame war coverage, coupled with the media's latent hard power bias and financial incentive to not appear unpatriotic to its audience, has been evidenced in many prominent examples of problematic coverage in just the 21st century alone. For example, elite newspapers such as *The New York Times* and *The Washington Post* ended up running lengthy *mea culpas* after providing uncritical megaphones for transparently bogus White House claims justifying the Iraq War. W. Lance Bennett et al. (2007) showed how the Bush White House was able to leverage news norms of "objectivity" to successfully persuade US news organizations to avoid using the word "torture" to describe the administration's torture regime. The press employed a premature victory frame seeded for months by elite Iraq War advocates in coverage of the toppling of the Saddam statue in Firdos Square on April 9, 2003 (Aday et al., 2005), setting the stage for Bush's infamous "Mission Accomplished" speech a few weeks later. Coverage of the US "surge" in Iraq in 2007 was largely uncritical and fawning, whereas coverage of the US withdrawal from that country and later from Afghanistan faced often withering criticism. While some of that negative press, especially in the latter case, was merited, the reflexive pattern of overly credulous coverage of pro-war arguments early in a crisis, but harsh skepticism of attempts to extricate from a disastrous conflict, is something that describes mainstream media coverage of war, especially in America, going back to Vietnam.

Yet with all that said, the story about war coverage is not all bad. First, as has been the case since people began chronicling war, some of the best, most impassioned, and most important reporting happens in wartime. This is when we still often see journalism perform its primary function as a source of accountability, especially in documenting war crimes. This was as evident in coverage of the liberation of the concentration camps in 1945 as it was during the Balkan genocides of the 1990s or in coverage of Russian atrocities in Ukraine in 2022. War coverage also can be excellent at telling stories of civilian suffering and, occasionally, official misconduct.

Finally, technological advances, especially digital media platforms and the ability to report using handheld devices including cell phones, are making it more economically feasible for news organizations to utilize foreign correspondents around the globe, and to tap into many more local voices and diverse sources of information than before. Ideally, these new developments will open the door for more culturally sensitive and less elite-driven reporting, as well as opportunities for local journalists to tell their own stories. A globalized yet often fractious 21st-century world requires it.

References

Aday, S. (2005). The real war will never get on television: An analysis of casualty imagery in American television coverage of the Iraq war. In P. Seib (Ed.), *Media and Conflict in the 21st Century* (pp. 141–156). Palgrave

Aday, S., Cluverius, J., & Livingston, S. (2005). As Goes the statue, so goes the war: The emergence of the victory frame in television coverage of the Iraq war. *Journal of Broadcasting & Electronic Media, 3*, 314–331.

Bennett, W. L., Lawrence, R., & Livingston, S. (2007). *When the press fails: Political Power power and the news media from Iraq to Katrina*. University of Chicago Press.

Hallin, D. (1986). *The "uncensored" war: The media and Vietnam*. Oxford University Press.

PART V

Challenges and Opportunities for Local News

Local news serves an important function in a democratic society, and addresses topics that have a direct impact on people's everyday lives. Yet, for years the local news sector has been in decline. Roughly 2400 newspapers have closed in the past 15 years, meaning that over 65 million Americans now live in counties with only one local newspaper, or none at all. It isn't just newspapers. Local television and radio news have similarly faded in many markets, and new upstart web operations are often unprofessional or lacking in credibility. The result is a local news desert that is growing by the year, and in which the public is deprived of the information needed to make intelligent, informed decisions.

There are many factors that have precipitated this trend. The most simple – and perhaps also most significant – is that the traditional subscription- and advertising-based business model that once supported local newspapers has become difficult to sustain. Increasingly fewer Americans hold print subscriptions, and many local news organizations have struggled to amass digital subscribers. Further, tech companies – especially Meta and Google – dominate the digital advertising space.

As a result, many local newsrooms find themselves in the impossible situation of trying to do more with less. In turn, the quality suffers, and people become increasingly disappointed with the reporting they see. The problem is cyclical; people turn away from local reporting, which results in the loss of revenue, which causes the quality to suffer, which in turn causes even more people to turn away from local news. Through Part V, we explore the crisis in local news and ways in which the news industry can potentially turn the corner.

DOI: 10.4324/9781003315605-21

13

LOCAL NEWS IN CRISIS

Bill Reader

Although the local news sector dominated the US news industry into the early 21st century, a combination of economic and socio-political changes over the past two decades have triggered significant declines in both the quantity and quality of local news, leading to what many industry watchers have dubbed "the local news crisis." That phenomenon has been noted worldwide, but the decline of local news in America has been particularly severe.

"Local news" is journalism that is focused on specific geographic locations, and constitutes the largest quantity of news outlets in the United States, encompassing the vast majority of newspapers, regional TV, and radio news, and professional online news outlets. Even so-called "national newspapers" such as *The New York Times* and *The Washington Post* have robust "local news" sections focused on their home cities. However, the term "local" is relative enough to include anything from hyperlocal websites devoted to specific neighborhoods to "your local news team" at a television station whose coverage area may span hundreds of miles. In that sense, the term "local news" cannot be assumed to apply only to "small" news outlets; it also includes large-audience media such as metropolitan news organizations that reach audiences across hundreds of neighborhoods and exurbs. In such large, urban regions, there has traditionally been a layered approach to local news, with the large "metro" news outlets providing broad coverage of their regions and smaller news outlets focusing more on distinct neighborhoods and suburbs. In most cities, there are additional niche publications focused on religious, ethnic, and subculture communities, providing an additional layer of local news. Those professional news operations are supplemented by amateur forms of local news, such as school newspapers, church and neighborhood newsletters, and direct messaging from governments. In smaller cities and rural communities, however, the layers tend to be fewer and thinner; by the turn of the 21st century, most small communities had regional TV and radio news, one regional daily newspaper, and perhaps its own weekly newspaper.

DOI: 10.4324/9781003315605-22

For decades, even those smaller exurbs and rural communities had at least some routine coverage of local governments, schools, economies, and culture. The onset of the local news crisis in the 2010s marked significant declines in both the amount of coverage provided to such communities and the ability (or willingness) of those communities to financially support local news operations. The result is that there are thousands of American communities without reliable sources of local journalism.

The underlying causes of the local news crisis are often simplified into two broad factors – diminishing audiences and dwindling advertising. Those factors are reflexive, as smaller audiences do not attract as many advertisers, and less ad revenue means news operations cannot provide quality news coverage to maintain or expand audiences. Complicating the issue is an array of other variables: competition from social media networks; direct marketing to customers by local businesses; consolidation of media ownership leading to deep cuts (or elimination) in local news coverage; declining interest in careers in local or community journalism among the next generation of journalists; and ideological/partisan denigration of the news media in general. The COVID-19 pandemic exacerbated the problem for the local news sector, with a combination of economic recession that hit local businesses (and their advertising budgets) especially hard, and hyperpartisan divisions that put mostly neutral local news media in the crossfire of the American culture war.

At the same time, there has been some adaptation and innovation within the local news sector aimed at finding sustainable models for both new and legacy news media. For example, most legacy media had been slow to embrace digital-first publishing in the 1990s and early 2000s, but such efforts ramped up in the 2010s, resulting in cost savings from reduced printing and print-distribution costs. The relatively low cost of digital publishing (compared to print and broadcasting) has also allowed for the development of nonprofit and low-profit "hyperlocal" news sites that aim to fill voids in coverage left by diminishing or disappearing legacy media, albeit mostly in metro or suburban areas with the socio-economic baselines to support such efforts. Many for-profit outlets, especially local newspapers, have diversified their operations to include more special sections, niche publications, and ancillary services to generate revenue, but those efforts reduce staff time to cover government and public affairs. Some for-profit local news outlets have converted to nonprofit status, which can reduce tax liabilities and also make the outlets eligible for grants and donations. Concerned about the deleterious effects of the local news crisis on democracy and civic engagement, a number of philanthropic organizations have created special programs to support local news coverage, including national efforts such as Report for America, The American Journalism Project, and The Fund for Local Journalism. Even some lawmakers have proposed solutions, such as the proposed Local Journalism Sustainability Act introduced to Congress in 2020 and again in 2021, but the effort was stalled as of this writing. The long-term viability of those innovations remains to be seen.

The local news sector of US media is a complex array of professional and amateur efforts; this chapter focuses on the professional side of the local news ecosystem, the sub-sector that is most imperiled by the local news crisis in America for economic and socio-political reasons.

Economic Collapse of the Local News Sector

Professional news media in the US have traditionally been operated as for-profit businesses, and the late 20th century created highly favorable conditions for local news media to be quite profitable, indeed. The reason was simple: with few exceptions, there was a lack of competition for dominant local news outlets. In all but the largest cities, most communities in 2000 had just one newspaper and access to just five broadcast TV news networks with regional affiliates, while online-only news sources were in their infancy and had small audiences.

Those limited local media options for audiences also applied to the car dealerships, real estate agents, grocery store chains and other regional businesses that relied heavily on mass advertising, particularly in non-metro and rural regions where small circulation newspapers (most of them weeklies) were often the only sources of truly "local" news. Network-affiliated TV stations had coverage areas so expansive that slogans such as "your local news source" were strained to credulity, but they delivered large audiences to regional advertisers. For businesses that relied on local advertising to attract consumers, there were few options other than those near-monopolies.

As such, the local news sector was a financial juggernaut by the turn of the 21st century, and for many newspaper and television-news conglomerates, the high profitability of their smaller-market properties buoyed the flagging or stagnating profits in major metropolitan areas. For example, when Rupert Murdoch's News Corp. bought the Dow Jones Co. in 2007, a purchase focused on *The Wall Street Journal* and *Barron's* magazine, it also included the Ottaway Newspapers subsidiary; although dismissed as "silly little Ottaway papers" by Murdoch, those two-dozen small-market daily newspapers at the time were posting 19% returns on operating expenses, compared to just 3.4% returns from the more prestigious titles (Weisman, 2007, D1). When stockholders forced the sale of Knight Ridder in 2006, at a time when the company made a $638 million profit on $3.1 billion in revenue, the buyer, McClatchy, quickly sold off some of the largest newspapers in the chain, including flagships such as *The San Jose Mercury News* and *The Philadelphia Inquirer*, while holding on to the more profitable mid-sized dailies. Warren Buffett's Berkshire Hathaway bought more than five dozen community newspapers in 2012, an investment many industry watchers thought, at the time, signaled the long-term financial health of the local newspaper sector. The underlying realities, however, were that the high profits of the local news sector at that time were unsustainable, as they were largely based on cost-cutting measures amid rapid declines in audience and advertising revenue.

By the mid-2010s, the once-profitable local news sector was in rapid decline. Between 2008 and 2018, a quarter of US newsroom employees were laid off, according to research by the Pew Research Center. McClatchy's purchase of Knight Ridder at a time of peak profitability saddled the expanded media company with so much debt that it cut its workforce by 10% in 2019 and, in 2020, McClatchy filed for bankruptcy. The 2019 acquisition of Gannett by GateHouse Media, which created the largest newspaper company in the US, included a promise to not reduce newsroom staff. But declines before and during the COVID-19 pandemic pushed the company to mandate furloughs and buyouts of hundreds of employees; by 2021, Gannett had shut down or sold nearly two dozen of its smaller newspapers. In January 2020, just months before the COVID-19 economic collapse, Berkshire Hathaway announced the sale of all of its newspapers, and the previous April, Buffett said in an interview that he lamented that the local newspaper sector "went from monopoly to franchise to competitive to... toast" (Ro, 2019, para. 13).

The number of local newspapers in the US declined by some 1800 titles from 2004 through 2015, most of them small-circulation weeklies serving distinct urban neighborhoods, suburbs, small towns, and rural regions (Reader, 2018). Consolidation of ownership in terrestrial radio also led to declines in local news coverage that was replaced with regional or national news and talk programming (Crider, 2012). One seeming bright spot was with local TV news, with the number of hours dedicated to local TV news trending upward from less than four hours a day in 2006 to more than six hours a day in 2020, according to the Pew Research Center; however, that coverage tended to be more regional than truly "local," with only about half of suburbanites and about 40% of rural residents saying local news media cover the areas in which they live (Pew Research Center, 2019). By the 2020s, the dominant source of local news for some two-thirds of Americans had become "other local residents," with "word of mouth" far more common (71%) than email, text, or social media combined (28%), according to Pew. The same body of research has shown that older Americans are most interested in local news and the most willing to pay for access to such news – and as the loyal audience for local news dies off, it is unlikely that younger generations will be interested in, let alone support, legacy local news outlets.

The economic decline of the local news sector had been predicted since the late 1990s by many industry watchers, long before the buzzwords of "news deserts" and "ghost newspapers" entered the lexicon. A primary concern was the shift in ownership from mostly local news companies with deep cultural ties to their communities to chain ownership by essentially absentee landlords and shareholders who had little-to-no commitment to the importance of quality local news. Local news operations were pressured to maximize short-term profits rather than invest in long-term strategies focused on sustainability. In his book *Community Journalism: The Personal Approach*, community journalism expert Jock Lauterer lamented the increasing number of "bottom feeders" in the local-newspaper business, deriding "A paper dominated by leadership dedicated only to the bottom line. The result is a tiny news hole, an unhappy newsroom and a predictably uninspired news product" (Lauterer, 1995, p. 232). Another professor of the era, Philip Meyer, wrote in his book *The Vanishing Newspaper* that corporate owners of newspapers failed to see "the futility of cutting the quality of their products in an attempt to maintain monopoly profits after the monopoly was gone" and that to survive financially, those newspapers should "transform themselves into business models based on public service and the facilitation of democracy... If they continue to slash and burn their existing businesses, all they will end up with are slashed, burned, obsolete businesses" (Meyer, 2009, pp. 2–3).

Dozens of research studies since the 1980s have analyzed the quantity and quality of local news against the variable of "ownership model," and most found notable declines in the local news product after owner-operated news outlets were purchased by large conglomerates. Cuts in newsroom staffing combined with consolidated coverage areas resulted in sharp declines in the coverage of local government, public affairs, and micronews such as property transfers, marriage/divorce filings, school bus routes and lunch menus, and the like.

The goal of maximizing profits at the expense of quality news coverage also led to some short-sighted, and ultimately disastrous, decisions. One of the worst mistakes of local newspapers especially was resistance to digital-first publishing, with many publishers viewing "the internet" as internal competition against their print editions, rather than as a fast-developing opportunity for expansion and building the audience of the future. By the time news aggregation and social media became ubiquitous in the media diets of most Americans, many local news outlets had underdeveloped "shovelware" websites that held little appeal for online audiences, and advertisers quickly shifted to direct marketing via those alternative channels.

At the same time, top-down edicts aimed at boosting revenue further alienated audiences – and also set the stage for external competition. A primary example of that was the shift toward "paid obits," in which a low-cost, high-demand form of local content – obituaries – were no longer published without charge as a public service, but instead sold as, essentially, display ads paid for by the grieving families. The ubiquity of "paid obits" set the stage for online memorial sites, most notably Legacy.com, which now dominates the obituary sector to such an extent that many local newspapers had to concede to share obituary revenue with the online giant. Another missed opportunity was for local newspapers to rethink the role of classified advertising. Online venues such as Craigslist.com and regional "shoppers" published such ads for free while most local newspapers would charge to run them – however, switching to "free classifieds" would have generated a low-cost stream of popular content that many people are willing to pay to access, which would have increased audiences and subscription revenue.

Although external pressures certainly played a role in precipitating the local news crisis, it is hard to ignore the self-inflicted damage the sector did to itself. While coasting on momentum of monopolistic profits in the late 20th century, too few local media companies used those windfalls to invest in the future and prepare themselves for the challenges of the 21st century.

Socio-Political Pressures

The economic shifts that crippled the local news sector in the early 21st century coincided with a dramatic escalation in the decades-old culture war in America, particularly in the years after the terrorist attacks of 9/11 in 2001. The hot-button national issues exploited by politicians to energize supporters and demonize opponents – such as abortion rights, gun ownership, and the separation (or conflation) of religion and government – had by the late 2010s moved to the local level, with a clear downward trajectory after the 2016 election of a populist, anti-media candidate to the nation's presidency. Largely unchallenged by a weakened local news ecosystem, hyperpartisan alternatives got a foothold in small-town and suburban America.

Partisan disapproval of local news was not equal, with Republicans tending to be far less supportive of local news media than Democrats and independents. A survey by the Pew Research Center (2021) found that overall trust in local news sources fell from 82% in 2016 to 75% in 2021; among Democrats surveyed, the decline was by just one percentage point (from 85% to 84%), but among Republicans, fueled by Republican President Donald Trump's rhetoric calling news media "the enemy of the American people," trust in local news declined from 79% in 2016 to 66% in 2021. That sharp decline is notable because the local news crisis is most prevalent in rural and micropolitan regions, where Republicans dominated local and state offices.

There is a reflexive connection between the increased partisan divisions in America and the decline of professional local news media. Numerous research studies have shown that a lack of local news coverage correlates with diminished civic engagement, decreased voter turnout, and increased malfeasance (even outright corruption) by local government officials. Profit-boosting cuts to newsrooms coincided with less emphasis on covering local government and public affairs in favor of expanded coverage of more popular content such as youth sports, weather, police/ fire reports, and entertainment. Traditionally, routine coverage of local government was the stock in trade of local news organizations, and often a local reporter was the only person in attendance of meetings by city councils, county commissions, and school boards. Local news reporters would make daily rounds to police stations, county courthouses, and city halls, and they would have weekly chats with mayors, council members, police and fire chiefs, school principals, and other local officials. Although such routine reporting often resulted in news articles that were, objectively, quite boring, the consistent coverage of local government also prepared journalists to cover exceptional events such as public crises, controversial proposals, and partisan discord – and that coverage would often spark more civic engagement by concerned citizens and greater meeting attendance by members of the community. Such routine coverage was largely abandoned by the 2010s, with understaffed newsrooms only covering meetings when "something big" was going on, and reporters lacking the background knowledge and context with which to provide meaningful coverage beyond transcribing what was said. Even worse, many local news outlets were caught off-guard when controversies erupted, which only provided more evidence to the citizenry that the news organizations were out of touch with the communities they served.

While many local news operations were disconnecting from their watchdog roles, national media (primarily radio and TV) were becoming more popular – and more ideologically biased. Fox News is well known for feeding confirmation bias to conservatives, and MSNBC similarly succeeds by feeding confirmation bias to liberals. Network TV news tends to be more neutral, but local affiliates often are pressured from their corporate owners to push ideological stances, such as mandated "must runs" and censorship by right-leaning Sinclair Broadcasting, the second-largest owner of TV stations in America. Likewise, talk radio – by far the most popular platform for terrestrial radio – also capitalized on overtly biased programming, most of it right-wing messaging supported by corporate owners such as iHeartRadio (formerly Clear Channel).

The confirmation bias industry also launched a new competitor for quality local news – news media that openly celebrate their ideological bias. Online giants such as *Breitbart News* and *Huffington Post* went all-in to pander to the ideological preferences of their audiences, and on their coattails rode phalanxes of even more ideologically strident websites, social media channels, and fringe "fake news" sites – many of them shallow "news fronts" funded and operated by partisan operatives. The business of feeding people lies they want to believe has become quite lucrative, especially online, where clicks turn to cash via mass advertising services run by Google, Facebook, and other digital giants. For example, a CNN Money report in 2017 titled "The Fake News Machine" found that more than 100 fake news sites targeting American audiences operated out of the small town of Veles in Macedonia, providing lavish incomes for the young staffs (one of the site operators, asked about publishing fake news, responded by saying "I don't care, because people are reading… At 22, I was earning more than someone will ever earn in his entire life.").

By far the most pernicious – and dangerous – threat to legitimate local news outlets has been the rise of "masquerade media" outlets that pose as legitimate news sites but are really fronts for partisan political groups and operatives. The Tow Center for Digital Journalism has identified more than 1200 such sites across America, a few of them backed by liberal organizations but the vast majority backed by right-wing operatives. Such sites supplement biased reporting (often written by underpaid, remote freelancers, many of them in developing countries) with innocuous local content scraped and republished automatically from other online sources, such as obituaries, local press releases, and public records. For example, the company Franklin Archer claims to be "the largest producer of local news in the United States," but is just one of several "masquerade media" companies owned by conservative businessman Brian Timpone (others include Locality Lab, Metric Media, and Local Government Information Services). In the absence of quality local news products, such masquerade media fill the news hole in many places without ever setting foot in those communities.

It is hard to tell whether masquerade media sites drive citizens to be more partisan or simply pander to an already radicalized and divided electorate. What is evident is that such outlets peddle in propaganda and divisive politics, neither of which benefit community cohesion nor sustainable democracy.

Conclusion: Local News Must Reinvest in 'The Personal Approach'

For all of the factors working against legitimate local news outlets, there are still many factors working in its favor. That is evidenced by the thousands of local news operations that are surviving (some even thriving) the local news crisis. It also is evidenced by innovative approaches to producing local news that help bring communities together in common purpose, rather than divide them in the name of cheap partisan hackery.

The most basic formula for success is what Jock Lauterer defined in the early 1990s as "the personal approach," which means "news is not events happening to sources. News is people, your people, and how the changing world affects their everyday lives" produced by professionals "who either know how, or want to learn how, to celebrate the ordinary and who want to have a lasting impact for good in a community" (Lauterer, 1995, pp. xiv–xv). That kind of connectivity cannot be achieved by large, national news outlets, nor by automated "news bots" and underpaid freelancers living in far-off cities, even halfway around the world. The "personal approach" can only be achieved by professional journalists living and engaging with the communities they cover – by journalists who cover communities from within, not from afar.

Surveys by Pew Research Center and other reliable sources have consistently shown that Americans generally have higher opinions and more trust in local news media than they do in national media, but that tendency matters little when local news does not invest in maintaining and expanding that trust. Pew Center studies since 2018 showed that 85% of Americans believed journalists should know about local history, 82% thought journalists should be engaged in local communities, and 65% valued accurate news coverage as the most important function of local media. That same body of research found deficiencies in coverage of news where audience members live, ranging from a high of 62% in urban areas to a low of 41% in rural areas. More than a third of all Americans felt that local journalists were out of touch with their communities – but among those who felt their local journalists were more in touch with their communities, favorability rates were in the 70% to 80% range. All of those metrics suggest that local news media hoping to survive the local news crisis should invest in boots-on-the-ground journalists who interact with people throughout their communities, and who are compensated with pay and benefits that encourage those journalists to settle in long enough to learn the local history and to engage in community life.

Those metrics also suggest that genuine local news media should embrace more long-term, sustainable business models rather than models that maximize short-term profits – such "bottom feeders," as Lauterer called them, are no better than the imitation new sites that peddle political propaganda as "news" with the support of partisan dark money. A hallmark of "masquerade media" is a conspicuous lack of transparency – those sites rarely provide any information about the owners, the writers, and the financial backers; legitimate local media, however, can embrace a more robust transparency with their audiences, especially online with informative "about us" pages, staff bios with contact information, and reasonable levels of fiscal transparency. Another tactic that can benefit true local news media is to move fact-checking from a behind-the-scenes practice to an aggressive form of local news coverage, especially when the fact-checking is aimed at divisive politicians, masquerade media, and blatantly biased national news outlets. Meanwhile, local news outlets can embrace some of the automation used by their more nefarious competitors to collect and package micronews, but with the benefit of pre-publication review and editing by trained professionals who live in those communities.

Ultimately, those local media that are struggling to survive in the early 21st century should begin by admitting their own failings, taking responsibility for their own missteps, and lowering profit goals to more sustainable levels. Mostly, they must invest in the trained journalists – in people – who are the only ones able to rebuild public trust and regain support for quality local news.

References

Crider, D. (2012). A public sphere in decline: The state of localism in talk radio. *Journal of Broadcasting & Electronic Media, 56*(2), 225–244.

Lauterer, J. (1995). *Community journalism: The personal approach.* Iowa State University Press.

Meyer, P. (2009). *The vanishing newspaper: Saving journalism in the information age* (2nd ed.) University of Missouri Press.

Pew Research Center. (2019). For local news, Americans embrace digital but still want strong community connection. https://www.pewresearch.org/journalism/2019/03/26/for-local-news-americans-embrace-digital-but-still-want-strong-community-connection/

Pew Research Center. (2021). Partisan divides in media trust widen, driven by a decline among Republicans. https://www.pewresearch.org/fact-tank/2021/08/30/partisan-divides-in-media-trust-widen-driven-by-a-decline-among-republicans/

Reader, B. (2018). Despite losses, community newspapers still dominate the US market. *Newspaper Research Journal, 39*(1), 32–41.

Ro, S. (2019, April 29). Warren Buffett says the newspaper business is 'toast', *Yahoo! Finance.* https://finance.yahoo.com/news/warren-buffett-newspapers-are-toast-exclusive-133720666.html

Weisman, R. (2007, July 26). Ottaway readers, advertisers cast wary eye on Dow Jones talks. *The Boston Globe,* D1.

14

PUBLIC ACCESS TELEVISION

An Untapped Resource for Local News

Antoine Haywood and Victor Pickard

The structural problems facing our news media today are becoming glaringly obvious, especially the lack of commercial support for local journalism.[1] The US newspaper industry has lost about a quarter of its papers and over 60% of its workforce since the early 2000s. A consequence of this collapse is the growing phenomenon of "news deserts," in which entire communities and regions lack access to any formalized local journalism whatsoever. As news deserts expand across the country, the social costs are considerable. Study after study demonstrates the negative effects of these closures: less voting and civic engagement among the local population, and higher levels of polarization and corruption.

At the same time, some impressive strides have been made to improve news and information conditions across the US. While Capitol Hill policymakers are crafting legislative frameworks to bolster legacy news organizations, we also are witnessing what appears to be a new golden age for grassroots nonprofit experiments. These initiatives include City Bureau in Chicago, Outlier Media in Detroit, and Resolve Philly in Philadelphia. Such experiments are typically more accountable to local communities in general, and communities of color in particular. They focus on serving critical information needs and engage residents in making their own media and telling their own stories. These kinds of journalism models show us what news outlets can do when they privilege public service and participatory democracy over profit imperatives.

While these efforts are worth celebrating, the US still lacks a systemic fix to addressing the information needs for which the market fails to provide. In particular, few attempts have been made to figure out how public access television – one of the country's oldest democratic communication systems – can help address the information needs that the market no longer – in some cases, has never – provides. Expanding on recent studies (e.g., Regan & Jones, 2016; Haywood et al., 2021;

DOI: 10.4324/9781003315605-23

Crittenden & Haywood, 2020), this chapter contends that public access television's infrastructure is an untapped resource for building local journalism.

Democratic Infrastructures

American journalism and public access television are two democracy-serving institutions that deeply value free speech and keeping citizens informed. But, surprisingly, the two have never mutually supported each other. Times have changed, though, and rethinking this vacant relationship is necessary. Both institutions suffer from the commercial sector's inability to maintain public service communication infrastructures. On a grassroots level, short-staffed local news outfits and public access channels both struggle with figuring out how to be relevant, engaging, and financially stable in the digital age. Blending local journalism and public access media can be productive, especially in high-stakes moments like elections, natural disasters, and public health crises. A glimpse of this unusual approach to local storytelling was seen at the onset of COVID-19.

In response to the pandemic, several hundred community media centers that operate public, educational, and government (PEG) access channels transitioned to become local news and information providers (Aufderheide et al., 2020). It is uncommon for PEG channels to function in a journalistic manner; however, during the pandemic their services became essential, particularly in communities with severely short-staffed newsrooms. Journalists used access channels to track municipal governments and relay public safety alerts. A few exceptional access operations also taught residents how to shoot, edit, and cablecast/stream neighborhood-level video reports. These journalistic interactions involving PEG channels ultimately begs the question: Can public access television's infrastructure, if adequately staffed and funded, serve as a viable option for local journalism?

Skeptics see public access television as an analog relic that has lost its way in the digital communication age. "Why do we need local access channels when there's YouTube?" is one of many irksome questions that cable access proponents struggle to answer while their infrastructure steadily erodes. Recent studies have shown, despite prevailing threats and skepticism, PEG's infrastructure is still relevant. Nevertheless, turning back to access television's roots, forged by activism, and its core principles – freedom of expression, media education, localism, and public service – serves as an important reminder of what we risk losing. Understanding how these principles have been developed, grappled with, and put into practice since the 1970s is key to any productive conversation about the medium's contemporary relevance.

The Shape and Roots of Public Access Television

Community television models anchored by cable revenue and local access channels have existed in the US for more than four decades. According to the Alliance for

Community Media, over 1600 operations currently facilitate local program production for 3000 PEG channels across the country. The nature of these operations varies, and their organizational identities range from "community access media" to "local access" to "(insert municipality name) television." Three-quarters of these operations are maintained by 1–3 fulltime employees who, with extremely tight budgets, offer an array of important communication services. Nonprofit organizations, public school districts, community/state colleges, and municipal governments typically provide fiscal oversight for PEG channels.

In places like Bedford, Massachusetts, Greater Northshire, Vermont, and Eureka, California, it is common to find one organization managing all the PEG channels for neighboring suburban, exurban, and rural communities. However, in large cities such as Philadelphia, multiple entities manage the PEG channels independently. PhillyCAM, for example, is the nonprofit that operates Philadelphia's public access channels; Temple University, Community College of Philadelphia, LaSalle University, Drexel University, and the School District of Philadelphia oversee educational channels; and the city government runs its own channel, PHLgovTV.

PEG channels have distinct programming functions. They do not produce conventional news, but they collectively play an important role in documenting community life. Government access (G) channels document local government meetings, municipal press conferences, and civic activities like holiday parades and ribbon-cutting ceremonies. Education access (E) channels stick to covering school board meetings, town halls, intermural sports, and public-school graduations. Public access (P) channels allow residents to self-organize and independently produce noncommercial programs, which range from bizarre variety shows to sobering personal documentaries. Community media centers that operate P channels distinctly provide residents access to noncommercial television production training, studio space, technical support, and channel time slots.

Out of the three channel types, Ps are the most scrutinized. Stereotypically offbeat, poor technical quality, and controversial programs have rendered the public access medium an easy target for pop culture satire. Vanity, hate speech, and kinky, late-night programs have also made it difficult for critics to find value in what P channels represent. But despite these blemishes, public access has virtues that stem from its roots in activism.

The seeds for public access television were planted in a pre-internet media landscape. Before cable television, news and information distribution was dominated by print, radio, and broadcast television media. Cable's expansion in the 1960s, however, provided new opportunities for localized public communication. Starting in the 1940s as community antenna television (CATV), cable technology was strictly used for relaying national broadcast signals, including a nascent public broadcasting service. As this educational programming model grew, so did its ability to capture and prioritize national audience attention. Community television visionaries saw a pathway to forge a cable media infrastructure that explicitly serves grassroots communication needs.

Small community/public access television experiments cropped up when geographically defined cable systems started dabbling in original content production also called "local origination programming." Some early experiments, like one in Dale City, Virginia, did not last long. They suffered from inadequate equipment, facility limitations, and maintenance problems. Nonetheless, in places like Pacifica, California, its community access television model, initiated in the 1960s, is still active today as Pacific Coast TV.

Distinct from public television broadcasting, public access cable television was designed to engage ordinary people in the process of making their own televisual messages, which was a "radical experiment in democratic communication" (Stein, 2001, p. 299). In the 1970s, this participatory approach to making television was heavily influenced by a new wave of social activism. New York City was a hotbed of many notable televisual experiments. For example, apartment associations used closed-circuit video technology to televise tenant meetings. Artist collectives and social justice activists used Sony's cumbersome but portable Portapak video rig (introduced in the mid-1960s) to document public protests and make electronic visual art. *Paper Tiger Television* and *Guerilla Television* also introduced their early versions of televised media literacy for inner-city audiences.

Demystifying and dismantling corporate media power was paramount for NY-based media activist matriarchs like DeeDee Halleck. As a founder of the Paper Tiger Television organization and Deep Dish TV satellite network, Halleck has often pointed to public access television as an effective tool that helps marginalized communities rethink and democratize television. While reflecting on her pedagogy, she noted, "It's one thing to critique the mass media and rail against their abuses. It's quite another to create viable alternatives" (2002, p. 111). Community media pioneers George Stoney and Red Burns, who founded New York University's (NYU) Alternate Media Center (AMC) in the early 1970s, also shared Halleck's sentiments.

Located above a small theater space in Greenwich Village, AMC was the cradle that nurtured young, emerging leaders in the US. public access television movement. As NYU professors and documentary filmmakers, Stoney and Burns used this space to develop a pedagogy they adopted from the Canadian participatory filmmaking program Challenge for Change. Stoney and Burns taught their students how to use Portapaks, two-way cable TV technology, and community viewing sessions in ways that initiated community dialogue. Facilitating social change by engaging neighbors in participatory media-making and collective storytelling was the foundational principle that motivated this movement.

Under the tutelage of Stoney and Burns, an "unlikely bunch of [women] revolutionaries" at AMC became enthralled by their mission to "make public access work" in a field traditionally dominated by men (Larkin, 2001, p. 22). These passionate interns used their collective knowledge, and National Endowment for the Arts funding, to help launch community television operations in places like Reading, Pennsylvania, and Dubuque, Iowa. They also forged a political organizing framework that established the National Federation for Local Cable Programmers (NFLCP) in 1976. This federation later became the Alliance for Community Media.

From AMC and NFLCP came the movement's extended guiding principles: *freedom of expression*, *media education*, *localism*, and *public service*. Proponents used these principles to rationalize the existence of a democratic communication infrastructure such as community access television. Although the nature of access media operations has varied over the years, facilitating hyperlocal communication that is energized by community participation remains a common, core characteristic.

The legitimate expansion of access television's infrastructure was also aided by a series of pivotal federal-level policymaking decisions and legal contests that involved the cable industry. Cable's expansive channel capacity appeared as prime real estate for diverse programs dedicated to amplifying social and cultural realities not seen in broadcast television. Hence, Stoney and Burns encouraged AMC's budding media activists to lobby the FCC and Congress for cable-anchored community television infrastructures that could be deployed and sustained across the country.

Before the NFLCP was established, the FCC issued a report and order that required cable companies in the top 100 markets to designate noncommercial local channels for public, educational, and government (PEG) purposes. The fledgling cable industry, however, resisted the FCC's local requirements and felt restrained by this obligation to manage PEG channel operations. These channels represented the community television movement's guiding principles, but their applications were inconsistent. After a series of circuit court-level disputes, the US Supreme Court decided, in 1979, the FCC overstepped its jurisdictional authority. Despite this temporary setback, the Cable Communications Policy Act (1984), also known as the "1984 Cable Act," codified PEG's infrastructure into law.

The 1984 Cable Act authorizes state and local governments to form Local Franchise Authorities (LFAs). Under this law, LFAs can enter into franchise agreements to collect up to 5% of revenue generated by fee-based cable services provided in a geographically defined area. Collected franchise fees serve as a type of rent that a cable company must pay for its commercial use of "public rights-of-way" (streets, poles, and sidewalks). Reallocating cable revenue into state and municipal general operating budgets is customary. Inclined LFAs can also use these arrangements to request community media funds and technological resources like PEG channels, wired network connections, and system maintenance.

Some 2500 PEG operations existed during the medium's heyday in the 1980s. However, these numbers dwindled from the 1990s to early 2000s as LFAs found them troublesome to maintain. Cable company mergers, a general disinterest in supporting noncommercial channels, shifts in state-level telecommunication laws, strained municipal budgets, swaying local politics, and other challenges have made it difficult for communities to keep their PEG-fee-funded community media operations alive. PEG's survival in this country has been largely aided by grassroots lobbying groups and national policy work spearheaded by the Alliance for Community Media (ACM) and the National Association of Telecommunication Officers and Advisors (NATOA). Although PEG's future is uncertain, opportunities for growth still exist.

Challenges and Opportunities

Early assessments interpreted public access programming on cable as a new form of citizen-made journalism. Outspoken citizens and movement-oriented groups have used access television to make their political grievances known. However, independent journalism never took hold and became widespread as some community media advocates hoped. Various factors have made it difficult for journalistic practices to thrive in public access television environments.

Cable revenue has sustained community media operations for decades. Managers use these funds to purchase equipment, pay staff, and cover other operational expenses such as building rent and organization insurance. But these resources are dedicated to serving a broad spectrum of community members and interests. Adding on local news production poses a financial burden that access organizations find hard to justify, especially as cable revenues decrease.

Furthermore, organizational leaders that carry traditional mindsets do not see journalism as pertinent to their mission. Generations of managers and board members have believed that largely avoiding editorial interventions and gatekeeping is the ideal way to achieve equitable, free speech communication. Passively facilitating local productions also helps buffer organizations from political repercussions that could jeopardize funding from LFAs. Content curation and deliberate outreach are two topics that access television proponents have debated passionately for years. Conservative attitudes, however, have started to shift as organizations struggle with demonstrating relevance and diversifying income.

More and more organizations are rethinking the passive, purist approach – if not completely abandoning it – to eliminate participation barriers, engage underrepresented communities, and produce journalistic reports on civic life. Public Media Network (Michigan), Access Humboldt (California), PhillyCAM (Philadelphia), and Akakū Maui (Hawaii) exemplify PEG-anchored media centers that have recently initiated journalistic productions. Boston Neighborhood Network News is one of the longest-running local news programs with support from Boston University interns. These centers have made strides, but additional funding, reporting collaborations, mentoring fellowships, and training curricula are still needed to grow local news programs in community media.

A lot can be gained by bridging gaps between local journalism and access media. As local newsrooms dwindle, access channels are potential partners for citizen-engaged journalism programs like City Bureau, which pays resident trainees to report on local government affairs. Cablecasted and streamed coverage of government meetings, town halls, and press conferences are valuable resources that reporters can use to promote civic action. Collaborative journalism networks could also benefit from community media reporters who cover local elections, public health issues, and neighborhood initiatives. Also, access channels managed by high schools, colleges, and universities are fertile training grounds that can yield budding young journalists.

Weaving local news and community media together can improve civic life in the long run, but significant policy and attitude shifts are in order. Access media advocates are worried about the steady decline of cable subscription revenue and the proliferation of unregulated streaming media services. Access operations use third-party, app-based streaming services to make content on their channels more accessible. Unlike PEG cable channels, these apps also collect viewership data. The caveat is, however, third-party platforms do not generate any revenue that supports PEG media services. In this scenario, the legislative power of the 1984 Cable Act is quite limited: local governments cannot collect PEG fees from broadband revenue earned by cable companies. Thus, there is a need for revised state and federal level policies that enable new revenue streams for community media.

Lastly, the time has come for local journalism and access media practitioners to see each other as beneficial partners. Journalists do not always take PEG access media seriously, seeing its infrastructure as incapable of generating credible news. Access media practitioners typically do not trust journalists who use extractive, biased reporting techniques that harm communities, especially communities of color. But as City Bureau co-founder Darryl Holliday eloquently noted, "A newsroom that connects existing civic assets around the participatory production and distribution of accurate, trustworthy, locally relevant information will build a future for local media as a true public good" (2021). Revamping a journalistic theory of change, as Holliday suggests, and reinvigorating the social change mindset that sparked the public access television movement are crucial to the advancement of local news practices in community media.

Conclusion

Access to local news and information is of vital importance. Instead of a commodity, journalism should be viewed as an essential public service, especially during pandemics, elections, and other critical moments. However, it is increasingly glaringly obvious that a profit-driven media system cannot support the minimal informational needs that a democracy requires. As local journalism's commercial model continues to collapse, public and nonprofit media institutions can serve as informational safety nets to support the media that all members of society need to navigate their daily lives and to conduct themselves as a self-governing populace.

Indeed, the worsening journalism crisis demands that we begin discussing how we might build this new system, one committed to universal service, building social solidarity, and providing diverse and reliable news and information that democracy requires. One starting point is to re-imagine and restructure already-existing public infrastructures that produce and disseminate vital information (Pickard, 2020). In addition to public broadcasting stations, libraries, and post offices, public access media outlets are another community infrastructure that deserves our attention and support. If we can scale up and radically democratize such infrastructures, we can create the kind of media system that serves all members of society. Throughout its history, and especially during the recent pandemic, PEG media have offered glimpses of what this new system might look like: participatory, radically democratic, and responsive to local communities' information and communication needs.

As a democratic society, we simply cannot afford to sit back and wait for the market to take care of the social and ecological crises facing us today. Without functioning news and information systems, such problems are insurmountable. Confronted by an ever-worsening journalism crisis, now is time to seriously reconsider how investments in PEG media could potentially provide for our local democratic necessities. We should leverage and expand these invaluable community infrastructures before we lose them altogether.

Note

1 This essay builds on an argument we first articulated in Antoine Haywood and Victor Pickard (2021). Public access television channels are an untapped resource for building local journalism, *NiemanLab*, November 10. https://www.niemanlab.org/2021/11/public-access-television-channels-are-an-untapped-resource-for-building-local-journalism/

References

Aufderheide, P., Haywood, A., & Santos, M. S. (2020). *PEG access media: Local communication hubs in a pandemic*. Center for Media and Social Impact. https://cmsimpact.org/report/peg/

Cable Communications Policy Act of 1984, Pub.L. No. 98-549, 98 Stat. 2779 (1984). https://www.govinfo.gov/app/details/STATUTE-98/STATUTE-98-Pg2779

Crittenden, L., & Haywood, A. (2020). Revising legacy media practices to serve hyperlocal information needs of marginalized populations. *Journalism Practice*, *14*(5), https://doi.org/10.1080/17512786.2020.1759124

Halleck, D. (2002). *Hand-held visions: The impossible possibilities of community media*. Fordham University Press.

Haywood, A., Aufderheide, P., & Santos, M. S. (2021). Community media in a pandemic: Facilitating local communication, collective resilience and transitions to virtual public life in the US. *Javnost-The Public*, *28*(3), 256–272. https://doi.org/10.1080/13183222.2021.1969617

Haywood, A., & Pickard, V. (2021, November 10). Public access television channels are an untapped resource for building local journalism. *NiemanLab*. https://www.niemanlab.org/2021/11/public-access-television-channels-are-an-untapped-resource-for-building-local-journalism/

Holliday, D. (2021, December 15). *Journalism is a public good. Let the public make it*. Columbia Journalism Review. https://www.cjr.org/special_report/journalism-power-public-good-community-infrastructure.php

Larkin, N. B. (2001). Pink Tulle: An unlikely bunch of revolutionaries. *Community Media Review*, *24*(2), 22–23. https://archive.org/details/CMRv24n2Sum_2001/mode/2up

Pickard, V. W. (2020). *Democracy without journalism? Confronting the misinformation society*. Oxford University Press.

Regan, J., & Jones, E. (2016). *New(s) access? Local news and alternative journalism at US community television stations*. https://www.academia.edu/31303039/New_s_Access_Local_News_and_Alternative_Journalism_at_U_S_Community_Television_Stations

Stein, L. (2001). Access television and grassroots political communication in the United States. In J. D. H. Downing (Ed.), *Radical media: Rebellious communication and social movements* (pp. 299–324). Sage.

15

THE ENGAGED STUDENT JOURNALIST

A Teaching Hospital Model for the 21st Century

Allison M. Frisch and Gina Gayle

It is a moment of peril for facts. In an age of misinformation and disinformation, well-trained student journalists may be the best hope for repairing community relationships torn apart by political polarization. The teaching hospital model of journalism education seeks to offer student journalists hands-on training and offers the opportunity for them to produce news stories for the communities surrounding their colleges. The model has many influential cheerleaders, including nonprofit journalism boosters such as the John S. and James L. Knight Foundation, which offers grants to college journalism programs that aim to provide news to "news deserts" and communities where "ghost papers" (Abernathy, 2020) are the only sources of civic information vital for a functioning democracy.

Yet the model also has its critics. Even those who champion the idea of a "teaching hospital" model disagree regarding whether that's the correct description of what journalism schools are currently doing and lament the fact that large higher education institutions may be too siloed and entrenched in old pedagogies to successfully pull practitioner-led faculty together to achieve a common goal. That goal is training the next generation of journalists by immersing them in work that results in quality, factually accurate reporting in communities that are, with the possible exception of questionably accurate social media content, devoid of local news.

The Ongoing Pedagogical Debate

The evolution of the teaching hospital experiential learning model is rooted in the post-Civil War era when professionalism came to the industrial world. It was applied to law, medicine, business, social work – and, eventually, journalism. Using this approach, students, professors, and newsroom editors and managers collaborate

DOI: 10.4324/9781003315605-24

to inform the public. Throughout history, however, the merits of the teaching hospital model in journalism have been debated, as have differing ideas regarding the correct pedagogical approach, if any, to take toward training journalists. Some saw journalism as a trade closely associated with working a printing press. Others, however, saw journalism as a profession that required academic training, and by the 1860s, schools such as Cornell University and Washington College established some of the first journalism courses.

This debate has continued over the decades, and one key question has highlighted competing approaches to journalism. It was the focus of intense debate at the turn of the century, and remains relevant today in the age of the citizen journalist: Is journalism a vocation born of the industrial printing press or a profession to be practiced by university-trained reporters versed in mass media research, liberal arts and social sciences? Is it a working-class endeavor, open to all citizens as their right established in the First Amendment of the Constitution, or is it a profession to be entered by way of a university degree?

This central issue is as germane today as ever, and, as Jean Folkerts (2014) notes, the debate over different approaches – experiential, liberal arts, research – remains relevant today. Most citizens in the United States have the power of the press in their pockets, in the form of a cellphone, equipped with text, photo and video tools and access to the masses via the internet. They have all the tools they need, even without a degree, to report from the field if they wish. This technology makes it easier to realize some of the goals established by leading voices in journalism education in decades past.

For instance, in 1908, when journalist and educator Walter Williams created the Missouri School of Journalism, he insisted student journalists learn by doing, and created the first journalism lab of its kind. As other schools began to emulate "Mizzou," employing "The Missouri Method" into their pedagogies, Williams created a code of ethics to help guide them. Later, in 1931, the dean of the Columbia Journalism School, Carl W. Ackerman, and a major journalism organization, the American Society of Newspaper Editors, similarly argued for "work simulation" over "superficial and routine" master's degree programs and warned journalism schools to respond, "intelligently to the requirements of the newspapers" (p. 240).

This perspective was adopted by some journalism schools, and the period of time from the mid-20th century to the dawn of the 21st century found schools such as those at Columbia University and Northwestern University also pursuing "a pure working journalist model, with students active in the local press, even to the point of skipping classes to work as reporters" (Folkerts, 2014, p. 246). This pedagogical argument plays out today amid rapid evolution of a digital news ecosystem that is seen today.

Others, however, pursued a different model toward journalism education, and many public universities applied a variety of approaches, including focusing on ethics, law, and history and branching out into broadcasting, photojournalism, and even public relations and advertising. During this time, professional organizations such as the American Association of Schools and Departments of Journalism and the American Society of Journalism School Administrators argued over accreditation while advocacy for federal and private funding for "communication study as an academic discipline" increased (Folkerts, 2014, p. 246).

At that time, during the community newspaper heyday of the 20th century, such debates around curriculum didn't center on the survival of the medium. Today, however – in the era of big tech and the swift decline of community newspapers and locally owned broadcast newsrooms – they take on greater significance.

Journalism Education at a Crossroads

At least 1800 communities that had local news outlets in 2004 had none at the start of 2020, creating "news deserts" and communities served by "ghost papers" (Abernathy, 2020). Most of those losses were weekly newspapers in economically struggling communities. To counter the rise of news deserts, journalism schools began to partner with local newsrooms. These reporting collaborations can be found at schools such as the University of California at Berkeley, Columbia University, Arizona State University, the University of North Carolina, the City University of New York, and others. Notably, the University of North Carolina's multimedia curriculum expanded and became interdisciplinary, drawing in complementary fields of study, and the school created a high-profile digital research news lab. Also, in 2005, the Knight Foundation announced the Carnegie-Knight Initiative on the Future of Journalism Education (Folkerts, 2014).

Such programs have had an impact. For instance, Nick Swyter, who went on to work for *The New York Times* as the program manager for its philanthropic partnerships, wrote about his experiences as a student who participated in the teaching hospital model while interning with the Knight Foundation as a junior at the University of Miami. He noted the experience he received as a student journalist "tracking down activists, undocumented immigrants and politicians to produce a documentary on immigration reform." However, Swyter estimated that such a teaching hospital model only existed "in bits and pieces at no more than 100 of the country's estimated 500 journalism schools and programs. For the most part, it still only exists as an aspiration" (Swyter, 2014, paras. 6–7).

Katherine Reed, associate professor of journalism at the University of Missouri, echoed Swyter's admonishment: Journalism schools must ask themselves tough questions and cast away old ideas of what journalism pedagogy looks like, moving away from entrenched and siloed systems in favor of a newer, bolder framework and a collaborative, convergent program. Integrating an "under one roof" (2014, para. 4) philosophy is vital to adopting the teaching hospital method successfully.

In a time of struggling legacy news providers and the rise of new opportunities – for community startups, nonprofit, independent and citizen journalism – the teaching hospital model in journalism is once again at the forefront of the conversation.

The teaching hospital model is, for some, our best hope to not only reinvigorate community news – helping it to survive and, hopefully, once again thrive – but to reinvigorate higher education as well.

Indeed, like newsrooms in the late 20th century, the halls of academia have been slow to evolve, and many colleges and universities now face financial challenges largely due to fewer students applying amid slowing population growth. The cost of college – and the resultant college debt – means more prospective students and their parents are questioning the value of a four-year education, and opting for less costly career and vocational training.

The lack of certainty about the value of a four-year education – combined with other societal factors, including concerns over the role of journalism in a climate of political polarization – may be the perfect storm that ushers in new ways of thinking about teaching journalism. Drastic times call for drastic measures, and this may prompt colleges and universities to rethink curricula that doesn't provide hands-on opportunities for students to graduate career ready, with experience in the news industry and a portfolio to prove it.

Accordingly, a fresh pedagogy might include staples such as newswriting, ethics and law combined with technology and niche offerings such as mobile and social journalism, and health, environmental, and social justice reporting. Student journalists might be assigned to contribute to a news site covering the region surrounding their college, starting with reporting about local and state elections, or community events, and then move on to produce investigative reporting podcasts and visual broadcast news packages.

Creating such opportunities, designed to prepare students for a new age of reporting, also means that senior leadership support, adequate funding and capable faculty are needed. As noted by the *International Journal of Communication*, "Professionals co-exist with scholars in law and medicine. They co-exist in art and music and business schools. They could do so in journalism as well. When they do, students and professors might be helping invent the future of news" ("The Promise and Peril," 2022, para. 20).

Encouraging Innovation and Entrepreneurship

Journalism and innovation seem at odds, in part due to the tenet of separating journalistic "church and state," in which anything associated with business growth and revenue is siloed from newsgathering. In reality, and historically, it has been challenging to actually live up to this ideal, and separate an advertiser from the copy.

A 21st-century approach to the teaching hospital model in journalism education must include an opportunity for students to experiment with new ways of both delivering and funding journalism. In the modern age – beset as it is with economic challenges – educators should no longer shy away from the conversation about funding journalism. After all, a public good, one that's integral to a functioning democracy, must include well-compensated practitioners.

Accordingly, a student journalist must be well versed in funding models such as subscriptions, membership models, live events, and more. If they are not offered options for funding their journalism and are instead forced to rely solely on corporate media for poorly paying mid-level jobs, the state of journalism will continue to decline. Instead, if they are equipped with the resources to start their own media organization, be it for-profit or nonprofit, they have a better chance of success. They have little chance, however, if they are tied to old ideas that no longer serve the community where they live and work.

Armed with such knowledge about how to succeed – and develop a sustainable business model – students can also be encouraged to go back to their hometown to start grassroots, niche newsrooms in the communities where neighbors know and trust them, rebuilding a public discourse damaged and undermined by big technology companies, polarization, and corporate ownership. To encourage and inspire enthusiastic student journalists, it is key to allow them to follow issues they are passionate about and explore new ways to fund and deliver their journalism to their neighbors. Such enthusiastic early-career journalists with proper training can supplement local news organizations as freelancers or start their own businesses. Perhaps they ultimately flood communities across the country with neighborhood news – and shore up relationships torn apart by social media–accelerated political polarization fueled with misinformation and disinformation.

The Value of Specialization

Historically, many journalists at newspapers and broadcast television and radio stations saw themselves as generalists, covering a wide variety of topics and dishing up bite-sized stories for a wide, and often affluent, audience. Yet, in the 21st century, an argument for specialization can be made. Journalism schools might offer curricula that supports more niche reporting, geographically or based on the issues of the day. Students might be trained to cover a geographic area (a city neighborhood or adjacent neighborhoods or a small rural town or village) and/or an issue of significance. Such a focus would encourage students just starting out in journalism to follow their natural curiosity and interests, and would lead to the development of the skills needed to do more in-depth reporting than a generalist agenda might allow.

The City College of New York's Newmark Graduate School of Journalism offers two examples of how this can be done. In 2022, the school announced its inaugural cohort of the Black Media Product Strategy Program, a "six-month, tuition-free program to train Black-owned newsrooms to build product strategies for digital transformation, audience growth and sustainability" (Newmark J-School, 2022, para. 1). The program is funded in part by the John S. and James L. Knight Foundation, whose aim is to strengthen journalism, communities, and the arts. Members of the inaugural cohort included *The Atlanta Voice*; *The Black Wall Street Times*, based in Oklahoma; and *The Haitian Times*, based in New York.

Newmark is also known for its NYCity News Service, which covers communities, including those in Brooklyn, Bronx, Queens, Staten Island and Manhattan.

The stories are reported, written and prepared by students, under the close supervision of the school's news director and professors, and supplied to newsrooms of all sizes for free.

Conclusion

Our evolving society and culture call for an evolution in journalism, one that reveres the tenets of journalism as a public good and the voice of the people, while imagining a healthy and fresh approach to this purposeful – and vital – work. There are myriad options for engaging students using an updated version of what is known as the "teaching hospital" model. We might move away from a staunch, "one-size-fits-all" definition of what engaged, practical journalism education is and infuse it with the flexibility our times call for. Entrenched hallowed halls that offer no opportunity for a student to explore and practice will continue to discourage student journalists to the point of leaving the discipline in favor of something more creative – or lucrative.

A new political and social paradigm calls for a new approach to inspiring student journalists. From the moment student journalists step into their inaugural college journalism course, to their final semesters, working together to complete a community news capstone or working in a newsroom as an intern training for a full-time career, it's imperative to inspire, as well as instruct. By introducing a pedagogy that recognizes a new generation of journalists and their approaches and concerns, journalism education may offer new opportunities and options and encourage students to return to their community and report on issues that resonate with their neighbors.

By expanding the possibilities of community journalism while student journalists are in training, we equip them to go home and independently report on the fullness of their community. That means recognizing unsung heroes, covering the school board and offering solutions-based journalism to uplift a community of which they have been a lifelong member. It means recognizing and respecting the way their work as a journalist is crucial to a healthy democracy, and speaking truth to power with integrity. Finally, it means building the credibility to facilitate difficult conversations, tell inconvenient truths, and ultimately strengthen the community, civically, socially, and democratically.

References

Abernathy, P. M. (2020). *News deserts and ghost newspapers: Will local news survive?* University of North Carolina Press.

Folkerts, J. (2014). History of Journalism Education. *Journalism & Communication Monographs*, *16*(4), 227–299. https://doi.org/10.1177/1522637914541379

Newmark J-School. (2022, March 16). *Announcing the first black media product strategy cohort - Newmark J-School.* https://www.journalism.cuny.edu/2022/03/announcing-the-first-black-media-product-strategy-cohort/

Reed, K. (2014). *Before the "teaching hospital model" of journalism education: 5 questions to ask.* Nieman Lab. https://www.niemanlab.org/2014/10/before-the-teaching-model-of-journalism-education-5-questions-to-ask/

Swyter, N. (2014). *A student's take on the teaching hospital model in journalism.* Knight Foundation. https://knightfoundation.org/articles/students-take-teaching-hospital/

The Promise and Peril of Teaching Hospitals. (2022). *Searchlights & sunglasses. International Journal of Communication.* http://www.searchlightsandsunglasses.org/the-promise-and-peril-of-teaching-hospitals/

ESSAY

Building Better Competitive News Environments

John-Erik Koslosky

It was mid-afternoon on a weekday when the phone rang. Another reporter from my newsroom had just returned from a hastily scheduled press conference held by local officials and their lawyers. Their aim was to discredit an investigative piece I'd written exposing the lax enforcement of local building codes.

The published work was solid, backed up by photos of crumbling facades and rusted-out fire escapes. But rather than address the evidence, the local officials went on the attack, demanding apologies. In this case, they knew they had at least five other news media outlets willing to do their bidding.

Montour County may be one of Pennsylvania's smallest counties by both size and population, but around the turn of the 21st century, it was home to one of the state's fiercest battles in local news. There were reporters from no fewer than seven news outlets working the beat. But for as many journalists as there were stalking the halls of government, a scant few dared to scrutinize the local establishment, preferring instead to maintain friendly relations and access.

At the *Press Enterprise*, a family-owned regional newspaper, we saw an opportunity. It was a vision shared by our newsroom and our business office, and for a stretch, we helped deliver the county's residents a surge of high-impact reporting. But the wave crashed, and when it rolled back out to sea, it left an expanse of dry land. Indeed, Montour County today finds itself on the list of "news deserts" published by the Tow Center, which has been tracking the disappearance of newspapers across the US.

This essay is a story of how that furious little competition came together, how it fell apart, and what we can learn from the unfortunate collapse of what may have been among of the country's hottest little news markets – at least for a little while.

I was first assigned to cover Montour in the late 1990s. The *Press Enterprise* had long staffed a small bureau in Montour but decided to make a serious push into the community and beef up staffing. The hometown paper there was *The Danville News*,

DOI: 10.4324/9781003315605-25

an afternoon daily that was distributed to more than half of all Montour County households. It was owned by a local family and edited by a former national sportswriter who married into the family. The larger *Daily Item*, a Dow Jones-owned paper in nearby Sunbury, PA, maintained a two-person news outpost in Montour. Three local broadcast outlets – a Christian radio station in town, a regional radio chain, and a locally owned cable network – sent reporters to public meetings, court proceedings and events.

Every one of those organizations vied for scoops day to day, but rarely dug into controversial matters or produced work that challenged what we might call the local power elite.

Then there was an on-again, off-again weekly, *The Danvillian*, run by a young 20-something, Matt Lysiak, better known today as dad of Hilde Lysiak, whose exploits as a daring kid news publisher earned her national attention and inspired the Apple TV series "Home Before Dark." Back then, Matt was nurturing his own budding ambition to break into investigative reporting. His tireless promotion of upcoming exposés injected excitement into the competition, even if his promised blockbuster reports often fell flat.

The *PE* was known at the time for aggressive watchdogging and enterprising news coverage – and as a training ground for young journalists later bound for papers in Philadelphia, Pittsburgh, Chicago, or Washington D.C. That helped the newspaper stand out among its competitors. Our management knew it, and they gave us the green light to patrol our beats with the zeal they deserved.

"Zig while the others zag," my managing editor would implore. For our three reporters assigned to cover Montour government and business, that meant searching for angles no one else was finding, sources no one else was talking to, and issues no one else was covering.

And zig we did. We revealed a sketchy separation agreement between high-ranking public school officials that sparked a state investigation and reprimand. We published an enterprise package on factory farm conditions that halted plans for a large-scale swine operation (and earned me a death threat from a very perturbed young farm operator with a violent past). We investigated the homicide probe of a dead Amish infant, helped clear the parents of suspected murder, and triggered statewide reforms in child and family services operations. And, of course, we shone light on those dangerous building conditions that left local officials feeling that they needed to mount an attack against our reporting.

But our aggressive watchdogging also ensured we got beat on important news stories promulgated from community-boosters and government offices and boardrooms cozier with our news rivals. Such is the nature of news competition.

Competitive news environments have significant benefits over their non-competitive counterparts. News organizations in competitive environments produce more news overall, are more likely to invest in innovation, more likely to engage in accountability journalism in covering local government and business, and more likely to follow up on news stories (Konieczna, 2018). Montour County's residents enjoyed those benefits.

But another type of competition threatened to tear it all down – and eventually did.

Let's pause and address an uncomfortable truth: The vaunted "wall" that exists to separate news matters from an organization's business matters has always been, to some degree, an illusion. The business office may not meddle in day-to-day editorial decisions like what to cover or what stories are chosen for the top of the front page or newscast. But it controls the purse strings of the operation, and it helps establish the boundaries in which a newsroom can operate.

All our watchdog reporting from Montour was possible only because the reporting mission found support in the newspaper's business office. Our newsroom was given the resources for our zigging because Montour offered something else besides government and business in need of watchdogging: It was the home of a fast-growing health system, which employed a population of doctors, nurses, scientists, and other professionals. And those were prime demographics for advertisers. As reporters raced to one-up their colleagues on the beat, the business department raced to monopolize local ad revenue.

In that push, we managed to double our circulation in the Montour County area in just a few short years, while the hometown *Danville News* saw its circulation plummet by some 40%. That helped our business office woo more advertisers and charge higher rates. But the *Danville News* sold to a rival competitor in 2001, and our publishers never did secure the monopolistic lock on advertising they sought. When ad revenue growth came to a halt, so did the great era of watchdog reporting in Montour.

As we look to rebuild our local news ecosystems, what happened in Montour County – and other places like it – can provide us with valuable lessons. Around the time that our news organizations were battling in Montour, scholar C. Edwin Baker was ringing an alarm over commercial news markets and media consolidation, and urging reform. Baker argued that the strongest local media system was one with the largest number of owners – "maximum dispersal," as he phrased it. That reflected the principles of democracy, was less corruptible, more durable, and ensured the widest array of ideas and voices.

But by this measure, Montour County had a model news system – a wide array of owners, mostly local. And still, it failed its residents.

To understand why, we need to address how organizations generate revenue and fund their reporting efforts. In Montour, with just one exception, every news organization was a commercial enterprise heavily reliant on advertising to pay its bills and produce profits for its owners. When the business office saw no more growth, it was not long before editors began deprioritizing labor-intensive enterprise and investigative reporting so reporters could focus on delivering shorter, more frequent news articles. Some were reassigned off of government beats or told to stop regularly attending meetings. News bureaus were shuttered. Some news organizations still claim to cover Montour today, but the watchdog was muzzled.

Still, hope is not lost for Montour and countless other places like it. In recent years, many prominent proponents of news media reform have all but given up on commercial news, concluding that a vast expansion of the public media system is the best solution to the local news crisis. Montour provides a dramatic illustration of how a commercial news market can fail the public, but if we take away one lesson from Montour, it's that our goal should not be to find a single form of ownership or revenue model to replace what has collapsed.

While an expanded government-funded news media holds promise in helping to address the public's informational needs – research has shown that public media tend to cover a wider array of issues and do so with more depth (Neff & Pickard, 2021) – it's far from a silver bullet. A local media system that is largely reliant on public funding – and one whose purse strings are controlled by elected leaders – is also vulnerable to corrupting influences, especially if stringent non-partisan guiderails are not established and respected. Every revenue model has its strengths and its weaknesses.

A local news media system will be strongest and serve the public best when it's built from the widest arrays of ownership types and revenue sourcing. For-profit advertising-based and subscription-based models, locally owned public benefit corporations, low-profit LLPs, small non-profit community-based news organizations, larger non-profit organizations with local or regional offices, and public media models all have a place in a strong news media system.

In areas of Pennsylvania not far from Montour, we see promising developments. Several of Pennsylvania's public media affiliates are expanding their news operations and watchdogging state and local governments. Non-profit news organizations like *SpotlightPA* and *PublicSource*, dedicated to public-service journalism, are adding to staff. Partnerships between public and non-profit media and legacy media outlets have flourished. And in several areas of Pennsylvania, including counties just west of Montour, fledgling for-profit news websites have sprung up, and some are venturing into accountability reporting. Smart policy – in the form of tax incentives as well as public funding – should nurture all these areas of potential new growth while providing support for legacy outlets.

Competition among news organizations is healthiest when every journalist looks to dig deeper and tell the stories that aren't being told. To zig while others zag. But it's also healthiest when one organization's rise is not dependent on another's financial demise.

As for that news conference, just as the local officials had hoped, several local news outlets published their allegations without so much as offering me a chance to respond. It was a Pyrrhic victory, however. We stuck by our coverage, and it wasn't long before a new slate of officials were elected and eventually ushered out the top municipal official who oversaw the lax code enforcement.

Several of the buildings in question met the wrecking ball and were replaced. But there isn't much to prevent it from happening again, as so little watchdog reporting emanates from Montour County today. The people there deserve better, and smart public policy choices that promote healthy competition could deliver something even better than they had before. There may not be as many reporters attending press conferences, but there can be a stronger and more diverse array of organizations serving the public.

References

Konieczna, M. (2018). *Journalism without profit: Making news when the market fails.* Oxford University Press.

Neff, T., & Pickard, V. (2021). Funding democracy: Public media and democratic health in 33 countries. *The International Journal of Press/Politics.* https://doi.org/10.1177/19401612 211060255

PART VI
The Real Impact of Fake News

There is nothing new about fake news. In fact, we've been dealing with fake news since the earliest days of journalism. Fake news was rampant in ancient Rome, where the imperial family frequently made use of *Acta Diurna* (*Daily Acts*) to promote their agenda and supply the public with favorable information. It was still a big problem during the Middle Ages, and so much so that two different popes, Pius V and Gregory XIII, issued decrees banning fake news and threatening both ecclesiastical and secular punishment in the form of forced labor or death. In colonial America, it was such a concern that the first newspaper published in North America announced a plan to publicly shame anyone found to be spreading fake news. It remained a problem after the revolution, in the young American republic, where John Adams complained, "There has been more new error propagated by the press in the last ten years than in an hundred years before 1798."

But when most people think of fake news today, they are not calling to mind such historical examples. Instead, the idea of "fake news" itself really burst onto the minds of contemporary Americans during the 2016 presidential election cycle. After that, the stage was set for the growth of a new information epidemic. Empowered by new digital platforms that gave a stage for voicing extreme views, the perfect conditions existed for the proliferation of false narratives, conspiracy theories, and propaganda. Just as troublesome as the growth of actual fake, untrue news, is the way in which the term "fake news" itself has been weaponized and used to discredit and attack any information – including that which is factual and valid – that one dislikes. Part VI begins with a consideration of the origins and history of fake news, and presents some ways in which it might be addressed moving forward.

DOI: 10.4324/9781003315605-26

16

UNDERSTANDING FAKE NEWS TODAY

Larry J. King

During the 2016 presidential campaign the term "fake news" became one of the most often repeated phrases by candidates and media figures alike, and many throughout the nation came to recognize that, as scholar Diana Owen (2017) claimed, the election that year was characterized by "the amount of misinformation, misleading stories, and boldface lies that were propagated" (p. 175). Further, the term "fake news" was used so often in 2016 that it became a campaign issue unto itself, and may have, according to some, influenced the outcome of the campaign. Hillary Clinton, the Democrat candidate in 2016, claimed in her first speech following the election,

> The epidemic of malicious fake news and false propaganda that flooded social media over the past year – it's now clear that so-called fake news can have real world consequences… It's a danger that must be addressed, and addressed quickly.

This "epidemic" did not end with the 2016 election cycle, and in some ways has only increased in the years that followed. Notably, the Collins Dictionary identified a 365% increase in the term's usage during the year following that election, leading both the Collins Dictionary and the American Dialect Society to name "fake news" the Word of the Year for 2017 (Graves, 2018). Similarly, an analysis of the use of the phrase "fake news" on the national television networks Bloomberg, CNBC, CNN, Fox Business, Fox News, and MSNBC showed that there was a dramatic increase in the use of the term following the election (Leetaru, 2017). Additionally, with the election of Donald Trump as the 45th president of the United States, accusations of Russian collusion with the Trump campaign, the Mueller investigation, and media investigations into the new president, fake news continued to garner attention. The term fake news became a favorite of President Trump, with one report claiming that he used the term more than 1900 times in public statements and social media posts between 2016 and 2020 alone (Woodward, 2020). During this time, the term also started to

DOI: 10.4324/9781003315605-27

take on additional meanings, as Trump increasingly used "fake news" to refer to news coverage that he did not like, that was negative toward him and his administration, that he perceived did not give credit for his success, or that used unnamed sources.

Though Trump had used the term "enemy of the people" in relation to the news media on numerous occasions, his relationship with the media appeared to reach a new low in October of 2018 when he claimed in a tweet that "… The Fake News Media, the true Enemy of the People, must stop the open & obvious hostility & report the news accurately & fairly" (Trump, 2018). His claim that the media was "the true Enemy of the People" seems to have led to a new level of antagonism between the president and some members of the news media, which first became especially evident in a fiery exchange between Trump and Jim Acosta, CNN's Chief White House Correspondent, during a November 2018 White House press conference. From this point on, President Trump's perspective on fake news seemed to spread internationally as leaders in other countries like Syria, the Philippines, Turkey, Cambodia, Myanmar, Venezuela, Malaysia, Israel, Hungary, Russia, and China began applying the term fake news to any unflattering media coverage, regardless of its accuracy.

The emergence of the COVID-19 epidemic in late 2019 again led to a surge of fake news and attention to the dangers of misinformation during a public health crisis. The problem became so prominent that the World Health Organization called it an "infodemic… that makes it hard for people to find trustworthy sources and reliable information" (World Health Organization, 2020). A 2019 Pew Research Center study found that Americans viewed fake news to be a more serious problem than racism, climate change, or terrorism, and a 2021 Gallop poll showed that public trust in the media in the US had fallen to the second-lowest level in the history of the poll (Brenan, 2021). Accordingly, given the prominence of fake news – in both reality and perception – it appears unlikely that related issues will diminish any time soon. Thus, it is important for media consumers and professionals to understand the origins of fake news, how to define fake news, and how to identify fake news. The remainder of this chapter will examine each of these critical topics.

The Origins of Fake News

Many media consumers and professionals likely believe that fake news is a recent phenomenon, attributing the term to Donald Trump or the wider events surrounding the 2016 presidential campaign. It's easy to see why media consumers and professionals would believe that Trump was the source of the term; after all, he took credit for introducing the term. During an October 7, 2017 interview with Mike Huckabee, Trump said,

> The media is really, the word, one of the greatest of all terms I've come up with, is 'fake,'… I guess other people have used it perhaps over the years, but I've never noticed it…

(Huckabee, 2017)

Later, in an Oval Office appearance on October 2, 2019, President Trump said, "… I'm the one that came up with the term [fake news]. I'm very proud of it …" (Woodward, 2020). Trump also used the term to refer not only to the media in general but also to a substantial number of media outlets and news stories. He used the term so often during and immediately after the campaign that it easily became associated with him and his campaign. However, it's important to understand that the term and concept of fake news predates Donald Trump or any of the events surrounding the 2016 election.

The Partisan Press

If fake news did not originate with Donald Trump or the 2016 presidential election, where did it begin? Notably, fake news – in some form – reaches back to the early days of the nation and the period of the partisan press. During this period, newspapers were closely affiliated with the political factions and parties of the day. There was no notion of an unbiased and nonpartisan press in America during the Revolutionary period and for many years following, and competing newspapers often printed outlandish and questionable claims against their political foes.

Not even George Washington was spared from the disparaging attacks of the partisan newspapers. Many of the attacks on Washington in the partisan press and pamphlets were based on a group of seven letters that first surfaced during the revolution. These letters had expressed Washington's devotion to the English monarchy and his doubts about the justification for the American Revolution, or its chances of success. When first published during the revolution, the letters caused significant consternation among the public in the American colonies. They also caused considerable public concern when they were once again published during Washington's presidency. Washington steadfastly denied authorship of the letters. While it is generally understood today that these letters were, indeed, forgeries, they became such a source of frustration for Washington that at the end of his second term as president he wrote to the secretary of state, who shared his comments with newspapers that had spread the misinformation, disavowing the "spurious letters," and – in a sense – fact-checking the newspaper coverage of the time.

Newspapers also promoted the fear that Washington, Hamilton, and the Federalists wanted to establish an American aristocracy and monarchy, such as existed in England. A celebration of Washington's birthday, for example, was cast as proof of Washington's desire to become a king. Hamilton's plans for the public debt were characterized as a plan to do away with the American Republic and replace it with a hereditary monarchy. Criticism later turned to John Adams, when he succeeded Washington as president. By the time he assumed office Adams was characterized as "old, querulous, bald, blind, crippled, toothless" (Shafer, 2018). One infamous pamphlet seemed to imply that Adams was a hermaphrodite, and a book labeled Adams the biggest fool on the continent.

Yellow Journalism

According to the Merriam-Webster Dictionary, the term fake news appears to have come into common use in the late 1800s, during the age of yellow journalism in the United States. Yellow journalism was characterized by the reporting of overly sensational and shocking news stories to attract readers and boost newspaper circulation. There are a few notorious stories that are often cited to illustrate the excesses of yellow journalism and fake news of the period. One of the earliest and best-known examples is sometimes referred to as the Great Moon Hoax of 1835. This consisted of a series of six articles published in the New York *Sun*. The articles claimed to be an account of a scientific discovery of life on the moon and reported the existence of batlike humanoids, structures including temples, and a fanciful landscape. The articles captured the attention of the public and led to widespread fascination with the series. Another, less-remembered, example is what has been called the New York Zoo Hoax. On November 9, 1874, *The New York Herald* published a grizzly and detailed story of animals escaping from the Central Park Zoo and the death and mayhem which ensued. Even though the story contained a disclaimer at the end noting that it was a fictitious account, it caused widespread public panic.

While these articles seemed to be harmless antics intended to draw public attention and readers, other fake news in the era of yellow journalism had more serious consequences. An example of this came in the period preceding the Spanish–American War. Notably, William Randolph Hearst of the *New York Journal* – along with rival publishers, including Joseph Pulitzer of *The World* – ran numerous stories promoting rumors and conspiracy theories regarding the sinking of the battleship USS *Maine* in the Havana harbor, seeking to sway public opinion, and helping to push the nation to declare war against Spain.

Fake News in the 20th Century

During the 20th century, a sense of journalistic professionalism and social accountability developed, due to a variety of factors including the growth of professional organizations of journalists, the development of college and university journalism programs, and public concern over past excesses of some newspapers and journalists. Also, during this century technological developments introduced a variety of new media. Even with these developments, journalism continued to be dogged by fake news. The propaganda campaigns of World Wars I and II caused widespread public concern over the accuracy and reliability of news and the governmental control of information in the media. Academic research and public information campaigns focused on how to identify and combat propaganda. Governmental disinformation propagated in the media during the Vietnam War created widespread disillusionment with both the government and media news sources.

Other examples of fake news during the 20th century can be found in the pages of tabloid newspapers, including the *National Enquirer* and the *Weekly World News*.

These tabloids battled each other and traditional newspapers for readership. Over the years the *National Enquirer* published several outrageous stories claiming that President John F. Kennedy was killed by a variety of conspirators, including, among others, the CIA, organized crime, Richard Nixon, Lyndon Johnson, and a Russian agent. The *National Enquirer* has also published several stories claiming to have evidence of sexual scandals involving Bill and Hillary Clinton over the years, yet the evidence has not surfaced. Even more outrageous, the *Weekly World News* claimed that, among other things, President Bill Clinton rode in a spaceship and had been endorsed by a space alien, Hillary Clinton had adopted an alien baby, Vice President Dick Cheney was a robot, and in one of its most popular series of stories, that a Bat Boy had been discovered in a cave in West Virginia.

Defining Fake News

Clearly, fake news was not invented by Donald Trump and did not have its genesis in the 2016 election. There is a long history of reporting information that is not based in fact in this country and the origin of the term in reference to American journalism can be traced back to at least the 1700s, if not much earlier. Today, many consumers of mass and social media likely have personal definitions of fake news that generally focus on the truth or the factuality of news stories. Similarly, numerous communication researchers and scholars have also focused on fake news and offered a variety of definitions. Edson Tandoc et al. (2017) conducted a comprehensive review of the definitions of fake news and identified six general categories. These six categories, in turn, can be understood as existing on a continuum involving the level of facticity – "the degree to which fake news relies on facts" (p. 146) – and the level of intentional deception – "the author's immediate intentions to deceive" (p. 147).

On one end of this continuum is "news satire," content that has a low level of facticity, but which is intended to be humorous, rather than deceitful, and which uses "non-factual information to inject humor" (p. 143). Such "news satire" might be seen in a television program such as *The Daily Show*. The second category, "news parody," is content that also has a low level of facticity, but which is intended to be humorous, not deceitful, and which "plays on the ludicrousness of issues and highlights them by making up entirely fictitious news stories" (p. 143). Such "news parody" might be seen in a television program like *Saturday Night Live*, or in the articles of *The Onion*.

At the other end of the continuum are types of fake news content that are much more insidious. Notably, a third category of fake news is "news fabrication," content that has a low level of facticity and which is intended to deceive. Often, fabricated news is false information presented in the style and form of legitimate news; while it may appear to the consumer to be legitimate, it is content that is intentionally presented to mislead or misinform. The fourth category of fake news, which focuses on "news manipulation," is content that is low in facticity and highly deceitful, and which is characterized by the alteration of images or videos to create a "false narrative" (p. 145).

"Native advertising" constitutes a fifth category of fake news. This involves content that is low in facticity and intended to deceive, and which involves presenting advertisements that appear to be legitimate news items or editorial content. Finally, the sixth category of fake news – also highly deceitful and low in facticity – is "propaganda," which is content that is "created by a political entity to influence public perceptions" (p. 147).

News consumers are not passive in the fake news creation process and, as Tandoc and colleagues noted, whether it is intentional or unintentional, fake news is "co-constructed by the audience" (p. 150). As Tandoc et al. (2017) note, "fakeness depends a lot on whether the audience perceives the fake as real. Without this complete process of deception, fake news remains a work of fiction" (p. 150). This process of co-creation becomes even more problematic when news consumers go further, and begin sharing fake news through social media, where such content is even more likely to be believed because of the social connections that exist on such platforms.

Responding to Fake News

The proliferation of, and increased attention given to, fake news has brought calls from media consumers, industry professionals, and politicians for action. Public opinion polls indicate that 50–70% of the American public see fake news as a problem, and 86% of online global citizens report that they have been exposed to fake news (Auxier & Arbanas, 2021; Mitchell et al., 2019; Simpson, 2019). Clearly, fake news is perceived as a problem, and numerous solutions have been suggested, including governmental action, intervention from social media companies, and educational initiatives involving public schools, universities, and the public. While the first option – governmental action – might seem like an obvious solution, any such governmental measures would border on censorship and easily run the risk of violating individual rights to free speech. More opportunities exist for intervention within the private sector, and in this regard some limited steps have been taken. Notably, the call for intervention from social media and technology companies led to the development of fact-checking organizations and networks. Poynter's International Fact-Checking Network (IFCN) was established to "bring together the growing community of fact-checkers around the world and advocates of factual information in the global fight against misinformation" (IFCN, 2021), and has partnered with Meta to review and identify problematic content on its Facebook, Instagram, and WhatsApp platforms. Various fact-checking websites have also been developed to help media consumers and organizations identify fake news.

As to the call for educational efforts, there have been several suggested approaches to training students and the public in evaluating information and news for truthfulness. One often-cited and widely used approach is the CRAAP (Currency, Relevance, Authority, Accuracy, Purpose) Test developed at California State University, Chico. The CRAAP Test encourages media and information consumers to analyze the following main points, and related questions, about any information they consider:

Currency: The timeliness of the information.
Relevance: The importance of the information for your needs.
Authority: The source of the information.
Accuracy: The reliability, truthfulness, and correctness of the content.
Purpose: The reason the information exists.

(Meriam Library, n.d.)

The CRAAP Test suggests that media and information consumers should be suspicious of any information or news that cannot pass the test and consider such information or news to be questionable and likely false or misleading.

Conclusion

As noted earlier, fake news is considered a serious problem by a sizable percentage of the public, and many believe that journalism has a special responsibility for solving the fake news problem (Mitchell et al., 2019). Because the existence and perception of fake news harms public trust in the media, journalists do well to take such public sentiments seriously and – to protect the integrity and future of their profession – respond appropriately to the fake news threat. Events from history demonstrate that fake news is not a new problem and has been around throughout the history of journalism and the media. That history also provides some indication of the conditions or environments when journalists and media professionals should be on their guard. In the past, fake news often surfaced in times of significant political power struggles, like the period of the partisan press and the 2016 election. Fake news also seems to appear when there is considerable competition for readers, viewers, listeners, or clicks, as during the period of yellow journalism, or such as existed in the 20th-century tabloid and television news markets.

History has also shown that journalists and media professionals need to respond to the demands of communication media with a sense of professional ethics. When such standards are neglected in favor of creating interesting or appealing content, the result can be the creation of fake or manufactured news.

Journalists and media professionals working to address the danger of fake news can draw inspiration from the public information campaigns developed to respond to 20th-century propaganda campaigns. For instance, social scientists, philanthropists, educators, and journalists worked together in the Institute for Propaganda Analysis (IPA) to inform and educate the public on how to identify and critically evaluate propaganda. The IPA published pamphlets, books, educational materials for schools, and supplied articles and op-eds for newspapers. Journalists and other media professionals should be activists in uncovering and publicizing fake news from any source. They should also actively work to educate media consumers on what fake news is and how it can be detected and evaluated. In these ways journalists and media professionals will provide a valuable public service.

References

Auxier, B. & Arbanas, J. (2021). Majority of news consumers see "fake news" as a big problem today. *Deloitte.* https://www2.deloitte.com/us/en/insights/industry/technology/study-shows-news-consumers-consider-fake-news-a-big-problem.html

Brenan, M. (2021, October 7). Americans' trust in media dips to second lowest on record. *Gallup.* https://news.gallup.com/poll/355526/americans-trust-media-dips-second-lowest-record.aspx

Graves, L. (2018, February 26). How Trump weaponized "fake news" for his own political ends. *Pacific Standard.* https://psmag.com/social-justice/how-trump-weaponized-fake-news-for-his-own-political-ends

Huckabee, M. (2017, October 7). Full interview President Trump [Video]. YouTube. https://www.youtube.com/watch?v=hVQPVGPAUtc&t=4s

IFCN. (2021). State of the fact-checkers 2021. https://www.poynter.org/wp-content/uploads/2022/01/IFCN_2022_StateFactChecking2021_v06.pdf

Leetaru, K. (2017, February 17). Did Facebook's Mark Zuckerberg coin the phrase 'fake news'? *Forbes.* https://www.forbes.com/sites/kalevleetaru/2017/02/17/did-facebooks-mark-zuckerberg-coin-the-phrase-fake-news/?sh=44771cfb6bc4

Merriam Library. (n.d.). Evaluating information – Applying the CRAAP Test. https://library.csuchico.edu/sites/default/files/craap-test.pdf

Mitchell, A., Gottfried, J., Stocking, G., Walker, M., & Fedeli, S. (2019). Many Americans say made-up news is a critical problem that needs to be fixed. *Pew Research Center.* https://www.pewresearch.org/journalism/2019/06/05/many-americans-say-made-up-news-is-a-critical-problem-that-needs-to-be-fixed/

Owen, D. (2017). Twitter rants, press bashing, and fake news. In L. J. Sabato, K. Kondik, & G. Skelley (Eds.), *Trumped: The 2016 election that broke all the rules* (pp. 167–180). Rowman & Littlefield.

Shafer, R. (2018, September 8). The thin-skinned president who made it illegal to criticize his office. *The Washington Post.* https://www.washingtonpost.com/news/retropolis/wp/2018/09/08/the-thin-skinned-president-who-made-it-illegal-to-criticize-his-office/

Simpson, S. (2019, June 11). Fake news: A global epidemic vast majority (86%) of online global citizens have been exposed to it. *Ipsos.* https://www.ipsos.com/en-us/news-polls/cigi-fake-news-global-epidemic

Tandoc, E., Lim, Z.. & Ling, R. (2017). Defining "fake news": A typology of scholarly definitions. *Digital Journalism, 6*(2), 137–153. https://doi.org/10.1080/21670811.2017.1360143

Trump, D. [@realDonaldTrump]. (2018, October). The Fake News Media, the true Enemy of the People, must stop the open & obvious hostility & report the news accurately [Tweet]. *Twitter.* https://twitter.com/realDonaldTrump/status/1056879122348195841?ref_src=twsrc%5Efw

Woodward, A. (2020, October 2). "Fake news": A guide to Trump's favourite phrase – and the dangers it obscures. *The Independent.* https://www.independent.co.uk/news/world/americas/us-election/trump-fake-news-counter-history-b732873.html#

World Health Organization. (2020, February 2). Novel Coronavirus (2019-nCoV) Situation Report-13. https://www.who.int/docs/default-source/coronaviruse/situation-reports/20200202-sitrep-13-ncov-v3.pdf

17

THE RETURN OF FAKE NEWS

J. D. Ponder

Fake news is a plague upon any functioning democracy. An endless supply of false information has infiltrated the current communication ecosystem, eroding trust in the pillars of society. As fake news creators have developed and honed their craft, they have gotten better at creating believable reports, videos, and stories that undercut the functioning of our democracy. In this chapter I will trace the history of fake news and disinformation, discuss how fake news evolved, outline the difficulties journalists face today, and address the research on how to best address fake news in the current media environment.

History of Fake News and Disinformation

Contrary to media reports and popular opinion, fake news is not a new phenomenon. Some of the earliest recorded misinformation dates back as far as 1450 BCE, when Egyptian Pharaoh Horemheb chiseled out references to previous pharaohs to make it seem as though he were the direct successor of Pharaoh Amenhotep III. This was common practice in the ancient world. As civilizations developed, they used fake news to organize for war, negotiate treaties, or even gain public support to rule. For instance, in Ancient Greece, emperors and military leaders used fake news to consolidate power. One such instance occurred around 480 BCE under the efforts of Athenian naval commander Themistocles during the Greek struggle against Persia, and involved spreading deceptive counterintelligence which effectively changed the outcome of the war in favor of the Greeks.

The Birth of the Printing Press and the Rise of False News

When Johannes Gutenberg invented the movable type printing press in 1450, the nature of fake news changed dramatically. Prior to Gutenberg's invention, leaders

DOI: 10.4324/9781003315605-28

relied on messengers to spread disinformation amongst the populace – a practice that took significant time and resources as the messengers traveled from town to town. As literacy spread through society, however, printed fake news became commonplace. Further, this technological evolution led to fake news featuring printed images. This change was highly effective as words and images worked together to convince audience members about the veracity of a story.

Fake News and Early America

America was not immune from the use of fake news as a political tactic. Many of the Founding Fathers were adept at fake news. For instance, Benjamin Franklin was one of the first modern practitioners of black propaganda – propaganda designed to look as though it came from one source while actually coming from another. Franklin handled much of the black propaganda used during the American Revolution, writing several noteworthy pieces of black propaganda, including The Sale of the Hessians, a letter that exposed the ruthlessness of German princes in their dealings with the British government. The contents of the letter featured two nonexistent German princes. In addition to creating and spreading black propaganda in Europe, Franklin also was tasked to fight against fake news spreading across Holland and France at John Adams' request.

The Rise of Yellow Journalism

Once Joseph Pulitzer bought the New York *World* in 1883, news reporting began to shift dramatically to a more sensationalized style that prized readership and conflict over truth and objectivity. After William Randolph Hearst bought the *New York Journal*, the two papers became the center of an all-out competition for circulation in New York. This style of journalism fostered significant innovation in terms of journalistic practices. Publishers urged writers and editors to use vivid descriptions in stories. Newspapers coordinated coverage of issues to provoke an outcome of their choosing, or reveal some wrongdoing or scandal. At times, newspapers even staged pseudo-events to increase readership. The most famous example of fake news in the era of yellow journalism came in 1898, when the battleship USS *Maine* was sunk in the Havana harbor. Both Hearst and Pulitzer published front-page stories stating that the *Maine* explosion was caused by a bomb or torpedo, despite official records which suggested the explosion was accidental. Such claims, coming on top of the years of coverage that fanned anti-Spanish sentiments, had an impact on their readers, and most historians agree this inaccurate coverage played a significant role in fomenting public support for the Spanish–American War. The yellow journalism style eventually lost popularity, but the lessons learned on how to encourage readership are influential over 100 years later.

Fake News Adapts to the Internet

The final piece of the fake news puzzle was put in place in the 1970s, when scientists at the Pentagon first began developing the system that eventually became the internet. As the constituent parts of computing evolved – growing smaller and faster – the use of computers and eventually the internet became more mainstream.

By the early part of the 21st century, most Americans had access to the internet and reported using it on a daily basis. As a result, news platforms began to leverage their existing infrastructure to fill this new information landscape and invested in different forms of storytelling. The competition for viewers increased as news organizations realized advertising content would not sustain their current budgetary needs. Many news outlets pivoted to increasingly partisan media approaches to compete for viewership.

As the electorate began choosing partisan outlets that reinforced their own biases, the American population began to splinter into distinct sub-groups, which only received news from echo chambers that reinforce already held beliefs. This ultimately led to increased distrust in the highly fragmented news environment. A recent Pew Research Center report outlined that some 72% of the public distrust media organizations (Gottfried & Liedke, 2021).

As social media became more prolific and widespread, a new wave of citizens began to move beyond just consuming news and began disseminating news as well. These so-called citizen journalists began commenting on current events. As these people became more comfortable in their role, they began to create and disseminate a new form of news that didn't adhere to traditional journalistic norms and practices. This massive influx of content soon outpaced traditional journalistic efforts, and ultimately also led to a further erosion of public trust in news.

Fake News in 2016

The 2016 United States presidential campaign cycle featured a perfect storm of contextual factors for fake news to flourish. Trust in media, government, and science were all at historically low levels. The public had normalized poor media literacy habits. News channels had fragmented to different platforms and increased exponentially. The population had become increasingly more partisan. Finally, social media, which could easily spread information among social networks, gained popularity.

Whether the stories were in favor of Hillary Clinton or Donald Trump, over one-quarter of voting age adults visited a fake news website during the election. One study reported pro-Trump fabricated stories were shared 30 million times and pro-Clinton fabricated stories were shared 7.6 million times, resulting in a potential 760 million clicks of fake news stories (Allcott & Gentzkow, 2017). The sheer quantity of disinformation in the 2016 election cycle was so great that the average citizen encountered more than three instances of fake news about each presidential candidate. After 2016, "fake news" was quickly co-opted by President Trump as a slur to describe news stories critical of him or his policy decisions, further eroding trust in media amongst a part of the population.

Difficulties Journalists Face Today

Currently, journalists face a significant set of challenges they must overcome in order to successfully combat fake news. These challenges can be understood as existing in several categories.

Environmental Challenges

One environmental, contextual challenge involves the vast and fragmented news environment. This fragmentation occurs as people routinely consume news across different communication channels (e.g., news sites, social media, newspapers, and television) and within channels (e.g., through different TV channels, radio stations, news sites, newspapers, and magazines). This increased fragmentation creates an intimidating information landscape where users are often overwhelmed by the sheer quantity of choices they face, and seek out trusted others to vet this information. Fake news disseminators play upon this fact by flooding online sources and social media accounts with disinformation, which is ultimately picked up by unsuspecting individuals and disseminated through their social networks, thereby increasing the likelihood others will find the fake news to be credible.

Structural Challenges

The very nature of the news-gathering process places journalists at a disadvantage when it comes to fake news. Verified news (or news hereafter) takes time. In the news-gathering process, journalists must source ideas, gather and vet sources, identify and interview stakeholders, determine the significance and relevance of information, analyze the information, compose drafts, solicit feedback, and finally publish the news report.

Conversely, fake news is easy to create. Fake news does not need to be verified. Fake news creators often rewrite news articles to suit their goals or edit video to misrepresent what actually happened. Technological advances in image manipulation, video editing, and search engines have made this job much easier for these creators. Whereas traditional journalists can spend months collecting and verifying information for one story, fake news creators can edit multiple stories in a single day. Further, many fake news creators are financed by adversarial governments. Leveraging the financial support of these governments, fake news creators can often employ hundreds of employees to reinforce a particular narrative.

The next issue journalists face is the 24/7 news environment. In the 24/7 news environment, journalists often face increasing pressure to be the first to report a given story. When the speed of reporting inevitably leads to errors in a news story, the public can lose trust in the very institutions it needs to rely on for accurate information. Additionally, as information is updated, news articles also report the changes in the story. While the transparency is a welcome addition to the news environment, this transparency can be a problem for some disillusioned consumers of news. The inclusion of these corrections and updates can reinforce that narrative that journalists make errors in their reporting.

Finally, when news organizations attempt to correct fake news, they often repeat the fake news as a part of the correction. However, there are mixed results when it comes to using the actual text of the fake news when rebutting the fake news. Some studies have reported backfire effects where the correction in fact led to increased acceptance of the fake news. What seems to be consistent across the literature is that as the time between the correction and final test of beliefs increases, so does the likelihood of a backfire effect.

Audience Challenges

Fake news is often designed to appeal to specific parts of society, and fake news is often targeted toward groups of people with low levels of objective knowledge on a given issue. As people interact with new information, they must rely on a strong foundation of existing knowledge to rebut any fake news they encounter. However, those who lack a solid foundation of objective knowledge are more at risk of accepting fake news. This is further problematic as people tend to evaluate future information based on previously accepted information.

Another audience-related challenge journalists face is that audience members have extremely poor information literacy habits. A significant body of literature in social science has demonstrated that people are, by and large, cognitive misers – meaning they are not likely to think about issues until they are directly affected by them. The research on information processing also indicates people tend to readily accept information presented to them without verifying it.

Further, several studies have reported the general population has abysmal habits when it comes to their news consumption. Numerous studies have reported that fact-checking information is atypical of the traditional news consumer. A recent Zignall Labs study reported that only 14% of those surveyed indicated they fact check the news they consume, and Maksym Gabielkov et al. (2016) stated that only 60% of participants even read the content of a news article before sharing it on social media. These poor media literacy habits set the stage for fake news creators to spread false news amongst a vulnerable electorate.

Motivated reasoning is another explanation for accepting fake news. Substantial social science literature suggests people are more likely to accept information that confirms pre-existing political biases. People are more likely to accept fake news if it attacks members of the competing party. People are also more likely to reject fake news if it attacks members of their own political party. Further, when fake news is repeated by leaders of their own political party, people are more likely to accept the fake news as correct.

Channel Challenges

The creation and widespread adoption of the internet also created numerous challenges journalists must address as they combat fake news. Fake news sites often use names that sound like legitimate news organizations. They also employ a similar visual format to that of news organizations and create legitimate-looking layouts, graphics, and embedded advertising. These tactics tend to trick readers into believing the site is legitimate.

Fake news is also highly likely to be spread via social media. Fake news disseminators rely on the relative ease of sharing information on social media. As people often do not read the information they post, and instead rely solely on the headline to inform their opinions, false information is three times more likely to spread than accurate information. Finally, fake news creators and distributors create false profiles on social media sites and develop accounts managed by bots (automated programs used to engage on social media) to spread a story through social media.

Message Challenges

Current research on disinformation suggests that it spreads faster, farther, and more deeply than verified, trustworthy information. The salacious nature of fake news tends to draw attention compared to mundane news stories. Whether the story is about a mysterious Washington insider, a secret tracking chip inside vaccinations, or a secret dossier about illicit sex acts, fake news has a way of drawing the public's interest.

Further, the salacious nature of the stories tends to create difficulties when attempting to combat it. Fake news is designed to reinforce particular narratives about political institutions and actors, or degrade trust in existing media, education, or scientific institutions. Instead of facts, expert testimony, and statistics designed to inform an audience about a given issue, fake news uses narratives about scandal, corruption, and conspiracy to persuade the audience. These narratives encode more deeply into people's memories, are more likely to be remembered, and are more difficult to rebut. Finally, these salacious stories also tend to encourage readers to post, comment, and share them more than traditional news stories.

How to Address Fake News

As fake news is so common in the current information landscape, contemporary journalists must develop an approach to address and correct fake news. There are several ways in which this can be done.

Understand the Audience

Numerous social scientists have proposed that people tend to follow some sort of dual-processing model when it comes to information evaluation. These models propose people can either effortfully evaluate messages and information – weighing the arguments and evidence of any given message – or choose from a variety of different mental shortcuts to make decisions on the information provided to them. In the current technological environment where there is high probability for information overload, people are most likely to seek out these shortcuts to help them keep pace with the information system. Such shortcuts can include accepting information that reinforces their views, following the advice of those in their social network or even opinion leaders in social groups with which they associate, accepting familiar information, or believing information that reinforces familiar narratives. These biased approaches to information gathering and acceptance often lead people to accept fake news. The best suggestion for helping audience members make sense of complex information, therefore, is to make it interesting and easy for the audience to understand, as they are unlikely to expend the energy needed to vet everything they encounter.

Framing and Agenda Setting

Recent examples of the Arab Spring in 2011, the Ukrainian Revolution in 2014, and the Black Lives Matter Movement in 2020–2022 have shown the importance of framing messages for media organizations and for social movements, as both have successfully leveraged the power of framing to influence public opinion. Framing is the process of focusing audience members' attention on particular aspects of an issue, and can be a powerful tool when leveraged by the political elite, news organizations, and fake news creators to influence the public's opinions on given issues. As such, news organizations and vested stakeholders must work together to monitor traditional and newer media channels to ensure frames and stories are not co-opted by the fringe elements of society intent on disturbing the social hierarchy.

As people still turn to media channels to inform them about current events, it is even more important for the press to continue to take its agenda-setting role seriously and install practices to ensure stories released to the public are correct the first time. Each instance of an error in a news story or report provides more examples for a skeptical public to cite as justification for seeking out alternative information sources.

Finally, in an era where journalists are continually told to ensure multiple sides of the story are told, it is important to avoid false objectivity. There are many issues where experts across multiple fields have already come to a scientific consensus – the Earth is round, vaccines are effective and safe forms of mitigating the effects of harmful viruses, human activity has an impact on the climate. When most of the scientific community agrees upon something, journalists should avoid portraying these issues as still under debate for the sake of ratings. At best this creates a false impression of what is and is not being debated; at worst, it undercuts the public's faith in those experts who provide guidance on public policy decisions.

Rebutting and Debunking Fake News

Rebutting and debunking false claims is vital for any information system. Without correcting false information, no one would be able to trust any information, and it would be extremely difficulty to create a functional society. Man-Pui Sally Chan and colleagues (2017), therefore, suggested journalists minimize the arguments of fake news, encouraging audience members to critically evaluate fake news, and providing evidence the fake news is incorrect.

Journalists should also minimize repeating fake news when debunking the disinformation. As discussed earlier, the repetition of false claims when debunking fake news increases the likelihood of a backfire effect. Put simply, repeated claims, narratives, themes, and stories (false or true) tend to be evaluated as more believable and trustworthy. For journalists and news organizations, this provides the opportunity to de-fragmentize the truth by continually repeating, cross-promoting, and sharing accurate stories.

Next, journalists should pay attention to partisan and ideological cues such as referencing the political party of candidates or repeating popular talking points when crafting news stories and rebuttals to fake news. Oftentimes, partisan audience members just look for these cues and use them as a foundation for decision-making.

Finally, journalists should work with verified experts to encourage their participation in helping change public opinion on given issues. Oftentimes these experts have significant experience in the given area and, with some coaching on how to effectively communicate the message, can combat the misperceptions amongst the public. Further, by normalizing the role of experts in news coverage, it can improve public perceptions of experts in the fields of medicine, science, education, and public policy.

Leverage Opinion Leaders

Trust and credibility are important parts of message acceptance. People tend to believe information from information sources they trust, including local or national opinion leaders, and local news organizations which, in the United States, are consistently rated as being more trustworthy than the national press. Therefore, news organizations should seek to partner with credible, trustworthy opinion leaders to correct fake news. Adam Berinsky (2015) demonstrated that corrections which come from unexpected sources (those who might otherwise be expected to benefit from the fake news) are most effective at correcting the rumors.

Reflection on the Status Quo

Political parties often blame each other for the state of the current information environment, and it is largely true that members of all political parties use fake news to their advantage. However, finger pointing will never solve the problem of fake news, especially as foreign actors take advantage of the current political environment to sow discord and distrust amongst the populace. As Tim Cooper and Jem Thomas (2019) pointed out, foreign governments like China and Russia are taking advantage of the divisions that already exist in our society. If politicians refuse to create a more hospitable environment when distrust runs rampant in our media system, they should be held accountable for these actions.

Further, as Bernard Berelson, Paul Lazarsfeld, and William McPhee (1954) noted, "Political information is to democratic politics what money is to economics; it is the currency of citizenship" (p. 8). This analogy is particularly important when it comes to fake news as it is can be conceptualized as counterfeit currency. If too much counterfeit currency enters a system, and the system lacks the requisite controls for identifying and removing the counterfeit currency, the entire system will collapse. This fact leads to the next suggestion increase efforts to monitor fake news.

Increase Efforts to Monitor and Track Fake News

Numerous corporations and think tanks have begun efforts to track and monitor fake news. Organizations like Factcheck.org, Politifact, and Snopes already have large followings online and maintain a social media presence. NPR's efforts to fact-check debates have also received widespread support. After facing intense public and political scrutiny following the 2016 election, Facebook and Twitter began efforts to identify misinformation. TinEye and Google Images are free tools that allow journalists and the public to search for images that have been manipulated in some way. News sources like C-SPAN, *The New York Times*, and CNN have either partnered with nonprofit organizations or developed educational materials on how to spot fake news and have repositories of fake news sources. As fake news becomes more prevalent, news organizations should continue to develop partnerships with other organizations to help track and monitor fake news.

Invest in Education

Many of these suggestions will be of little use if the public does not adjust their own behaviors. While the United States has invested heavily in the infrastructure that supports the internet, education about media literacy lags far behind. Many of the issues surrounding fake news can be remedied with more critical stances by the public.

Citizens must be informed to participate in the democratic process. While this includes a working knowledge of current events, it should also include media literacy training. This type of training typically features education on how the media industry works, how media messages affect people, and how to critique and critically analyze arguments and their evidence. It is imperative for national, state, and local governments to invest heavily in this type of curriculum in order to prepare the citizenry to use digital technology, understand its nature, and develop approaches to acquire, analyze, and verify information in an increasingly digital and interconnected world.

Conclusion

In the short term, fake news and disinformation are likely to continue as long as political leaders see the benefits of deceiving the public, technology platforms conduct only half-hearted approaches to controlling the spread of fake news, and the public maintains its appetite for scandal at the expense of facts and evidence while simultaneously achering to poor media literacy habits. Certainly, the suggestions offered in this chapter will not provide an immediate fix to fake news, but continued and concerted efforts from journalists, political leaders, nonprofit organizations, and the citizenry can begin address the current fake news crisis.

References

Allcott, H., & Gentzkow, M. (2017). Social media and fake news in the 2016 election. *Journal of Economic Perspectives*, *31*(2), 211–236.

Berelson, B., Lazarsfeld, P., & McPhee, W. (1954). *Voting*. University of Chicago Press.

Berinsky, A. J. (2015). Rumors and health care reform: experiments in political misinformation. *British Journal of Political Science*, *47*, 241–262.

Chan, M. S., Jones C. R., Jamieson, K. H., & Albarracín, D. (2017). Debunking: A meta-analysis of the psychological efficacy of messages countering misinformation. *Psychological Science*, *28*, 1531–1546.

Cooper, T., & Thomas, J. (2019). *Nature or nurture: A crisis of trust and reason in the digital age*. Albany Associates.

Gabielkov, M., Ramachandran, A., Chaintreau, A., & Legout, A. (2016). Social Clicks: What and who gets read on Twitter? *ACM SIGMETRICS/IFIP Performance*. https://hal.inria.fr/hal-01281190

Gottfried, J., & Liedke, J. (2021). Partisan divides in media trust widen, driven by a decline among Republicans. *Pew Research Center*. https://www.pewresearch.org/fact-tank/2021/08/30/partisan-divides-in-media-trust-widen-driven-by-a-decline-among-republicans/

18

THE EVOLUTION OF FAKE NEWS ON FACEBOOK

Truth Disagreements and a Loss of Common Knowledge

Danielle R. Mehlman-Brightwell

"Today and every day, the American people must make decisions on which their whole survival may depend. To make sound decisions, the people must be informed" (Brydon, 1958). Although this was spoken on the TV show *Press and the People* in the late 1950s, the premise remains relevant today: an informed public is imperative for decision-making. Yet technology has changed how people receive information, and today traditional models of gatekeeping have been eroded. Whereas in the past, the validity and accuracy of news reports were vetted by professional editors and news organizations – the gatekeepers – news and information content is now increasingly delivered via social media platforms where human judgment has been replaced with automation and algorithms. Such algorithms are designed, not to promote factuality, but rather to maximize user engagement. In such a social media environment, there is no control over potential dangers or verification of content, and users are left to be their own gatekeepers. Accordingly, the question is raised: as people rely on platforms like Facebook, will users differentiate between real and fake news?

The lack of an informed citizenry can have harmful societal impacts. The consequences of an uninformed public are not agreeing on the truth or a loss of common knowledge, both of which can cause further divisions in America and threaten democracy. This chapter discusses these issues in-depth by examining fake news on Facebook.

The Term "Fake News"

Contemporary American journalism is being impacted by fake news. An article written by Craig Silverman on BuzzFeed helped popularize the term "fake news" in recent years (Benkler et al., 2018). The article discussed the influence of fake

DOI: 10.4324/9781003315605-29

news on Facebook users' engagements, including shares, reactions, and comments. Specifically, the BuzzFeed analysis found that between August 2016 and election day, fake news articles received more engagements on Facebook than did 19 major legitimate news outlets combined (Silverman, 2016). Further, while engagement with the top 20 fake news stories nearly tripled during 2016, engagement with legitimate mainstream news decreased by nearly one-third. This demonstrates social media's potential to reach masses of users even if the content is false or misleading.

The term "fake news" has now become ubiquitous. Many academics have written books about fake news, misinformation, propaganda and disinformation, and post-truth. Although the term fake news is used widely in society, scholars have not agreed on its proper definition. Instead, it is now often used as a blanket term for various contexts. Accordingly, scholars have defined fake news by using subgroups to describe these contexts. For example, Edson Tandoc, Zheng Lim, and Richard Ling (2018) separated fake news into six groups: satire, parody, fabrication, photo manipulation, propaganda, and advertising and public relations. But, with so many types of fake news, it makes sense that scholar Nick Anstead raised the question, "if we can identify six types of fake news, do we have a definition at all?" (2021, p. 4). Similarly, a "Fighting Fake News" workshop comprised of the Information Society Project and Floyd Abrams Institute for Freedom of Expression at Yale Law School (2017) asked: if the term fake news is used in so many contexts, is the term worthless?

Instead, some have opted not to use the term fake news. For instance, after noting that the term fake news has "taken on a variety of meanings, including a description of any statement that is not liked or agreed with by the reader," the United Kingdom Parliament instead recommended using the terms misinformation and disinformation (House of Commons, 2019, p. 10). Similarly, some scholars have also opted to define fake news through the categories of misinformation and disinformation. Claire Wardle and Hossein Derakhshan (2017) define misinformation as false information not created to cause harm and define disinformation as false information deliberately created to harm a person, social group, organization or country.

Anstead (2021) identifies three motivations for the creation of fake news: 1) profits, 2) geopolitics and 3) partisan/ideology (p. 44).

Fake News for Profit

First, an example of using fake news for profits is shown through teens from the Republic of Macedonia, who created nonfactual news content, which they posted on misleading US political websites they created, with names that appeared legitimate like WorldPoliticus.com, TrumpVision365.com, USConservativeToday.com, DonaldTrumpNews.co, and USADailyPolitics.com, and shared on pro-Trump Facebook groups. For example, one story falsely claiming Hillary Clinton would be indicted in a 2017 email scandal generated over 140,000 shares, reactions, and comments on Facebook (Silverman & Alexander, 2016).

Similar to the Macedonian teens, Jestin Coler, CEO of Disinfomedia, also profited from the creation of fake news websites such as: *National Report* and the *Denver Guardian*. In a *60 Minutes* interview, Coler disclosed making over $10,000 a month writing fiction posing as fact (Pelley, 2017). Coler made these large profits through his massive audience reach. For instance, the *Denver Guardian*'s fake news story about Hillary Clinton entitled, "FBI Agent Suspected In Hillary Email Leaks Found Dead In Apparent Murder-Suicide" was shared on Facebook 568,000 times, and generated over 15.5 million impressions (Grenoble, 2016).

Such deceptive and sensualized content may entice and lure a user into becoming a victim of clickbait and, as the examples of Macedonian teens and Coler showcase, the combination of fake news and immense audience reach can lead to massive profits.

Fake News for Geopolitical Goals and Russian Foreign Interference

A second motivation for the creation of fake news involves geopolitics, where a state undermines another state by exploiting pre-existing ideological divisions. Such efforts can include foreign election interference involving "attempts by foreign governments or entities to influence election results" (Mehlman–Brightwell, 2021, p. 4). Governments have long tried to influence international politics, and fake news is one of many ways in which this is done. An example of this is the Russian foreign interference in the 2016 US Presidential election.

After extensive investigation by US Special Counsel Robert Muller, it was determined that Russian operatives from the Internet Research Agency (IRA) attacked the 2016 US Presidential election in a "sweeping and systematic" manner (Mueller, 2019, p. 1). The IRA operatives sought to undermine the US political system, including the 2016 US Presidential Election, in what they called a social media "information warfare" campaign that involved creating and posting disinformation to distract and inflame US voters by sowing discord on social networking sites. Social media served as a tool to weaken the ties of democracy in the US by deceiving its users, and amplifying contentious societal and ideological divisions already existing in the US. For example, Russian operatives purchased political advertisements on social media in the names of American persons and entities without disclosing their Russian association (Mueller, 2019).

The IRA included content and pages directed at politically right-leaning and left-leaning viewpoints. Politically right-leaning content included immigration policy, the Second Amendment, and Southern culture; politically left-leaning content focused on police brutality, race, and sexual identity (US Senate Select Committee on Intelligence, 2019). The IRA posted disparaging content about several candidates, including Hillary Clinton, while posting ads that favored

Donald J. Trump (Mueller, 2019). An example of content favoring Trump is illustrated in this Facebook ad, which stated,

> Today, Americans are able to elect a president with godly moral principles. Hillary is a Satan, and her crimes and lies had proved just how evil she is. And even though Donald Trump isn't a saint by any means, he's at least an honest man and he cares deeply for this country. My vote goes for him!
>
> *(US House of Representatives Permanent Select Committee on Intelligence, 2018)*

Such efforts were widespread, as became known after Facebook disclosed the IRA's ad purchases. Russian entities purchased $100,000 in political advertisements over two years on Facebook alone (US Senate Select Committee on Intelligence, 2019). This purchase consisted of nearly 3400 advertisements on Facebook, to which more than 11.4 million Americans were exposed. In addition, the IRA created 470 Facebook pages, which exposed over 126 million Americans to the organic content (US House of Representatives Permanent Select Committee on Intelligence, 2018).

The IRA used different approaches to conceal their identities while spreading misleading content. These different approaches consisted of trolls and bots. To help conceal the trolls' true identities, the IRA set up a server in the United States, and posed as anti-immigration groups, Tea Party activists, and Black Lives Matter protestors (Mueller, 2019). As a result, trolls appeared as real American accounts.

The IRA also used bots to assist with social media "information warfare" campaigns. Social media bots algorithmically operate independently, imitating real social media users. The bots post information and interact with human social media users without the human user knowing they are corresponding with a bot. Although bots operate at a higher rate than human users, human social media users – knowingly or unknowingly – assist bots with spreading information when they engage with its content by liking, commenting, or sharing.

Fake News for Partisan and Ideological Goals

One example of fake news that is created to promote a partisan or ideological agenda involves 2020 US election fraud claims, in which false information was spread rapidly through fake news, conspiracies, and political lying. Some researchers have called these voter fraud claims the "most consequential misinformation campaigns in modern history" (Abilov et al., 2021, cited in Hendrix, 2021, para. 1). False narratives of the election being stolen and Joe Biden illegitimately winning the 2020 US presidency were spearheaded by Trump and flooded social media. Researchers from Technion and the Social Technologies Lab at Cornell Tech found keywords such as "voter fraud" and the #stopthesteal hashtag in 7.6 million tweets with 25.6 million retweets (Abilov et al., 2021).

Many Americans echoed Trump by casting doubt on the legitimacy of Biden's victory. A poll a month after the 2020 election revealed that 34% of Americans did not trust the election results (Marist Poll, 2020), and some Americans turned to social media groups to find information. While some safeguards were applied on Facebook to protect against misinformation in the months preceding the election, they were dismantled after the election. As a result, far-right conspiracy theories flourished on social media, inciting an attempted coup. Notably, Facebook groups related to election fraud conspiracies increased between election day and the January 6, 2021 siege of the US Capitol with at least 650,000 posts attacking Biden's legitimacy and the 2020 US Presidential Election (Silverman et al., 2022). While court rulings and independent analyses have confirmed the election results, truth disagreements remain about who the 46th president is.

Another example of fake news that is created for partisan or ideological goals involves COVID-19 vaccine misinformation, which has been spread widely in recent years. The COVID-19 pandemic amplified social anxieties and trust issues, leading many people to feel skeptical about COVID-19 vaccines and believe in the falsehoods that they saw presented online. A October 2021 study found 78% of the public either believed, or were unsure about, at least one COVID-19 falsehood, including the ideas that pregnant women should not get the vaccine, that people can contract COVID-19 from the vaccine, and that the COVID-19 vaccines cause infertility (Palosky, 2021). COVID-19 vaccine misinformation has led to further skepticism about other vaccines as well.

Partially resulting from such ideologically driven fake news about the pandemic, many people came to make decisions about getting the COVID-19 vaccine along party lines. A Pew Research Center study found that – with some exceptions related to age and education – Democrats were far more likely than Republicans to have received at least one dose of a COVID-19 vaccine (Funk & Gramlich, 2021). Public health has become political despite the loss of many lives due to COVID-19.

Attempts to Develop Regulations

Various types of regulation have been suggested to address fake news and misleading content. Some suggestions focus specifically on online political advertising. Notably, in the runup to the 2016 election, the IRA was able to purchase online advertising discreetly because online political advertising regulation does not exist. Under the Federal Election Campaign Act of 1971, the purchaser of radio and television political advertisements must be disclosed; however, online political advertising does not require revealing who paid for the ad. Many wonder why online political advertising does not have the same regulation as other media. The answer is simple; laws have not kept up with changing technology. To help prevent foreign interference in future elections and keep regulations fair among different media through improved transparency of online political advertisements, the Honest Ads Act was introduced in the United States Senate on October 19, 2017.

This bipartisan bill was eventually incorporated into the For the People Act, which intended to expand election access, election security, campaign finance transparency, campaign finance empowerment, and ethical standards. The House of

Representatives passed the bill on March 3, 2021; however, the bill was not passed by the US Senate because Senate Republicans blocked the bill with a filibuster. Another bill, the Prevention of Foreign Interference with Elections Act of 2019, intended to prohibit foreign interference in elections, was also introduced; however, its passage, too, was blocked by procedural delays.

In light of this inaction, others have looked to industry to police itself. Notably, Facebook (which has since rebranded as Meta) updated its policy on countering inauthentic behavior. The new policy update took place on October 21, 2019 and was a response to the 2016 US Presidential election foreign interference. The new policy established that Facebook would identify inauthentic behavior when actors use deceptive behavior to conceal their identity, make the organizer appear more popular or trustworthy, or evade law enforcement efforts, and then respond to coordinated inauthentic behavior by finding and stopping coordinated campaigns that seek to manipulate public debate (Gleicher, 2019).

Yet, despite the new policy designed to combat foreign interference, evidence has shown that the company has been slow to implement the policy. In 2021, Facebook whistleblower Frances Haugen secretly copied and leaked thousands of pages of Facebook's internal research to Congress and the Securities and Exchange Commission. The internal documents showcased how Facebook knowingly contributed dangerous harm to its users, through allowing the spread of misinformation, hate speech, and content that incited violence. As Haugen stated in congressional testimony, "Facebook's products harm children, stoke division, weaken our democracy and much more."

These problems have been confirmed repeatedly by Facebook's own internal research, and Haugen claimed Facebook CEO Mark Zuckerberg has at times contradicted, downplayed or failed to disclose company findings on its products and platforms (Haugen 2021).

Another potential way to combat the spread of disinformation in social media involves reforming Section 230 of the Communications Decency Act, which protects internet speech. This act specifically guards internet companies from legal liability from users' posts. Congress enacted Section 230 to encourage online growth and internet development by removing legal barriers. Section 230 states, "No provider or user of an interactive computer service shall be treated as the publisher or speaker of any information provided by another information content provider" ("47 US Code § 230," 1996).

Yet, in light of changes that have occurred in the decades since the act's passage, members of Congress of both parties agree that Section 230 should now be modified; however, the two sides have been unable to agree about what to change. Generally speaking, Democrats primarily want to make platforms liable for harmful content, while Republicans want to prohibit platforms from removing content. However, in Haugen's testimony, she stated that the issue is not with the content but with Facebook's algorithm. Haugen urged Congress to amend Section 230 to make Facebook responsible for its algorithms which are used to rank content, and which determine the content and its order on users' feeds.

As Haugen stated in her testimony,

> Modifying Section 230 around content is very complicated because user-generated content is something that companies have less control over. They [Facebook] have 100% control over their algorithms. And Facebook should not get a free pass on choices it makes to prioritize growth, virality and reactiveness, over public safety.
>
> *(Haugen, 2021, cited in Reardon, 2021, para. 7)*

Post-Truth Era

Fake news is affecting American journalism by delegitimizing voices of expertise. As a result, society is moving toward a post-truth era because of fake news, conspiracies, and political lying. This post-truth era can be seen through social and political circumstances in which citizens, audiences, and politicians "no longer respect truth but simply accept as true what they believe or feel" (Harsin, 2018, p. 1).

Divisions remain beyond 2020 US Election fraud claims and COVID-19 misinformation. These polar opposite divisions have two sides. One side is technocratic with evidence-based policymaking, and the opposite view is rooted in populist political ideas stemming from conspiracy theories and mistrust (Anstead, 2021). Ideological polarization, political lying, and social media have helped to contribute to an overall lack of trust. In order to combat the devaluing of truth, restoring trust is critical. However, mending societal trust will have challenges. The continual lying of politicians will keep citizens misinformed and isolated in conspiracy theories. Another challenge is social media's capitalistic belief that profits trump public safety. Facebook does use third-party fact checkers to help with fake news; however, if the engagement-based ranking algorithm is not addressed, it will continue to put users at risk of social media addiction and continual exposure to confirmation bias.

As long as people rely on platforms like Facebook, the risk remains that users will continue to not differentiate between real and fake news. The implications are serious; the public discourse necessary for a functioning democracy cannot happen without an informed public, and credible information is critical for citizens to make informed decisions. However, in a world where so many people rely on new and social media platforms that lack traditional gatekeepers and fact-checking procedures, there is a growing lack of trust in media and information itself. Additionally, fake news websites and false and misleading stories run rampant, and engagement-based ranking algorithms amplify ideological divisions, keeping users in filter bubbles and echo chambers. The result is a spiral of false information, leading to the contemporary infodemic and post-truth era, in which skepticism, conspiracy theories, and tensions involving real-world issues grow stronger. Truth disagreements and a loss of common knowledge cause like-minded groups to gather together, furthering divisions and threatening democracy. Addressing these issues is not easy, yet the importance cannot be overstated. If they are not, it is unlikely that new technologies and media platforms will do anything other than continue to perpetuate existing problems and foster a society based more on feelings, beliefs, and ideology than on reality and truth.

References

47 US Code § 230. (1996, February 8). Legal Information Institute. https://www.law.cornell. edu/uscode/text/47/230

Abilov, A., Hua, Y., Matatov, H., Amir, O., & Naaman, M. (2021). VoterFraud2020: A multi-modal dataset of election fraud claims on Twitter. *ArXiv:2101.08210 [Cs]*. http://arxiv.org/abs/2101.08210

Anstead, N. (2021). *What do we know and what should we do about fake news?* Sage.

Benkler, Y., Faris, R., & Roberts, H. (2018). *Network propaganda manipulation, disinformation, and radicalization in American politics* (Vol. 1). Oxford University Press. https://doi.org/10.1093/oso/9780190923624.003.0001

Brydon, L. (1958). Press and the People (No. 2). In *Washington and the Press*. WGBH-TV. https://openvault.wgbh.org/catalog/V_F3669EDCE0044D9C97FD3661EF031D95

Haugen, F. (2021). Statement of Frances Haugen. https://www.commerce.senate.gov/services/files/FC8A558E-824E-4914-BEDB-3A7B1190BD49

House of Commons. (2019). Disinformation and "fake news": Final report. https://publications. parliament.uk/pa/cm201719/cmselect/cmcumeds/1791/1791.pdf

Funk, C., & Gramlich, J. (2021, September 20). 10 facts about Americans and coronavirus vaccines. *Pew Research Center*. https://www.pewresearch.org/fact-tank/2021/09/20/10-facts-about-americans-and-coronavirus-vaccines/

Gleicher, N. (2019, October 21). How we respond to inauthentic behavior on our platforms: Policy update. https://about.fb.com/news/2019/10/inauthentic-behavior-policy-update/

Grenoble, R. (2016, Novewmber 16). Here are some of those fake news stories that Mark Zuckerberg isn't worried about. *Huffington Post*. https://www.huffpost.com/entry/facebook-fake-news-stories-zuckerberg_n_5829f34ee4b0c4b63b0da2ea

Harsin, J. (2018). Post-truth and critical communication studies. In J. Harsin, *Oxford Research Encyclopedia of Communication* (pp. 1–32). Oxford University Press. https://doi.org/10.1093/acrefore/9780190228613.013.757

Hendrix, J. (2021, January 22). Researchers release massive Twitter dataset of voter fraud claims [Tech Policy Press]. https://techpolicy.press/researchers-release-massive-twitter-dataset-of-voter-fraud-claims/

Information Society Project. (2017). Fighting fake news workshop. https://law.yale.edu/isp/initiatives/floyd-abrams-institute-freedom-expression/practitioner-scholar-conferences-first-amendment-topics/fighting-fake-news-workshop

Mehlman-Brightwell, D. R. (2021). *Facebook users' social media dependency, news credibility, and concerns of foreign interference in 2016 and 2020 US presidential elections* (Publication Number 28647376) [Doctoral dissertation, Indiana University of Pennsylvania] ProQuest Dissertation Database.

Mueller, R. S. (2019). Report on the investigation into Russian interference in the 2016 Presidential Election. *US Department of Justice*. https://www.justice.gov/storage/report.pdf

Marist, Poll. (2020). NPR/PBS NewsHour/Marist Poll Results: The Transition, Trump, & COVID-19. *Marist Poll*. https://maristpoll.marist.edu/polls/npr-pbs-newshour-marist-poll-results-the-transition-trump-covid-19/

Palosky, C. (2021, November 8). COVID-19 Misinformation is Ubiquitous. *KFF*. https://www.kff.org/coronavirus-covid-19/press-release/covid-19-misinformation-is-ubiquitous-78-of-the-public-believes-or-is-unsure-about-at-least-one-false-statement-and-nearly-at-third-believe-at-least-four-of-eight-false-statements-tested/

Pelley, S. (2017, March 26). How fake news became a popular, trending topic. 60 Minutes. https://www.cbsnews.com/news/how-fake-news-find-your-social-media-feeds/

Reardon, M. (2021, October 6). Section 230: How it shields Facebook and why Congress wants changes. *Cnet*. https://www.cnet.com/news/politics/section-230-how-it-shields-facebook-and-why-congress-wants-changes/

Silverman, C. (2016, November 16). This analysis shows how viral fake election news stories outperformed real news on Facebook. *BuzzFeed.News*. https://www.buzzfeednews.com/article/craigsilverman/viral-fake-election-news-outperformed-real-news-on-facebook#.bp90yKJ1W

Silverman, C., & Alexander, L. (2016, November 3). How teens in the Balkans are duping Trump supporters with fake news. *BuzzFeed. News*. https://www.buzzfeednews.com/article/craigsilverman/how-macedonia-became-a-global-hub-for-pro-trump-misinfo

Silverman, C., Timberg, C., Kao, J., & Merrill, J. B. (2022, January 4). Facebook hosted surge of misinformation and insurrection threats in months leading up to Jan. 6 attack, records show. *ProPublica*. https://www.propublica.org/article/facebook-hosted-surge-of-misinformation-and-insurrection-threats-in-months-leading-up-to-jan-6-attack-records-show

Tandoc, E. C., Lim, Z. W., & Ling, R. (2018). Defining "fake news": A typology of scholarly definitions. *Digital Journalism*, 6(2), 137–153. https://doi.org/10.1080/21670811.2017.1360143

US House of Representatives Permanent Select Committee on Intelligence. (2018). Exposing Russia's effort to sow discord online: The Internet Research Agency and advertisements. https://intelligence.house.gov/social-media-content/

US Senate Select Committee on Intelligence. (2019). Russian active measures campaigns and interference in the 2016 US election Volume 2: Russia's use of social media with additional views. https://www.congress.gov/congressional-report/116th-congress/senate-report/290/1

Wardle, C., & Derakhshan, H. (2017). Information disorder: Towards an interdisciplinary framework for research and policy-making. *Council of Europe*. https://rm.coe.int/information-disorder-toward-an-interdisciplinary-framework-forresearc/168076277c

Inoculation Theory and Fake News

Josh Compton

Throughout the COVID-19 global pandemic, there was a lot of talk about fake news about vaccines – conspiracy theories about the vaccine's development, promotion of suspect alternative treatments, and specious attacks questioning the credibility and motivations of vaccine scientists and other members of the medical community. But fortunately, along with these conversations about vaccine fake news, there were also conversations about vaccines *against* fake news – intervention approaches based on insight from communication and psychological science that might help to thwart the influence of fake news, often by preempting its damage much like medical vaccines preempt damage from viruses.

Perhaps the most promising approaches to preempting dangerous effects of fake news are those based on inoculation theory – a classic theory of resistance to influence first introduced 60+ years ago by the social psychologist William McGuire (McGuire, 1964). Inoculation theory has been around for some time, but it has had a resurgence of interest and research in just the past few years, rising to meet the challenges of new forms, types, and approaches of fake news.

I have been studying inoculation theory for more than twenty years, trying to figure out how this theory works in application to politics, health, education, science, sport, and other domains. My colleagues and I have shown how applications of this theory can protect politicians against persuasive attacks launched in political debates and television commercials (Compton & Ivanov, 2013), how it can be used by companies to develop campaigns that protect their reputation from unflattering news stories and crises (Compton et al., 2021), and how it can promote better health (Compton et al., 2016). Inoculation messaging can work in all of these areas and more. Across issues and contexts, across demographics and media, inoculation messaging confers resistance to influence.

This is why I am so encouraged by the possibilities of inoculation theory to help people work through the complicated challenges of fake news: It has an impressive

DOI: 10.4324/9781003315605-30

track record. I am also encouraged by the evidence we have so far about inoculation theory's efficacy in fighting fake news, from the work with inoculation in the form of online games (e.g., Roozenbeek & van der Linden, 2019) to new insight into how inoculation treatments can be fine-tuned to specifically target common reasoning fallacies in fake news (e.g., Cook et al., 2017). The challenges of fake news remain many – and they are daunting – but we do have some tools that can help, including inoculation theory.

One of the things I appreciate about inoculation theory is that its moniker not only names it, but also, its name explains it. Inoculation theory is what it sounds like. Inoculation theory shows how resistance to influence can be conferred in much the same ways as medical inoculation leads to resistance to viruses – through preexposure to weakened forms of the future, stronger threat (McGuire, 1964). A conventional way of introducing a weakened form of a future, stronger threat in terms of attitudes and beliefs is to present a two-sided message – a message that raises and refutes counterattacks, with the refutations weakening the counterattacks so that they can function as training of sorts against stronger, unrefuted counterattacks in the future. This is how many medical inoculations work, too: a virus is weakened enough to motivate protective reactions from the body, preparing it to fight of stronger viruses later.

When McGuire first introduced his theory in the early 1960s, he showed how it worked against noncontroversial issues – things he called cultural truisms, like the benefits of daily teeth brushing. But soon after, scholars found that inoculation-based messages could also confer resistance to attacks on contested issues, too, and this broadened the potential of inoculation to a wide range of important issues across contexts (Ivanov et al., 2020).

The most common explanation for how inoculation messages confer resistance to influence centers on threat and preemptive refutation. In inoculation, threat means that the inoculation messages make recipients aware that a position that they hold is surprisingly vulnerable (Compton, 2013). This effect of an inoculation message causes people to start shoring up their defenses in advance of the impending attack. Inoculation messages can elicit threat by including a forewarning ("You have the right idea about this issue, but there are people who are going to try to mislead you"), by including sample counterarguments and refutations ("They might say that you can't trust medical experts when it comes to vaccine safety, but you should consider the years of training and experience that lead to medical expertise"), or both.

Preemptive refutation is the raising and refuting of counterarguments to a position or raising and explaining the tactics or fallacies people will use to try to change their minds. For example, a classical refutation of a counterargument in the context of fake news might be to raise misinformation about an issue, like questioning the expert consensus on climate change (Cook et al., 2017), and then correct this misinformation. To refute an argumentation strategy, an inoculation message could explain a common reasoning fallacy, like ad hominem attacks (name-calling) or hasty generalizations (making broad claims without sufficient evidence), and why that strategy is unsound (Roozenbeek & van der Linden, 2019).

There are a couple of features of inoculation that make it a particularly powerful strategy for conferring resistance. First, one doesn't need to raise and refute every potential challenge someone will encounter to confer resistance. Raising and refuting a few challenges has been shown to confer protection against other challenges – ones not even mentioned in the inoculation message. (Otherwise, the strategy would be very limited – only working when every challenge could be predicted and refuted in advance.) Especially in the fast-moving environment of news, this ability of inoculation to protect against more than the specific attacks or strategies mentioned in the inoculation message is critical for it to work.

Another feature that makes inoculation particularly effective is that inoculation messages seem to improve critical thinking about the issue, not just simple resistance. This seems especially true when the inoculation messages are teaching about reasoning fallacies or specific propaganda strategies (Cook et al., 2017).

These features, plus others, are what make inoculation theory such a promising antidote to fake news. Inoculation messages can raise and refute specific stories, like conspiracy theories about vaccination risks, but they can also preemptively teach how to identify and reject conspiracy theories in general when used as a propaganda strategy. Approaches like these shift the benefits of inoculations from individuals (e.g., politicians using inoculation-based strategies during campaigns to win more votes) and corporations (e.g., businesses using inoculation-based marketing strategies to fend off competitors' claims) to larger societal and democratic benefits, like a more informed citizenry and more savvy news consumers.

One of the most encouraging examples of how inoculation theory can help to fight fake news is the free online game, *Bad News*. This game puts players into the role of an unscrupulous fake news creator, which teaches players how to recognize fake news strategies, like impersonating credible sources and misusing emotional appeals (Roozenbeek & van der Linden, 2019). The game not only entertains, but also helps players become more media-savvy. Because of this game and other exciting applications of inoculation theory, I'm optimistic about what the future holds for inoculation theory in the context of fake news.

I think it is wonderfully apt that a theory named for medical inoculation is poised to protect against fake news about medical inoculation – and more. My hope is that inoculation theory research and application will continue to show ways that news consumers can equip themselves to protect against fake news, and as a result, lead to a healthier journalism ecosystem all around.

References

Compton, J. (2013). Inoculation theory. In J. P. Dillard & L. Shen (Eds.), *The Sage handbook of persuasion: Developments in theory and practice* (2nd ed.; pp. 220–236). Sage. http://dx.doi.org/10.4135/9781452218410.n14

Compton, J., & Ivanov, B. (2013). Vaccinating voters: Surveying political campaign inoculation scholarship. *Annals of the International Communication Association, 37*(1), 251–283. https://doi.org/10.1080/23808985.2013.11679152

Compton, J., Jackson, B., & Dimmock, J. A. (2016). Persuading others to avoid persuasion: Inoculation theory and resistant health attitudes. *Frontiers in Psychology*, 7(122). https://doi.org/10.3389/fpsyg.2016.00122

Compton, J., Wigley, S., & Samoilenko, S. (2021). Inoculation theory and public relations. *Public Relations Review* 47(5). https://doi.org/10.1016/j.pubrev.2021.102116

Cook, J., Lewandowsky, S., & Ecker, U. K. H. (2017). Neutralizing misinformation through inoculation: Exposing misleading argumentation techniques reduces their influence. *PLOS ONE 12*(5). https://doi.org/10.1371/journal.pone.0175799

Ivanov, B., Parker, K. A., & Dillingham, L. (2020). Inoculation theory as a strategic tool. In H. D. O'Hair & M. J. O'Hair (Eds.), *Handbook of applied communication research* (Vol. 1, pp. 13–28). Wiley. https://doi.org/10.1002/9781119399926.ch1

McGuire, W. J. (1964). Inducing resistance to persuasion: Some contemporary approaches. In L. Berkowitz (Ed.), *Advances in experimental social psychology* 1, (pp. 191–229). Academic Press. https://doi.org/10.1016/S0065-2601(08)60052-0

Roozenbeek, J., & van der Linden, S. (2019). Fake news game confers psychological resistance against online misinformation. *Palgrave Communications*, *5*(1), 1–10. https://doi.org/10.1057/s41599-019-0279-9

PART VII

Journalistic Trust and Accuracy in an Era of Hostility and Partisanship

Criticizing the press isn't new, and the American public has long had a love/hate relationship with its news media. Often, we applaud the news when it tells us what we want to hear, and ridicule it when stories challenge our preexisting beliefs. But, today, dislike, disdain, and even hatred of the press are on the rise in alarming ways. This hostility is openly encouraged by political leaders the world over. Everyday people take note, and many agree; a recent survey by the Edelman Trust found that 59% of people across 28 nations reported feeling that journalists deliberately mislead the public and intentionally spread false reports. In a world of rampant politicization and polarization of nearly everything, the press has become an especially convenient scapegoat.

This mistrust becomes even more concerning because skepticism has blurred the line between rhetorical attacks and physical attacks, leading to unprecedented levels of violence against members of the news media. In the United States alone, there were 144 documented assaults on journalists in 2021; in 2020, there were 446. Often these assaults happen while reporters are covering innocuous stories and just going about their everyday business. Unsurprisingly, the US Press Freedom Tracker declared that US press freedoms are "in crisis."

This trend is alarming within the United States, and it is even worse in many nations around the world, where the climate of hatred is leading to targeted assassinations, and the open encouragement of mob violence against journalists. A recent analysis by Reporters without Borders shows that just 7% of countries now offer "favorable environments for journalism," and that the situation is bad or very bad in 41% of the world's countries. Reporters are attacked on a regular basis, and their work is hampered by increasing legal restrictions and multiplatform disinformation campaigns.

Part VII explores some of the challenges associated with building trust and reporting accurately in the contemporary cultural, political, and media landscape, and also presents ideas for building a better relationship between journalists and the publics they serve.

DOI: 10.4324/9781003315605-31

19

HOSTILITY TOWARD THE PRESS

Background and Steps Forward

Kelsey Mesmer and Kaitlin Miller

For many journalists, sifting through sexist and racist tweets and posts to find meaningful reader comments to engage with is part of the everyday work routine. A bullet-proof vest, helmet, pepper spray, goggles, and a first aid kit are kept alongside journalists' notebooks and spare recorder in their go-bags. And it's becoming harder for journalists to find community members to act as sources because so many Americans distrust the press and do not want to interact with them. This is true for political stories and polarized topics, but also for human interest stories. When journalists approach members of their community while reporting, they are often called "fake news" and accused of being biased. This falls under what scholars refer to as "hostility toward the press," which is defined as "unwanted abusive behaviors" (Miller, 2021a, p. 4), which can include verbal abuse and threats, physical assault, sexual harassment and sexual assault, and other behaviors that make reporters feel uncomfortable and vulnerable.

Hostility toward the press is on the rise globally, leading to increased attacks toward journalists online and offline. Although the naming of the press as the "enemy of the people" by former US President Donald Trump is often thought of as a point of escalation, in which anti-media rhetoric and hostility drastically increased, hostility has always been a reality for journalists. Indeed, presidents have criticized and tried to undermine the credibility of the press for as long as there have been presidents, and hostility toward the news media predates the American Revolution. In his seminal work on violence against the press throughout US history, John Nerone (1994) positions hostility as a "familiar theme in US history" (p. 9) – a constant pressure and consequence of journalism – and chronicles how hostility has changed in form over time. Just five years after the printing of the first American daily newspaper in 1794, Benjamin Franklin suggested members of the press should be cudgeled as a form of punishment when they printed insults and

DOI: 10.4324/9781003315605-32

unflattering information. Although Franklin was joking, violence against editors and even those working at the printing house was common. News editors of the late 1700s and 1800s frequently encountered violence by readers (often those who were written about in the papers) and even by other journalists, as early partisan newspapers used to feud with each other. Mob violence was also common throughout the 1800s, and newspaper offices were ransacked or vandalized by large groups enraged by content that dissented from majoritarian political views. Newspapers that supported abolition were targets of mob violence leading up to and during the Civil War. Although mob violence and attacks on whole newsrooms lessened near the end of the 1800s, Southern African American newspapers that reported on lynchings, and specifically published stories about white women desiring Black men, were still targets. Among these cases was the mobbing of Jesse Duke's newspaper, the Montgomery, Alabama *Herald* in 1885 and Ida B. Wells' newspaper, the Memphis *Free Speech*, in 1892. In the early 1900s, upticks in the number of newspaper mobbings correlated with labor movements and wartimes. Of the most notable of these, the *Los Angeles Times* was bombed in 1910 after publishing antiunion sentiments, and the prominently antilabor *Denver Post* was mobbed in 1920 during a riot in response to the Tramway Company railroad workers' strike.

The *Capital Gazette* newspaper shooting in 2018, in which a gunman entered the newsroom and opened fire, killing five, is the most infamous case of recent violence inflicted upon a newsroom. Aside from this case and a handful of other exceptions, individual journalists became the more common target of violence in the latter half of the 20th century, and this tends to remain the case today. Personal violence can include verbal harassment, sexual harassment, intimidation and assault, and perpetrators are usually politicians, athletes or other celebrities, and people whose alleged crimes have been written about in the news. Journalists reporting on organized crime have been the targets of physical violence, with some being killed in relation to a story they published or were pursuing. Some high-profile cases include Don Bolles, of the *Arizona Republic*, who was killed by a car bomb in 1976 after angering local contractors with his reports of their land fraud schemes, and Charles DeVetsco, of the *Harrisburg Patriot-News*, who was murdered in 1980 by a man who, in a previous interview with DeVetsco, had admitted to a robbery. The number of journalists killed in the United States is relatively low when compared to violence in other countries (globally, 48 journalists have been killed and 181 have been arrested on average each year since 1992, according to the Committee to Protect Journalists), but other forms of hostility are more commonplace. For example, Lisa Olson, a sports reporter for the *Boston Herald*, was sexually harassed by New England Patriots football players in the team's locker room in 1990. When Olson's case garnered national attention, several other women sports writers came forward to relate similar accounts. Sexual harassment has also been a problem for women political reporters in Washington, DC, where 60% of those surveyed said they had been harassed by a source (McAdams & Beasley, 1994). Another survey in 1996 found that of women journalists across a variety of news beats, more than 25% had experienced physical sexual harassment and 70% had experienced verbal sexual harassment (Walsh-Childers et al., 1996). Reporters have also been subject to verbal hostility, as readers write mean-spirited letters to the editor targeting specific reporters for their stories and editorials, and write letters directly to reporters and call newsrooms with complaints, criticism, and, sometimes, threats.

Contemporary Challenges

While journalists have faced hostility from the public for decades, how they experience abuse, harassment, hostility, and violence has shifted over time. In contemporary journalism, the internet – particularly through social media avenues – has facilitated a rise in the abuse journalists receive. This occurs for several reasons. First, journalists are highly visible on social media. As a near-ubiquitous professional norm, journalists are tasked with branding themselves on social media. Personal branding on social media is any post "that is self-referential, be that a notice of an upcoming television appearance, a link to one's own story, or positive or negative discussion of oneself" (Molyneux, 2015, pp. 931–932). This can include selfies, the sharing of direct messages from viewers (good or bad), and promotion of news content for oneself or one's news organization (Molyneux, 2015). In addition to branding one's personal identity, journalists are also tasked with using social media as tools to connect with readers and viewers in an interactive way – with the hope of building trust and developing meaningful story ideas. However, those interactions with audiences often turn negative and destructive. With these activities comes visibility and accessibility that make journalists' personal and professional lives open for the public to criticize and attack, making it easier to abuse a journalist without having to see them in person.

Second, social media has created a platform for politicians and the public to attack journalists in highly visible and overt ways. Matt Carlson, Sue Robinson, and Seth Lewis (2021) began using the term *digital press criticism* "as a descriptor to indicate the use of non-journalistic platforms as a means for critiquing journalism" (p. 737). This often means celebrities, politicians, and activists can take to their personal social media accounts to attack journalists – often sending their large followership after them to further the attack. This influx of online attacks causes many journalists to have their accounts flooded by name calling, verbal harassment, and even violent threats. In a study looking at online harassment of journalists, 37% of attacks came from political actors, with another 57% coming from anonymous or unknown attackers. The study, which looked specifically at women journalists around the world, found that 73% of respondents had experienced online violence (Posetti et al., 2020).

The abuse journalists experience online is not mutually exclusive of the hostility they face offline. In one global study, 20% of journalists said "they had been attacked or abused offline in connection with online violence they had experienced" (Posetti et al., 2020, p. 2). This abuse can range from name calling, threats, and physical intimidation, to throwing objects, hitting, and chasing. In fact, as populism rises globally, so has a surge in protests around the world, especially in the

US. At these protests, journalists have reported verbal and physical attacks that have left them both mentally and emotionally injured. The perpetrators of hostility at protests also often include law enforcement, who do not distinguish between protesters and those with press credentials when deploying smoke bombs or rubber bullets, or when making arrests.

Indeed, there is a wide range of effects that hostility against the press can have on individual journalists. For example, harassment can affect their job satisfaction, psychological wellbeing, and even contribute to burnout. And more than how it affects journalists' personally, many studies also show that hostility can have a chilling effect on journalists in the work they produce. Based on the way journalists experience harassment, they are sometimes dissuaded from covering certain topics or interviewing certain sources to help head off harassment. Many will even turn off messaging or change how they act on social media to avoid harassment. This ultimately becomes a problem for democracy.

Hostility and Intersectionality

Scholars are becoming increasingly aware of how journalists' identity has the potential to intensify and create opportunities for hostility. Statistics about violence and hostility toward the news media often show that men are the usual victims of violence. According to the Committee to Protect Journalists, only 100 women working in journalism have been killed since 1992. However, gendered biases in the journalism field result in more men working as war reporters, specifically in conflict areas, which helps explain why statistics on violence toward journalists show a higher number of men than women killed each year. When looking at all forms of violence and hostility, including sexual harassment, online abuse and microaggressions, women have far more negative experiences than men (Posetti et al., 2020). Journalists of color are also subject to more online abuse and microaggressions than their white colleagues who are men (Chen et al., 2020). Microaggressions, which are statements slipped into otherwise harmless conversation that subtly attack a person's identity, can be sexist, racist and ageist in nature, or a combination of all three.

Hostility toward journalists is context-based, as the journalists' gender, race, age, (dis)ability and other aspects of their identity operate as sites of oppression, including their professional identity, which is often villainized (Miller, 2021a). In a study of hostility directed at journalists from their sources – the people journalists interviewed, or tried to interview for a news story – it was found that "The specific mix of a journalists' perceived demographics, story topic and geographic region can often lead to hostility from news sources" (Mesmer, 2022, p. 157). For example, an Indian-American broadcast reporter said she was put in an unsafe situation when she was asked to interview people on the street about former President Donald Trump's immigration ban. She was working in a rural, conservative county, and experienced hostility from sources who assumed she was an immigrant. One became so aggressive that he got in his car and followed her as she drove away. Also contributing to hostility is the form of reporting and journalists' tenure in their job. In man-on-the-street interviews, reporters are approaching people they know nothing about, which can put them in unsafe situations. This is also the case when reporters are asked to go to people's homes unannounced and knock on their doors. Although many younger journalists have said they feel unsafe conducting these types of interviews alone, they are reluctant to talk to their editors and turn down the stories for fear of appearing unprofessional or too timid to be a reporter. The reluctance often lessens as reporters gain more tenure. For example, a Black reporter with 30 years of experience at the same newspaper said he no longer takes story assignments in which he must knock on people's doors, and he advocates for younger Black reporters who are asked to do so. This comes after years of begrudgingly accepting those assignments, which often resulted in someone calling the police on him.

Additionally, younger women journalists often dealt with sources who crossed professional boundaries in ways that made them feel uncomfortable and vulnerable. Professional boundary crossing included calling the journalists at all hours on their personal phones and sending inappropriate messages to their social media accounts, posting hostile and/or defamatory content about the journalists online, and trying to get the journalists fired by complaining directly to their editors or bosses (Mesmer, 2022). Boundary crossing occurred with routine sources on a reporter's beat, meaning the journalists had to interact with these perpetrators of hostility on a regular basis. This affects journalists' routines as they actively try avoiding these sources to prevent more hostile interactions, and has the potential to cause burnout. Ultimately, younger white women and women of color are more likely to leave the journalism profession because of routine hostility they experience on the job.

Normalizing Hostility

Perhaps one of the more troubling effects of such frequent hostility toward journalists is a normalization of the abuse. Indeed, many journalists, especially women and journalists of color, have come to expect harassment from those external to the newsroom, viewing it as what many call an "occupational hazard." In some cases, this leaves journalists to feel helpless both in the field and in their newsrooms. When hostility is expected, management often does little to stop or even prevent it. This normalization of abuse in journalistic work has led to two distinct outcomes. First, "it is plausible that journalists are becoming increasingly desensitized to the most common forms of online harassment, like being insulted or called names, perhaps to the point where they do not consciously think of it as harassment" (Lewis et al., 2020, p. 1061). In this sense, harassment is glossed over and internalized as typical. In some cases, this harassment may even be revered as a sign that one is doing their work effectively. This is the result of journalists who feel that when reporting stories that spread truth and hold people accountable, someone is going to naturally be upset – signaling that the journalism is sound.

Another form of normalization is a belief that harassment is inherent to journalistic work because of hate and bigotry, and thus cannot be avoided. These journalists tend to see harassment as a normal effect of doing journalism no matter what. Because harassment has been viewed as such an intrinsic part of journalistic work by some, one study found that nearly 30% of journalists considered leaving journalism altogether because of the harassment they experienced (Miller, 2021b). Instead of ignoring or even praising the abuse, they feel burdened and injured by the abuse, and see no avenue in which it will stop.

While harassment is indeed considered by many as a normalized part of doing journalistic work, many have found ways to cope. Research shows that 60% of people who experience online harassment simply ignore it (Lewis, Zamith, & Coddington, 2020). Another survey found that 25% of US journalists said they avoided covering certain topics because of harassment, while another 15% said they changed a story angle (Miller, 2021b). Moreover, nearly half of all journalists surveyed (49%) said they had to change how they acted on social media because of harassment, with 24% saying they turned off messaging on their media apps.

These proactive measures to minimize the abuse do not consider the often unhealthy ways in which journalists cope with the effects of consistent hostility. For example, many journalists note that because of the stress and mental health effects of harassment, they have taken to drinking alcohol, binge eating, exercising, and on some occasions seeking therapy. While some of these coping mechanisms are considered unhealthy and others productive, the primary takeaway is that journalists are affected personally and professionally by harassment that they experience (Miller, 2021a).

Looking Forward

While hostility affects journalists differently and is experienced with varying frequency, it is perhaps a blind spot of current journalism education that hostility is not discussed more in the classroom. Future journalists, especially women and journalists of color, need to understand the reality they are about to enter. This means educating journalism students on how to stay safe, as well as how to prevent abuse. For example, students should be empowered early on to speak up when they do not feel safe. There is often a culture for young reporters to want to appear as team players and go-getters who will do anything to get a story, and are therefore scared to make clear when a situation feels unsafe, even though they often receive the most harassment and hostility (Miller, 2021b). By empowering students to speak to managers and supervisors when experiencing hostility, they can be better advocates for themselves early on, not after a situation escalates to potentially dangerous levels. Furthermore, students should be taught proper online security. As journalists spend increasingly more time on social media interacting with audiences, there are several avenues in which they can be bullied, threatened, doxed, or hacked. Organizations like Troll Busters and resources such as the Society of Professional Journalists' Journalist Safety Toolbox and Digital Security Toolbox should be utilized to provide students with tools to protect themselves from online threats and abuse.

Additionally, as studies have consistently found that journalists feel unsupported by newsroom management, a culture shift is needed within newsrooms so journalists' wellbeing is prioritized. Some newsrooms have met this call in regard to covering protests, as they provided personal protection equipment for reporters and photographers, mandated buddy systems so no reporters were in the field alone, and explicitly told reporters to stay out of the action at protests and to leave the scene if they feel uncomfortable. However, hostility occurs during routine journalistic work as well. Soon-to-be-published research found that when reporters deal with routine hostile sources and confide in their editors about what they are experiencing, editors often either pay lip service to their concerns — showing empathy in the moment but not offering tangible support and steps forward — or disregard their concerns as an expected job hazard and therefore not important (Mesmer, 2022). This has been shown to occur even when reporters provide specific suggestions for how their editors might support them. Editors need to demonstrate that safety is an issue they take seriously, and that reporters will receive help when they ask for it.

Since harassment is a rampant problem on social media, newsrooms should also rethink their social media policies, many of which require engagement on platforms such as Twitter, Facebook, and Instagram. There is evidence that managers are becoming more attuned to this issue. In April 2022, the executive editor of *The New York Times* announced that the paper's journalists would no longer be required to have a social media presence, in part due to concerns about online harassment and threats that jeopardize reporters' wellbeing. The *Times* also announced it would be implementing training workshops to teach reporters how to prevent and respond to online abuse. Hopefully, other newsrooms will follow suit with similar policy changes and support mechanisms. Ultimately, newsroom management should adopt an ethic of care toward reporters, photographers, and other staff members, which should be practiced on a regular basis, not only when a hostile situation arises and makes caring necessary.

References

Carlson, M., Robinson, S., & Lewis, S. C. (2021). Digital press criticism: The symbolic dimensions of Donald Trump's assault on US journalists as the "enemy of the people". *Digital Journalism, 9*(6), 737–754.

Chen, G. M., Pain, P., Chen, V. Y., Mekelburg, M., Springer, N., & Troger, F. (2020). 'You really have to have a thick skin': A cross-cultural perspective on how online harassment influences female journalists. *Journalism, 21*(7), 877–895.

Lewis, S. C., Zamith, R., & Coddington, M. (2020). Online harassment and its implications for the journalist–audience relationship. *Digital Journalism, 8*(8), 1047–1067.

McAdams, K. C., & Beasley, M. H. (1994). Sexual harassment of Washington women journalists. *Newspaper Research Journal, 15*(1), 127–139. https://doi.org/10.1177/073953 299401500113

Mesmer, K. (2022). An intersectional analysis of US journalists' experiences with hostile sources. *Journalism & Communication Monographs, 24*(3), 156–216. https://doi.org/10. 1177%2F15226379221116640

Miller, K. C. (2021a). Hostility toward the press: A synthesis of terms, research, and future directions in examining harassment of journalists. *Digital Journalism*. https://doi.org/10.1080/21670811.2021.1991824

Miller, K. C. (2021b). Harassment's toll on democracy: The effects of harassment towards US journalists. *Journalism Practice*. https://doi.org/10.1080/17512786.2021.2008809

Molyneux, L. (2015). What journalists retweet: Opinion, humor, and brand development on Twitter. *Journalism*, *16*(7), 920–935.

Nerone, J. (1994). *Violence against the press: Policing the public sphere in US history*. Oxford University Press.

Posetti, J., Aboulez, N., Bontheva, K., Harrison, J., & Waisbord, S. (2020). Online violence against women journalists: A global snapshot of incidence and impacts. *United Nations Educational, Scientific and Cultural Organization*. https://www.icfj.org/our-work/icfj-unesco-global-study-online-violence-against-women-journalists

Walsh-Childers, K., Chance, J., & Herzog, K. (1996). Sexual harassment of women journalists. *Journalism & Mass Communication Quarterly 73*(3), 559–581.

20

PARTICIPATORY JOURNALISM

A New Approach for Increasing Public Trust and Engagement

Mirjana Pantic

To new generations of journalists who are preparing to enter the media industry and those who have joined it in the past decade, it would be inconceivable to work in a news environment in which it was not possible to establish direct communication with readers and viewers via diverse digital intermediaries. Interaction with audiences through email and social media has become an integral part of the daily routine of media professionals. New technologies have not only allowed this two-way communication between news producers and news consumers to emerge and flourish; they have also paved the way for a blurring of the boundaries between the two groups of actors. Due to a vast array of digital tools at their disposal, audiences have taken an active role in news production and the dissemination of information. In a contemporary news ecosystem, digital platforms have empowered ordinary citizens to supply media organizations with real-time information, breaking news, videos from remote areas, still images of natural disasters, and other items that could contribute to more comprehensive coverage of events across the globe. Their deeper engagement with media, which enables the audience to not only consume but also create news content, is labeled participatory journalism.

Development and Flourishing of Participatory Journalism

Although the term participatory journalism is tied to the practice that emerged with the arrival of new technologies in newsrooms, traces of this form of audience engagement in news creation could be found in the pre-digital era. Stuart Allan, who has dedicated considerable research attention to journalism produced by amateurs, suggests that "the notion of citizen journalism is really as old as journalism itself" (Hájek, Štefaniková, & Allan, 2014, p. 175). Furthermore, before email and social media platforms became essential tools in the news ecosystem, face-to-face

DOI: 10.4324/9781003315605-33

interactions, along with telecommunication devices, allowed readers, listeners, and viewers to contact newspapers, radio, and TV stations, to signal news to them or share newsworthy information.

However, other than sharing stories with media professionals in person and via telephone, or in rare cases delivering a filmed depiction of events, citizens did not have sophisticated technologies to produce content and disseminate it in real time. A series of occurrences in different parts of the globe at the beginning of the 21st century changed the game. While various events at that time led to increased audience participation, ranging from natural disasters to acts of terrorism, scholarly literature most frequently heralds the Indian Ocean earthquake and tsunami of December 26, 2004 as the start of modern participatory journalism. When the tsunami slammed into the coasts of multiple countries, tourists started photographing and video-recording what was later described as one of the deadliest natural disasters in history. The first accounts of such a devastating event were published on holidaymakers' blogs and web pages (Allan, 2009), and shortly thereafter established news organizations began integrating such content into their own coverage of the unprecedented event.

Another tragic event that uncovered the importance of citizen storytelling was the London terrorist bombing that happened on July 7, 2005. Many Londoners and others – people Allan described as "citizen witnesses" – who directly observed this crisis event documented it with their phones and shared the information they had with news media. The prominence of this engagement is reflected in 22,000 emails and texts, including 300 photographs and several videos portraying the terrorist attacks, which citizens sent to the BBC (Douglas, 2006). Their records of the London suicide bombings were invaluable. As Douglas (2006) pointed out, "with events happening largely underground, far removed from the eyes of the media professionals, the mobile phone camera came into its own, helping illustrate the day's horrific events in a way that would not have been possible before" (para. 5).

During this period of the rise of modern-day citizen journalism, CNN launched a platform called "CNN iReport" to encourage its viewers and readers to practice amateur journalism by supplying stories, still images, and videos. Pieces produced by ordinary citizens were welcomed and celebrated for documenting important events, such as Hurricane Sandy and the Israel-Gaza conflict, as well as "personal stories that put a face on complex issues like mental illness and gay rights" (CNN, n.d., para. 1).

Participatory vs. Citizen Journalism

Participatory journalism has been used interchangeably with the term "citizen journalism" among both academics and journalism practitioners. Multiple scholars have, however, recommended a distinction between the two, particularly in the areas concerning citizens' autonomy to publish content and the necessity of professional engagement in facilitating information selection, production, and distribution. For instance, Nip (2006) noted that citizen journalists are able to collect, craft, and disseminate information independently, without the assistance of paid, professional journalists. They find a home for the content they produce on alternative websites, blog platforms, or social media. Furthermore, citizen journalists can use diverse digital platforms to break news from remote places or create websites and have full autonomy to disseminate information. On the other hand, participatory journalism is facilitated by news organizations and involves the "active involvement from many parties, not just production of a single (news) entity" (Lewis, 2010, p. 63). As an illustration, participatory journalism could manifest itself in specialized sections on news websites for user content, poll responses, social media posts embedded in articles, comments posted as users' reactions to news stories, or other content created by readers but made available to the public after being approved by media professionals.

Challenging Times for Participatory Journalism

Regardless of whether we draw a line between citizen and participatory journalism or treat them as indistinguishable concepts, it is evident that these phenomena have gained more prominence with the rise of social media. When digital platforms began to spread, they allowed more people to disseminate information and reach a broader spectrum of internet users. In 2010, at a time when citizen journalism was flourishing, the number of social media users in the world was almost 1 billion. This transformation of the media ecosystem also empowered audiences to have conversations with news producers, and social media supplied citizens with opportunities to collect information, recommend articles, post comments on diverse issues, and disseminate news. While this gave journalists access to a wide array of information, however, it also posed multiple challenges to traditional publishers. As more people started establishing social media accounts and expanding their networks, they no longer needed media organizations to increase the visibility of their posts, photographs, or other newsworthy information. As such, by the second decade of the 21st century, optimism about the role of citizens in news production and citizen journalism began to fade, and news media became less willing to "facilitate a public discourse – in the form of comments – on their sites" (p. 301). Similarly, participation in live-blogging, a journalistic phenomenon that is recognizable by its strong emphasis on user participation, decreased, even when established media organizations offered citizens opportunities to share their perspectives or information (Pantic, 2020a). By 2017 much engagement had shifted toward what Thorsten Quandt (2018) labeled as "dark participation." This type of participation does not mean the absence of it. Rather, "dark participation" is depicted in trolling, offensive comments on news stories, and attacks on other users or groups of people.

Other than this form of non-meaningful and detrimental participation or the lack of willingness to participate, during the second decade of the 21st century, some successful participatory journalism projects ceased to exist. Notably, declining visitor participation pushed CNN to retire iReport after almost a decade of operation, and instead encourage citizens to share stories on Facebook, Twitter, and

Instagram, adding the hashtag #CNNiReport. This initiative, however, was not as successful as the original idea of citizen contributions via the iReport site. Posts on Twitter with #CNNiReport hashtag are comparatively rare. By this time social media had overpowered CNN as a disseminator of user content.

A New Approach to Participation

The loss of interest in nurturing diverse participatory components on news websites co-occurred with the shift in audiences' news consumption habits, as they started gravitating toward social media to obtain and share news. With the continual global growth of social networks, it would be almost inconceivable to reimagine participatory journalism taking place outside of the space dominated by social networking sites. Social media have been an integral part of citizen participation for more than a decade and will continue to play an important role in the contemporary media ecosystem, pressing news organizations to further embrace these platforms to maximize engagement. The problem, on the other side, is that these platforms have also contributed to certain problematic relationships between news organizations and citizens, including the spread of fake news and increased lack of trust in news media. Notably, a recent report by the Reuters Institute for the Study of Journalism suggests that trust in the news people use is 44%, while the overall level of trust in news is just 29% (Jenkins & Graves, 2021). Pew Research Center data show that this lack of trust is particularly strong among Republicans, dropping from 70% to 35% between 2016 and 2021, compared to a 5% drop, from 83% to 78%, among Democrats (Gottfried & Liedke, 2021).

Evidently, lack of trust in the media and fake news are the two most common carcinogens in the contemporary news ecosystem. Participatory journalism, a phenomenon that connects two major stakeholders in the news production and consumption process – journalists and audiences, could help to address the problem of public distrust in the media. Involving citizens in news creation and fighting misinformation is critical as an engaged public is "an important prerequisite for deliberation and participation" (Karlsson et al., 2015, p. 298). There are already available tools for the revival of participatory journalism and certain successful elements of reader engagement that should be further developed to reestablish trust between news organizations and citizens. Most notably, participatory journalism can fight misinformation and rebuild trust by: 1) encouraging readers to report fake news; 2) launching new initiatives via social media to build a stronger connection with citizens and organizing participation around topics rather than sections; 3) live blogging; and 4) hosting both virtual and in-person events to connect with readers. The key to the new approach to participatory journalism is flexibility.

Fighting fake information has been proposed as the first step in the process of revitalizing participatory journalism due to its enormous impact not only on the people's perception of news media, but also on democracy itself. Creators of fake news deliberately spread made-up stories to deceive internet users and lead them to make uninformed decisions about important aspects of their lives, including who they are going to vote for in presidential elections or whether they would get or reject a COVID-19 vaccine. Even though a media strategy to fight false information that involves amateur news producers, like other participatory journalism initiatives, might not elicit high engagement, it could serve the purpose of debunking fake news and creating a sentiment among readers that they joined forces with journalists in the mission of combating misinformation.

Creating a pact with citizens to identify and prevent the spread of fake news could be initiated by news organizations through social media. As noted above, reimagining participatory journalism in an information ecosystem dominated by social networking sites is difficult to envisage without platforms such as Twitter, YouTube, or TikTok. Segments that represented the hallmark of participatory journalism in its blooming stages, such as comment threads, sections for user content, or blogs, could be succeeded by new strategies that involve more meaningful interaction with readers. Hence, participation could be organized around specific topics rather than sections for citizen journalism. More frequent social media posts that ask users to share information or opinions about a specific issue or event, or that simply asks them to participate in an opinion poll, could lead to a stronger connection between citizens and news media. A potential obstacle to successfully implementing this strategy could be a lack of resources in news media and the tendency of debates on social media to take a form of dark participation that causes more harm than good.

Additionally, it would be beneficial for news organizations to focus on reinforcing forms of participation that have proven invaluable in a digital media ecosystem, one of them being a live blog. This journalistic genre supplies readers with updates on events in motion, such as breaking news or sports games, and is recognizable by its capacity to serve as a platform for various voices and information providers. Live blogging enjoys the prominence in digital journalism that the inverted pyramid format has in print media. It has been around for more than two decades and has manifested resilience over time, remaining the same at its core, by providing updates about rolling events and accommodating diverse sources. As technological advancements have facilitated the introduction of new multimedia elements, live blogs have become more diversified to include a greater variety of photographs, videos, embedded Twitter posts, and other media items (Pantic et al., 2017). Due to its digital nature, the live blog can incorporate a vast array of multimedia elements and allow new microforms of storytelling in the future. Even though it might suffer from a lack of enthusiasm or reader engagement – problems also common to other forms of participatory journalism – this journalistic format benefits from being engaging and responsive to the demands of modern news consumers who want to receive information about events in real time (Pantic, 2020a; Pantic, 2020b). Furthermore, the live blog allows meaningful participation, because it hosts opinions from both official and unofficial sources, while being moderated by professional journalists who can prevent "dark" modes of participation or other harmful user engagement. Live blogs also allow journalists to preserve their authority over the newsmaking process by deciding on the pieces of content that will be embedded into the live coverage of events.

Last but not least important, news organizations could host both virtual and in-person events to connect with readers. This practice has been embraced by multiple prominent news media that have established themselves as trustworthy and reader-engagement-focused outlets. Organizing events for readers, such as panel discussions, opportunities to meet journalists, book clubs, or quiz nights, contributes to relationship-building between readers and media representatives. Therefore, such practices could pave the way to regaining audiences' trust. Due to the expansion of digital media, events that gather readers and journalists could be hosted not only in person but also virtually. Currently, Twitter spaces are becoming popular among users of this social media platform. News organizations should take advantage of this trend by hosting Twitter spaces on defined topics, and inviting users to participate in discussions. Through such discussions, they can learn how to better serve citizens in an era marked by numerous challenges facing both journalism and democracy.

Conclusion

Participatory journalism has gone through diverse stages over decades, reaching its peak at the beginning of the 21st century, with the emergence of digital media. It has provided citizens with opportunities to voice their opinions and share information about major events they witnessed through mainstream media platforms. Professional journalism has embraced user participation as it has increased engagement and contributed to more comprehensive coverage of events that might otherwise not have been reported.

Participatory journalism is the bridge that meaningfully connects media professionals and their audiences. In these turbulent times, when the relationship between the two stakeholders faces multiple challenges, this form of journalism could serve as a building block in rebuilding trust. The new approach to participatory journalism discussed in this chapter does not propose a revolutionary change in how journalism engages citizens in the news production process. Rather, it suggests that news organizations should further develop successful forms of participation and be flexible to adopt new practices that arise with technological advancement. Embracing such an approach is not solely focused on utilizing content from audiences that news media would not be able to acquire otherwise, or content that allows them to supplement stories with information provided by amateurs. Investing in participatory journalism should pave the way for news organizations to restore public trust by engaging and empowering audiences to share meaningful viewpoints, join forces with journalists to debunk fake news, and prevent noise and misinformation from dominating our digital media space.

References

Allan, S. (2009). Histories of citizen journalism. In S. Allan & E. Thorsen (Eds.), *Citizen journalism* (pp. 17–31). Peter Lang.

CNN. (n.d.). *Behind the scenes.* http://edition.cnn.com/ireport-awards/how-it-works

Douglas, T. (2006, July 4). How 7/7 'democratised' the media. *BBC News*. http://news.bbc.co.uk/2/hi/uk_news/5142702.stm

Gottfried, J., & Liedke, J. (2021, August 30). *Partisan divides in media trust widen, driven by a decline among Republicans*. Pew Research Center. https://www.pewresearch.org/fact-tank/2021/08/30/partisan-divides-in-media-trust-widen-driven-by-a-decline-among-republicans/

Hájek, R., Štefaniková, S., & Allan, S. (2014). Citizen journalism is as old as journalism itself: An interview with Stuart Allan. *Mediální Studia, 2* 174–181.

Jenkins, J., & Graves, L. (2021). *United States*. Reuters Institute. https://reutersinstitute.politics.ox.ac.uk/digital-news-report/2021/united-states

Karlsson, M., Bergström, A., Clerwall, C., & Fast, K. (2015). Participatory journalism – the (r)evolution that wasn't. Content and user behavior in Sweden 2007–2013. *Journal of Computer-Mediated Communication, 20*(3), 295–311.

Lewis, S. C. (2010). Citizen journalism: Motivations, methods, and momentum. In M. McCombs, A. W. Hinsley, K. Kaufhold, & S. C. Lewis (Eds.), *The future of news: An agenda of perspectives* (pp. 59–76). Cognella.

Nip, J. Y. (2006). Exploring the second phase of public journalism. *Journalism Studies, 7*(2), 212–236. https://doi.org/10.1080/14616700500533528

Pantic, M. (2020a). Engagement with live blogs: When passive consumption overpowers participation. *Electronic News, 14*(1), 22–36. https://doi.org/10.1177/1931243120910449

Pantic, M. (2020b). Gratifications of digital media: What motivates users to consume live blogs. *Media Practice and Education, 21*(2), 148–163. https://doi.org/10.1080/25741136.2019.1608104

Pantic, M., Whiteside, E. E., & Cvetkovic, I. (2017). Politics, conflict generate more live-blog comments. *Newspaper Research Journal, 38*(3), 354–365. https://doi.org/10.1177/0739532917722979

Quandt, T. (2018). Dark participation. *Media and Communication, 6*(4), 36–48.

21

OF SOUNDER MIND

Considering the Well-Being of Professional Journalists

Avery E. Holton and Valérie Bélair-Gagnon

In front of a large international crowd at the 2022 International Symposium for Online Journalism at the University of Texas at Austin, Luisa Ortiz Pérez asked the audience to consider how they felt in their personal lives, how they felt in their journalistic lives, and what impact those feelings combined to have on their personal well-being (Ortiz Pérez, 2022). The question from the Vita Activa founder and executive director was met with comments from the globally diverse audience about a constant state of anxiety and exhaustion. Some members of the audience even openly shared that they wrestled with tensions between their commitment to journalism as a profession and the emotional and mental degradations they were experiencing.

These sentiments are part of a growing – or at least now more publicly shared and acknowledged – challenge facing journalists and those who are counted on to amplify their voices and to find pathways to support them (e.g., publishers, news organizations, academic researchers, civil society organizations, and policymakers). This comes amid a call in journalism studies to look at the role of emotions in journalism (Goyanes & Cañedo, 2021; Pantti & Wahl-Jorgensen, 2021; Stupart, 2021) and the well-being of journalists (Deavours et al., 2022; Holton et al., 2022). This matters for many reasons, including the ability for news organizations to attract and retain talented journalists who can produce impactful stories and provide unique perspectives and positionalities. A number of global media scholars have highlighted the mounting difficulties journalism as a profession, and particularly journalism engaged through social media platforms, has placed on journalists without support mechanisms in place to address the many traumas they increasingly face in coverage and in audience engagement (Waisbord, 2020).

While the profession has for decades been synonymous with long hours, inflexible schedules, low pay, job insecurities, and professional precarity, the rise in social media accessibility across the globe has pressed journalists to become near-ambient

DOI: 10.4324/9781003315605-34

laborers (Hermida, 2014). Congruent with this temporal pressure, journalists have also been guided by their news organizations to engage more frequently and personally with audiences, often without clear organizational policies (Bossio et al., forthcoming; Nelson, 2021). Journalists have thus been asked, if not pushed, to be more present online and engaged with audiences than ever before without systematic scaffolding or protections against professional slip ups or, and arguably more concerningly, new stressors from audiences including harassment, trolling and abuse among others.

In the sections below, this chapter highlights a recent rise in reports of harassment and other forms of abuse among journalists that have fueled an exodus from social media by some (Mathews et al., 2021), disconnection strategies for others (Storm, 2020; UNESCO, 2021), and untenable burnout for many of those remaining (Bedai, 2021; Bossio & Holton, 2021). This is happening as news organizations and various actors involved in journalism, including tech-oriented actors, continue to wrestle with the need for innovative business models, engagement with emerging and fast-paced technology and social media platforms and policies that can promote sustainable workplace well-being. As Diana Bossio et al. (forthcoming) noted, journalists are learning new ways to protect themselves professionally and personally and, when pushed, choosing more frequently to invest in their personal futures rather than in those of unsteady organizations. In the absence of personal well-being – which can be linked to broad support from news organizations – journalists may continue in their retreat from the profession.

Harassment, Abuse, and Other Harms

While journalists have traditionally experienced moderate levels of harassment from news audiences, visible attacks, both on- and off-line, have heightened in recent years, especially against journalists identifying as women and people of color. Such harassment has shown up as threatening comments to online stories in Sweden (Nilsson & Orneberg, 2016), suggestions of violence in social media exchanges in the United States (Chen et al., 2020; Lewis et al., 2020), social media mobs terrorizing women journalists in the Philippines (Tandoc et al., 2021), and sexual harassment and attacks on women journalists in Pakistan and Ghana (Boateng & Lauk, 2021; Jamil, 2020). While journalists may weather these attacks, normalizing them as professional expectations in some cases, they nonetheless are in need of a cultural shift among news organizations that values journalists alongside, if not ahead of, the journalism they produce (Deavours et al., 2022; Holton et al., 2021).

Public attacks by news audiences against journalists have moved beyond angry letters to the editor and into social media spaces that privilege mob attacks and hate speech and encourage the demonization of journalists (Waisbord, 2020). An alarming number of journalists report social media abuse spilling over into their private lives and elevating fears for themselves, their families, and those around them (Holton et al., 2022; Westcott, 2019). As Kaitlin Miller (2021, 2022) noted, increases in harassment may be in part due to political alignments and motivations, access to journalists through social media spaces and other platforms and the evolving and diffused identities of journalism as a community of practice. This is complicated by a news environment wherein harassment against women journalists and journalists of color by others within their news organizations and in journalism is well-documented (see Ferrier & Garud-Patkar, 2018; Walsh-Childers et al., 1996) and where organizational responses have tended to be sluggish and palliative (Holton et al., 2022).

In the face of harassment from all sides, and without resources in place to prevent harassment or to even open safer, destigmatizing dialogues about personal well-being, journalists are now shouldering the fragility of journalism as an industry along with the "precarious professionalism" required to maintain their profession (Matthews & Onyemaobi, 2020). They appear to be at times asked to assume all of the risks of being more public, engaged, and reciprocal (Lewis et al., 2020) with little to no protections from news organizations that tend to swoop in after harassment has reached insufferable levels. And while some journalists have been able to lean into one another for support or to find comfort in friends and colleagues outside of journalism, the devastating toll of the mental and emotional labor now being required of journalists is immutable.

Absences Through Individualized Practices

More than a decade ago, Scott Reinardy (2011) found that journalists, and young journalists in particular, were more exhausted by their work than at any point in history. That warning came just as news organizations were pushing into social media spaces, pressing their journalists to take the plunge while they worked to develop policies and approaches to platforms such as Facebook and Twitter. To innovate, often through engagement with technology already adopted by news audiences, news organizations risked fatiguing and professionally burning out their journalists (Anger, 2019). They opted instead to ask their journalists (and other journalistic actors) to become innovators and risk-takers, creating gendered work environments and imbalanced, if unsustainable, workloads for journalists and particularly women journalists and journalists of color, leading to what Silvio Waisbord (2020) named "mob censorship."

Edging closer to burnout, and beating back harassment, journalists have found some solace in managing absence strategies in ways that calm, even if briefly, their professional and personal lives (Bossio et al., forthcoming). Without organizational resources to inform coping mechanisms, journalists have found some individual relief in allowing themselves small absences, or disconnections, from social and digital media. These intentional practices of disconnection within the continuum of connective practices may be a bit of the kind of scaffolding journalists need to remain thoughtfully absent at times without completely disengaging from journalism.

Journalists have noted that being less reciprocal and less reactive in social media spaces has afforded them micro-breaks from the anxieties that such engagement can bring (Bélair-Gagnon et al., 2022; Henrichsen, 2021). Coupled with less time spent on social media, either by simply walking away from devices, blocking certain users or platforms, or by creating break times that are conveyed to colleagues, management, and supervisors (and even family in some cases), this approach may help journalists create boundaries with and around social media use for professional and personal purposes (Bossio & Holton, 2021). This also creates space between would-be harassers and journalists – again, even if briefly so – allowing journalists to reset and recenter. Yet, these micro-absences still place the burden of self-protection and personal well-being solely on individual journalists (Bélair-Gagnon et al., 2022).

Absence strategies such as temporary disconnection – though it is but one approach journalists may use to address their own mental health and well-being – signals a greater need for news organizations and other actors mentioned above to rally behind journalists and, ultimately, journalism. They also call for the recognition of these labor-ridden practices to be acknowledged as work by journalism and their media organizations (Bossio et al., forthcoming). Globally, journalists have said that facing harassment, trauma, burnout, fatigue, and other stressors take a significant toll on their personal well-being. News organizations and other actors would be wise, and perhaps revolutionary in a "journalism as profession" sense, to take more even seriously the issues facing journalists and the ways in which journalists are self-medicating what is a systemic problem.

Some organizations have been successful in taking the lead in creating intentional spaces of well-being, including the news website company Axios, or professional bodies like the Association for Health Care Journalists and the Dart Center for Journalism and Trauma, among others. For those who still are considering such a shift, solutions cannot be individually sustained. Journalists have made it clear that such a burden is becoming too much to bear and that exchanging their personal well-being for a profession that does not offer much in the way of support is a lost battle.

Well-being in Journalism Practice and Studies

Journalists, as with other professions in contemporary workplace environments, are frequently and willfully (at least until it's too much) blurring the boundaries of their professional and personal lives for the sake of journalism. They do so at great peril to themselves, those around them, and the institution of journalism itself. While there is evidence to suggest journalists are finding ways to maintain their well-being, as we have shown in the previous section, news organizations have been slow to take up the call for action.

In this concluding section, we call for key practical and academic approaches in journalism practice, pedagogy, and scholarship which should be considered for the personal well-being of journalists and arguably for the more holistic health of journalism as a profession. These approaches to personal well-being for journalists include: (1) the need for a *systemic approach* as opposed to an individualist approach; (2) the *situatedness of well-being in time-space*; and (3) the *professionally and normatively driven* nature of well-being in journalism/journalist contexts building from *epistemology* and *reflexivity* in journalistic *knowledge production* of professionals' pursuits of *truth* and *knowledge.*

First, practice and research has shown the need for an understanding of well-being from a *systemic perspective* as opposed to a "single-problem," or individualist, approach. That is, in the case of news organizations, a systematic effort to build and maintain organizational leadership that destigmatizes mental health and well-being in the workplace and openly acknowledges the roles of experience and positionality to support engagement between leadership and journalists. This is evidenced in several recent studies of journalists and news organizations, including the work of Maja Šimunjak and Manuel Menke (2022). In interviews with journalists in Germany and the United Kingdom, they found journalists in want of leadership that could be more transparent and compassionate in developing resources for journalists' well-being. Edson Tandoc and his colleagues (2021) found similar results among women journalists in the Philippines, who said they wanted more professional and structured support from news organizations. Diana Bossio and her colleagues (forthcoming) proposed a systemic approach from news organizations that should be "reflected in clear policies, support mechanisms, training awareness that are centralized in approach" (n.p.).

Scholars have considered the nuances news organizations may face when deploying a systematic approach to personal well-being. These scholars have advocated that personal well-being for journalists could be improved through preventative and palliative care. Rather than continuing to support environments where journalists do not feel safe talking about issues such as harassment, abuse, or trolling and find little, if any, preventive actions or resources to support their well-being through difficult professional times, calls to build and sustain systematic support for well-being that can become part of a broader systemic perspective (and enactment) for the profession of journalism are becoming louder both in practice and for researchers.

Second, research and practice has pointed to the importance of the *situatedness of well-being in time-space* for journalists. Researchers have taken lessons from journalism, psychology, organizational and management studies that have used varied methodological approaches, including textual and historical analyses, surveys, interviews and observations, to explore issues such as harassment and trauma among journalists. Many of these studies have also indicated that happiness, personal well-being, and quality of life are less social constructs and more psychological constructs impacted by a number of factors within journalists' professional and personal environments. This suggests the need for research and practice to engage journalists' well-being more deeply as a psychological construct, which itself requires acknowledgement of work that could inform this space as well as gaps that need addressing.

Claudia Mellado and Maria Luisa Humanes (2012) provided insights into the elements that can impact psychological constructs such as well-being. In their study of journalists in Chile, they found factors predicting professional autonomy among journalists depend on media political organizations, geographical locations, newsbeats/assignments and editorial positions within the media. This suggests that organizational and spatial factors are key in understanding the autonomy of journalists, the latter of which is a key aspect of journalists' personal well-being and professional sense. Gina Chen et al. (2020) found common ground for women journalists who work or have worked in Germany, India, Taiwan, the UK, and the US in terms of experience with harassment but also uncovered differences in how online engagement (and perceptions of online engagement with audiences) impacted their sense of well-being. Women journalists in the Philippines described different resources of support, or the want of such resources, at personal, peer, and professional levels (Tandoc et al., 2021). Such support, even if unaccompanied by sustained action, can be connected to positionalities in news organizations and nuanced cultural values that, too, are ingredients of personal well-being. Mariateresa Garrido (2020) observed that journalists in Venezuela faced increased harassment and violent confrontations as government protections and support for journalists diminished, indicating that well-being, or at least certain aspects of it, may often be affected by influences acting on news organizations and journalism more broadly.

Third in our proposed approaches is a call for research studies that address well-being as a crisis facing journalists. Well-being is part of the *epistemological*, meaning how do we know what we know, and also the *reflectivity* of journalism and journalists, referring to individual or collective examination of feelings, reactions, and motives. Well-being exists within journalistic knowledge production – through practices including verification, sourcing, and distribution – and with recollections through memory, perceptions, and metajournalistic discourses. Well-being is part of the journalistic pursuit of truth and the knowledge, beliefs, and understanding of society. In terms of journalism, numerous studies have shown that professional norms and ethics are key in harnessing one's well-being, especially in trauma journalism (see Newman & Miller, 2021). As an example, journalists covering trauma rely on principles and practices of journalism for their own mental health and well-being and to help them avoid sensationalizing stories, promote the privacy of photographers during interviews, and fact-check before publishing (Karki, 2017).

Conclusion

Situatedness, a systemic view, and epistemological, reflective, and knowledge production in the way that they are represented in practice and in the metajournalistic discourses, consciously or otherwise, are key in developing an understanding of, and practical approaches toward, journalistic well-being. What may be bolstered with these approaches is the notion of power and visibility, meaning for whom and by whom systematic support structures for journalistic well-being are talked about and enacted. Who is muted by this process and potentially alienated in journalism research and practice? And how can such voices be given more agency in more sustained ways so that well-being does not become a privilege for some but rather an affordance for all? Addressing such questions will be important to the sustainability of journalism as a profession and the overall well-being of individual journalists.

References

Anger, J. (2019). Time to step away from the "bright, shiny things"? Towards a sustainable model of journalism innovation in an era of perpetual change. In *Journalism Innovation Project*. Reuters Institute for the Study of Journalism. https://reutersinstitute.politics.ox.ac.uk/our-research/time-step-away-bright-shiny-things-towards-sustainable-model-journalism-innovation-era

Bedai, C. (2021). Taking time off to recover from trauma or burnout. *International Journalists' Network*. https://ijnet.org/en/resource/taking-time-recover-trauma-or-burnout

Bélair-Gagnon, V., Bossio, D., Holton, A. E., & Molyneux, L. (2022). Disconnection: How measured operations from journalistic norms and labor can help sustain journalism. *Social Media + Society*. Advance online publication. https://journals.sagepub.com/doi/10.1177/20563051221077217

Boateng, K. J. A., & Lauk, E. (2021). Proclivity of sexual harassment and blame attribution in journalism: Experiential narratives of Ghanaian female journalists. *Observatorio (obs★)*, *15*(2), 157–173.

Bossio, D., & Holton, A. E. (2021). Burning out and turning off: Journalists' disconnection strategies on social media. *Journalism*, *22*(10), 2475–2492.

Bossio, D., Bélair-Gagnon, V., Holton, A. E., & Molyneux, L. (Forthcoming). *The paradox of connection: How digital media is transforming journalistic labor*. University of Illinois Press.

Chen, G., Pain, P., Chen, V., Mekelberg, M., Springer, N., & Troger, F. (2020). 'You really have to have a thick skin': A cross-cultural perspective on how online harassment influences female journalists. *Journalism*, *21*(7), 877–895.

Deavours, D., Heath, W., Miller, K., Viehouser, M., Palacios-Plugge, S., & Broussard, R. (2022). Reciprocal journalism's double-edged sword: How journalists resolve cognitive dissonance after experiencing harassment from audiences on social media. *Journalism*. Advance online publication. https://journals.sagepub.com/doi/epub/10.1177/14648849221109654

Ferrier, M., & Garud-Patkar, N. (2018). TrollBusters: Fighting online harassment of women journalists. In R. Vickery & T. Everbach (Eds.), *Mediating misogyny: Gender, technology, and harassment*. Springer International Publishing.

Garrido, M. (2020). The pitfalls and perils of being a digital journalist in Venezuela. In S. Jamil (Ed.), *The handbook of research on combating threats to media freedom and journalist safety* (pp. 319–337). IGI Global.

Goyanes, M., & Cañedo, A. (2021). The dark side of journalism: Understanding the phenomenology of conflicts in the newsroom and the mechanisms intended to solve them. *Journalism*. Advance online publication. https://doi.org/10.1177/146488492110147

Henrichsen, J. R. (2021). Understanding nascent newsroom security and safety cultures: The emergence of the 'Security Champion'. *Journalism Practice*. Advance online publication. https://doi.org/10.1080/17512786.2021.1927802

Hermida, A. (2014). Twitter as an ambient news network. In K. Weller, A. Bruns, J. Burgess, M. Mahrt, & C. Puschmann (Eds.), *Twitter and Society*. Peter Lang.

Holton, A. E., Bélair-Gagnon, V., & Royal, C. (2021). The human side of (news) engagement: Emotion, platform and individual agency. *Digital Journalism*, *9*(8), 1184–1189.

Holton, A. E., Bélair-Gagnon, V., Bossio, D., & Molyneux, L. (2022). 'Not their fault, but their problem': Organizational responses to the online harassment of journalists. *Journalism Practice*. Advance online publication. https://www.tandfonline.com/doi/abs/10.1080/17512786.2021.1946417

Jamil, S. (2020). Suffering in silence: The resilience of Pakistan's female journalists to combat sexual harassment, threats and discrimination. *Journalism Practice*, *14*(2), 150–170.

Karki, A. (2017). Covering trauma: Six tips for protecting your mental health. Dart Center for Journalism and Trauma. https://dartcenter.org/blog/2017/11/covering-trauma-six-tips-protecting-your-mental-health

Lewis, S. C., Zamith, R., & Coddington, M. (2020). Online harassment and its implications for the journalist-audience relationship. *Digital Journalism*, *8*(8), 1047–1067.

Mathews, N., Bélair-Gagnon, V., & Carlson, M. (2021). 'Why I quit journalism:' Former journalists' advice giving as a way to regain control. *Journalism*. Advance online publication. https://doi.org/10.1177/14648849211061958

Matthews, J., & Onyemaobi, K. (2020). Precarious professionalism: Journalism and the fragility of professional practice in the global south. *Journalism Studies*, *21*(13), 1836–1851.

Mellado, C., & Humanes, M. L. (2012). Modeling perceived professional autonomy in Chilean journalism. *Journalism*, *13*(8), 985–1003.

Miller, K. C. (2021). Hostility toward the press: A synthesis of terms, research, and future directions in examining harassment of journalists. *Digital Journalism*. Advance online publication. https://doi.org/10.1080/21670811.2021.1991824

Miller, K. C. (2022). The 'price you pay' and the 'badge of honor': Journalists, gender, and harassment. *Journalism and Mass Communication Quarterly*. Advance online publication. https://journals.sagepub.com/doi/10.1177/10776990221088761

Nelson, J. N. (2021). A Twitter tightrope without a net: Journalists' reactions to newsroom social media policies. Tow Center for Digital Journalism. https://www.cjr.org/tow_center_reports/newsroom-social-media-policies.php

Newman, E., & Miller, N. S. (2021). Resources for Journalists Coping with Trauma. Dart Center for Journalism and Trauma. https://dartcenter.org/resources/journalists-coping-trauma

Nilsson, M. L., & Orneberg, H. (2016). Journalism under threat: Intimidation and harassment of Swedish journalists. *Journalism Practice*, *10*(7), 880–890.

Ortiz Pérez, L. (2022). Mental health and the wellbeing of journalists in an era of online harassment, extreme polarization, denialism and pandemic [Conference presentation]. International Symposium for Online Journalism, Austin, TX.

Pantti, M., & Wahl-Jorgensen, K. (2021). Journalism and emotional Work. *Journalism Studies*, *22*(12), 1567–1573.

Reinardy, S. (2011). Newspaper journalism in crisis: Burnout on the rise, eroding young journalists' career commitment. *Journalism*, *12*(1), 33–50.

Šimunjak, M., & Menke, M. (2022). Workplace well-being and support systems in journalism: Comparative analysis of Germany and the United Kingdom. *Journalism*. Advance online publication. https://doi.org/10.1177/14648849221115205

Storm, H. (2020). It's time for newsrooms to tackle taboos about mental health. Here's how. Reuters Institute. https://reutersinstitute.politics.ox.ac.uk/risj-review/its-time-newsrooms-tackle-taboos-about-mental-health-heres-how

Stupart, R. (2021). Tired, hungry, and on deadline: Affect and emotion in the practice of conflict journalism. *Journalism Studies*, *22*(12), 1574–1589.

Tandoc, E., Sagun, K. K., & Alvarez, K. P. (2021). The digitization of harassment: Women journalists' experiences with online harassment in the Philippines. *Journalism Practice*. Advanced online publication. https://www.tandfonline.com/doi/full/10.1030/17512786.2021.1981774

UNESCO. (2021). The chilling: Global trends in online violence against women journalists. https://en.unesco.org/sites/default/files/the-chilling.pdf

Waisbord, S. (2020). Mob censorship: Online harassment of US journalists in times of digital hate and populism. *Digital Journalism*, *8*(8), 1030–1046.

Walsh-Childers, K., Chance, J., & Herzog, K. (1996). Sexual harassment of women journalists. *Journalism & Mass Communication Quarterly, 73*(3), 559–581.

Westcott, L. (2019). 'The threats follow us home': Survey details risks for female journalists in USA, Canada. Committee to Protect Journalists. https://cpj.org/2019/09/canada-usa-female-journalist-safety-online-harassment-survey/

ESSAY

Predatory Publishing

What Every Science Journalist Needs to Know

Amy Koerber

In 2015 John Bohannon, along with three coauthors, submitted an article with known scientific flaws to twenty journals, all of which he believed to be fake (Bohannon et al., 2015). Bohannon's belief in the poor quality of these journals was proven correct when the "paper was accepted for publication by multiple journals within 24 hours" (Bohannon, 2015, The Inside Man section, para. 2). One of these was *International Archives of Medicine*, where the authors submitted a credit card to pay the 600-euro publication fee, and the article was published within two weeks. Even though this journal's website suggests its articles are "double blind peer reviewed," Bohannon attests that his team's article was accepted without peer review: "Not a single word was changed" (Inside Man section, para. 3).

Bohannon and his coauthors' article, "Chocolate with High Cocoa Content as a Weight Loss Accelerator," was later acknowledged as a hoax carried out in partnership with a team of filmmakers making a documentary about the "junk-science diet industry" (Bohannon, 2015, The Setup section, para. 1). To implement the hoax, Bohannon and his coauthors had created an "Institute of Diet and Health" that existed only as a website, and he assumed the name "Johannes Bohannon" as lead author. The researchers enrolled fifteen participants, divided them into three groups, with a different diet assigned to each group, and concluded that "Subjects of the chocolate intervention group experienced the easiest and most successful weight loss" (Bohannon et al., 2015, p. 1). Bohannon attests that his team's research was conducted and accurately reported (Bohannon, 2015, The Con section, paras. 1–4). However, the study enrolled only fifteen participants, so its conclusions were not statistically sound, and nowhere in the article was the sample size mentioned.

After the article was revealed as a hoax, the journal editors retracted it and published a statement that characterized its publication as a "mistake" (Editorial Office, 2015). However, before retraction, the article's findings were reported by several media outlets with headlines such as "Slim by Chocolate" and "Why You Must Eat

DOI: 10.4324/9781003315605-35

Chocolate Daily" (Bohannon, 2015, para. 1). Thus, the Bohannon case presents us with some important questions about the ethical obligations of science journalists, who often must report expert information on subjects they are not familiar with. It also draws attention to the relatively recent emergence of "predatory" publishing practices. With the proliferation of journals that falsely claim to practice peer review – such as in the Bohannon case – science journalists' risk of spreading false scientific findings is greater than ever. Thus, in this essay I will introduce predatory publishing and offer some suggestions to help science journalists navigate a landscape of scholarly publishing that is becoming increasingly complex.

What is Predatory Publishing?

Jeffrey Beall (2012), a librarian at the University of Colorado-Denver, coined the term "predatory" in 2008 to characterize a small number of open access journals and publishers that he included on a "blacklist" published on his website. Along with its many benefits, the open access movement had also ushered in new practices, such as "gold" open access, meaning that the publication cost is shifted to authors to enable free online access. Beall used the term to characterize journals and publishers that he believed were exploiting this model to accept more articles, purely for the sake of increasing profits, without conducting peer review.

When it first appeared in 2008, Beall's list identified a handful of journals and publishers as predatory. However, as the list grew, so did the controversy that surrounded it. Beall took his list offline in 2017, amidst accusations that it was too reliant on anecdotal evidence and personal judgment. However, as the Bohannon hoax illustrates, many years after the demise of Beall's list, predatory practices continue to be a concern for scholars, policymakers, research funders, and the general public. Although most stakeholders agree on the seriousness of this problem, a great deal of confusion exists about the term *predatory* and how best to deal with it. In 2019, an international group of stakeholders developed the following consensus definition:

> Predatory journals and publishers are entities that prioritize self-interest at the expense of scholarship and are characterized by false or misleading information, deviation from best editorial and publication practices, a lack of transparency, and/or the use of aggressive and indiscriminate solicitation practices.
> *(Grudniewicz et al., 2019, The Definition section)*

Why Should Science Journalists Care about Predatory Publishing?

In the Bohannon hoax, the defining characteristics of a predatory journal are made quite visible. The article included no indication of the number of study participants and no indication that the research protocol had been reviewed by an Institutional Review Board. With these obvious flaws, the article never would have withstood peer review at a legitimate journal. Science journalists who reported the article's findings based on the assumption that the article had been peer-reviewed allowed these flawed scientific findings to be disseminated to public audiences who depend on science journalists to report accurate and credible information.

Some have argued that science journalists have traditionally operated from a different starting place than other journalists. From this perspective, it has been assumed that science journalists have to worry less than other journalists about verifying the accuracy of facts that they report because, as long as they are reporting findings published in a peer-reviewed journal, they can assume "that, within allowable limits for error, research is being properly conducted, peer-reviewed journals reliably publish only papers that have met high epistemic standards, and consensus opinion is a reliable indicator of which hypotheses are most highly confirmed by the evidence" (Figdor, 2017, para. 4). Furthermore, Carrie Figdor asserts, science journalists have seen their goal as promoting science rather than serving as critics, and it is hard to expect science journalists to adopt a more critical stance as long as they are not trained experts in the scientific subject matter on which they report.

Because predatory journals give the impression that their articles are peer-reviewed without actually conducting peer review, they make these assumptions no longer viable. However, the rise and proliferation of these journals must be understood as only one component of a complex situation. As I have argued elsewhere (Koerber, 2021), our entire infrastructure of scientific knowledge production and communication is being transformed. To a greater extent than ever, we are learning to navigate a situation in which tidbits of scientific data can circulate and become understood as gospel truth or, just as easily, be dismissed as fake, depending on the audience who happens to receive them. In addition to the rise and proliferation of predatory journals, new developments such as the growing prevalence of preprint publication and the use of social media to disseminate preprint findings before peer review are pushing the boundaries of our current understanding of the role that science journalists play in scientific discovery (Kupferschmidt, 2020). In the Bohannon chocolate hoax, science journalists were made painfully aware of these new realities. In Bohannon's (2015) opinion, these journalists made an embarrassing error that future science journalists should learn from.

Specific Recommendations for Science Journalists

The National Association of Science Writers' Code of Ethics states that "Science writers should strive to be accurate and unbiased in their professional work including verifying the accuracy of their information, checking sources' credentials and any potential conflicts of interest" (2014, para. 2). While this code's principles may be understood as timeless, science journalists today require new skillsets to apply them. Specifically, science journalists should

1. Be aware of predatory journals and other forms of suspect publishing practices. Just because an article is labeled as "peer-reviewed," this does not mean it has actually been peer reviewed.

2. Know the difference between preprint publications and peer-reviewed published findings and be aware that that it is increasingly frequent for preprint findings to be disseminated via social media (Kupferschmidt, 2020).

3. Not rely exclusively on press releases, but also use available resources to assess the quality of a journal where an article is published. A wide array of such resources exist. Be aware of these resources, but also be aware of their limitations (Koerber et al., 2020).

4. Whenever possible, contact an independent expert in the relevant subject matter – someone who was not on the research team – and ask them to assess the research reported in the article.

5. Use mechanisms such as DOI, ORCID, and CrossRef to verify the identity of scientific authors and articles.

References

Beall, J. (2012, November). *Predatory publishers and opportunities for scholarly societies*. Paper presented at the American Educational Research Association meeting, Washington, DC. http://eprints.rclis.org/18044/1/AERA%20paper%202.pdf

Bohannon, J. (2015, May 27). *I fooled millions into thinking chocolate helps weight loss. Here's how*. Gizmodo. https://gizmodo.com/i-fooled-millions-into-thinking-chocolate-helps-weight-1707251800

Bohannon, J., Koch, D., Homm, P., & Driehaus, A. (2015). Chocolate with high cocoa content as a weight-loss accelerator. *International Archives of Medicine*, 8(55), 1–8.

Editorial Office. (2015, June). Retraction notice on "Chocolate with High Cocoa Content as a weight-loss accelerator." *International Archives of Medicine*. http://imed.pub/ojs/index.php/iam/article/view/1087

Figdor, C. (2017, February). (When) is science reporting ethical? The case for recognizing shared epistemic responsibility in science journalism. *Frontiers in Communication*, 2(3). https://doi.org/10.3389/fcomm.2017.00003

Grudniewicz, A., Moher, D., Cobey, K. D., Bryson, G. L., Cukier, S., Allen, K., ... & Lalu, M. M. (2019). Predatory journals: no definition, no defense. *Nature*, *576*, 210–212. https://doi.org/10.1038/d41586-019-03759-y National Association of Science Writers. (2014, October 17). Code of ethics for science writers. https://www.nasw.org/code-ethics-science-writers

Koerber, A. (2021). Is it fake news or is it open science? Science communication in the COVID-19 pandemic. *Journal of Business and Technical Communication*, 35(1), 22–27.

Koerber, A., Starkey, J. C., Ardon-Dryer, K., Cummins, R. G., Eko, L., & Kee, K. F. (2020). A qualitative content analysis of watchlists vs safelists: How do they address the issue of predatory publishing? *The Journal of Academic Librarianship*, 46(6), https://doi.org/10.1016/j.acalib.2020.102236

Kupferschmidt, K. (2020). Preprints bring "firehose" of outbreak data. *Science*, 367(6481), 963–964.

National Association of Science Writers. (2014). Code of ethics for science writers. Retrieved from https://www.nasw.org/code-ethics-science-writers#:~:text=Science%20writers%20should%20refrain%20from,not%20acceptable%20under%20any%20circumstances

INDEX

Aday, Sean 131
advocacy 21, 59, 73
Afghanistan 114, 117, 122, 131
African American newspapers 27, 71–79, 204
Alien and Sedition Acts (1789) 6, 19, 21, 110

Baleria, Gina 15
Bélair-Gagnon, Valérie 218
Biden, Joe 77, 190, 191
Bill of Rights 1, 15, 16, 18, 19, 22
Biswas, Masudul 71
Black Lives Matter 40, 74, 75, 88, 94–96
Black press 52, 71–74, 78, 79, 99, 100
Boyd-Barrett, Oliver 116
Boynton, Lois A. 24
Brannock, Jennifer Cox 88

civil rights 11, 27, 40, 71–74, 93, 100
Civil War 8, 106, 154, 204
Claussen, Dane S. 33
climate change 55, 59, 60, 97, 170, 197
CNN 11, 12, 94, 96, 113, 143, 169, 212
Compton, Josh 196
confirmation bias 26, 142, 193
Constitution 1, 6, 15–19, 155
COVID-19 55, 60, 71, 74, 78, 94, 122, 138, 140, 147, 170, 191, 193, 196, 215
Cronkite, Walter 112

Daily Acts 3, 167
disinformation 22, 120, 154, 158, 172, 177, 179, 180, 182, 184, 188, 189, 192

education 7, 28, 31, 52, 78, 85, 99, 117, 147, 148, 150, 154–157, 174, 182, 185, 196, 208
equity 49, 52, 81, 82, 84, 86, 100
Espionage Act 109, 110

Facebook 94, 129, 143, 174, 185, 187–193, 209, 213, 220
fake news 17, 107, 143, 167, 169–175, 177–186, 187–193, 196–198, 203, 214, 214
false equivalency 11, 50
feminism 81, 84
feminist 64, 81–85, 97
First Amendment 17–22, 28, 30, 45, 155
Franklin, Benjamin 5, 13, 16, 178, 203
Frisch, Allison M. 154

Gayle, Gina 154
Gulf War 12, 113, 114, 119

harassment 81, 84–86, 203–209, 219–223
Haywood, Antoine 146
Hearst, William Randolph 8, 9, 108, 172, 176
Heckman, Meg 81
Hernandez Florez, Nicolas 55
Hernández, Leandra H. 63

Holton, Avery E. 218
hostility 170, 201, 203–209
Hutchins Commission 24, 25, 30–32
hyperlocal 137, 138, 150

Iraq 114, 117, 118, 121, 123, 131, 133

King, Larry J. 169
Koerber, Amy 227
Korea 10, 110, 111
Koslosky, John-Erik 161

local news 7, 12, 22, 31, 58, 131, 135,
    137–145, 146–147, 151, 152, 154, 156,
    158, 161, 163, 164, 184

masquerade media 143, 144
McIntyre, E. S. 47
Mehlman-Brightwell Danielle R. 187
Mellinger, Gwyneth 99
Mesmer, Kelsey 203
Miller, Kaitlin 203
misinformation 22, 55, 59, 60, 154, 158,
    169, 170, 171, 17–, 177, 185, 188,
    190–193, 197, 214–216

news desert 135, 140, 146, 154, 156, 161
news literacy 50
news value 56, 57, 58, 63, 65, 66, 85

objectivity 13, 20, 34, 37, 47–53, 55–61,
    63, 65–67, 96, 99, 111, 133, 178, 183
Office of Censorship 110, 111
Office of War Information 110, 111

Pantic, Mirjana 211
participatory journalism 211–216
partisan press 50, 171, 175
Patterson, Maggie Jones 39

penny press 7, 20, 55, 56
Pickard, Victor 146
Ponder, J. D. 177
post-truth 188, 193
*Publick Occurrences, Both Foreign and
    Domestick* 4
Pulitzer, Joseph 8, 9, 83, 84, 108, 172, 178

Reader, Bill 137

Schmidt, Hans C. xii, xiv, 1, 3, 37, 69, 103,
    105, 135, 167, 201
Sedition Act (1917) 21, 109, 110
Spanish-American War 108, 172, 178
symbolic annihilation 82

terrorism 116, 117, 121, 125–129,
    170, 212
Trump, Donald 60, 77, 128, 142, 169, 170,
    171, 173, 179, 203
trust 31, 42–45, 50, 57, 91, 142, 144, 152,
    158, 170, 175, 177, 179–184, 193, 201,
    205, 211, 214, 216
Turcotte, Jason 55

Vietnam 11, 40, 112, 113, 119, 121, 132,
    133, 172

watchdog 18, 28, 53, 142, 162–164
women journalists 82–86, 204, 205, 207,
    219, 220, 222, 223
World War I 25, 49, 109, 110
World War II 10, 12, 24, 73, 110,
    111, 132

Yang, Yiyi 125
yellow journalism 9, 20, 172, 175, 178

Zenger, John Peter 5